THE NEW
and the OLD

Published in Australia by
Vaughan Publishing
32 Glenvale Crescent
Mulgrave, VIC 3170

vaughanpublishing.com.au
A joint imprint of BBI – The Australian Institute of Theological Education
and Garratt Publishing

Copyright © 2023 Jim & Therese D'Orsa
All rights reserved. Except as provided by the Australian copyright law, no part of this book may be reproduced in any way without permission in writing from the publisher.

Text Design by Mike Kuszla, J&M Typesetting
Cover image iStock
Cover design © 2023 Garratt Publishing
Edited by Juliette Hughes

ISBN 9780648524656

Nihil Obstat:	Reverend Gerard Diamond MA (Oxon), LSS, D Theo/Diocesan Censor
Imprimatur:	Very Reverend Joseph Caddy AM Lic.Soc.Sci VG Vicar General Archdiocese of Melbourne
Date:	1 February 2023

The Nihil Obstat and Imprimatur are official declarations that a book or pamphlet is free of doctrinal or moral error. No implication is contained therein that those who have granted the Nihil Obstat and Imprimatur agree with the contents, opinions or statements expressed. They do not necessarily signify that the work is approved as a basic text for catechetical instruction.

 A catalogue record for this book is available from the National Library of Australia

The authors and publisher gratefully acknowledge the permission granted to reproduce the copyright material in this book. Every effort has been made to trace copyright holders and to obtain their permission for the use of copyright material.

The publisher apologises for any errors or omissions in the above list and would be grateful if notified of any corrections that should be incorporated in future reprints or editions of this book.

THE NEW
and the OLD

Christian Communities Recontextualise Faith in a Change of Era

Jim and Therese D'Orsa

VAUGHAN PUBLISHING
A joint imprint of BBI - TAITE
& Garratt Publishing

OTHER VAUGHAN TITLES

Mission & Education Series
- *Explorers, Guides and Meaning-makers: Mission Theology for Catholic Educators*
- *Catholic Curriculum: A Mission to the Heart of Young People*
- *Leading for Mission: Integrating Life, Culture and Faith in Catholic Education*
- *New Ways of Living the Gospel: Spiritual Traditions in Catholic Education*
- *Now with Enthusiasm: Charism, God's Mission, and Catholic Schools Today*
- *Pedagogy & the Catholic Educator*
- *Stirring the Soul of Catholic Education: Formation for Mission*

Educator's Guides
- Educator's Guide to *Catholic Identity*
- Educator's Guide to *Catholic Curriculum: Learning for 'Fullness of Life'*
- Educator's Guide to *Immersion for Mission: Formation and Transformation through Immersion*
- Educator's Guide to *Mission in Practice: Discipleship in Action in Catholic Schools*
- Educator's Guide to Service Learning: *Service learning, experiential, and whole school transformation*

This book is dedicated to the memory of
Bishop Hilton Deakin (1932-2022) in appreciation for his
friendship and confidence in entrusting the authors of this
volume with the preparation of his memoir
Bonded through Tragedy: United in Hope.

We appreciate especially Hilton's capacity to bring together
the new as well as the old in living his faith in the context
of Australia and Timor L'Este. His life is a case study
in mission in practice and a storehouse of insights into
pursuing faith in the public square. We have been richly
blessed by a life very well lived for others.

ACKNOWLEDGEMENTS

The authors are grateful to the following for their expert advice on aspects of the text: Kevin Lenehan, Francis Moloney and Jim Quillinan. Any errors remain the responsibility of the authors.

Celebrating the sixteen hundredth anniversary of the death of Saint Jerome (30 September 420), Pope Francis wrote, 'One of the problems we face today is illiteracy: the hermeneutic skills that make us credible interpreters and translators of our own cultural tradition, are in short supply' (*Sacrae Scripturae Affectus*, 30 September 2020). Therese and Jim D'Orsa's book shows a third millennium Christian audience how to face that problem. Text without context is pretext. The biblical and magisterial traditions that make God and God's ways known to us (texts) have been written, read, and repeatedly read and rewritten for over 2000 years (differing contexts). Each moment of interpretation and translation is profoundly shaped by its many contexts. Vatican II was a significant recontextualisation of the Catholic tradition in a never-ending process. I heartily endorse this outstanding contribution. It places the shifting contexts of each articulation of the Word of God and the Magisterium at the very heart of the act of interpretation.

– **Francis J Moloney, SDB, AM, FAHA**
Catholic Theological College, University of Divinity
Melbourne, Victoria, Australia

The authors of this book have a passion for the mission of Jesus. Drawing upon many different sources they present quite significant ideas in very simple terms. From the Old Testament through to the writings of recent religious education experts, we are gifted with a grand overview of how human beings have struggled to understand and to communicate the revelation of God in the world that they live in. This book continues this work within the context of Australia today.

– **Trevor Trotter SSC**
Director of St Columbans Mission Society in Oceania

Jim and Therese D'Orsa never cease to open horizons for those engaged in the mission of the Church, and this new book is no exception. *The New and the Old: Christian communities Recontextualise Faith in a Change of Era*, studies the cultural landscape of our time. As the Church continues to receive the Constitutions and Decrees of the Second Vatican Council this latest contribution echoes profoundly *Lumen Gentium* and *Gaudium et Spes*. At the heart of this work is the question: How are we to proclaim the Good News in the context and culture of our time? Profoundly this book engages with the observation of Pope Francis; 'It can be said that today we are not living in an era of change as much as a change of era' (Pope Francis, Florence, 2015).

In exploring the rich work being undertaken in the Enhancing Catholic School Identity project, the authors continue their legacy as dedicated Catholic educators and theologians. Through the lens of missiology, and placing their review through the prism of the Australian context, they lead us to bring into conversation the world of scripture and tradition with a contemporary vision of proclaiming the life, death and resurrection of Jesus Christ. As the Church's compass is clearly set toward the way of synodality, this inspirational book is timely for followers of Christ and the ever-ancient, ever-new mission entrusted to the Church.

— **Most Reverent Greg Bennet LST DD**
Bishop of Sale

Jesus invited the disciples to 'cast their nets out into the deep for a catch'. In response to the call of Christ, nets are still being cast wide across the world. In parishes, hospitals, schools and a multiplicity of good works, people commit to share their Christian faith in a way that is meaningful for those they serve.

Faith-based organisations nail their colours to the mast through visible signs – logos, statements, custom and practice. Responsive to the realities of their particular place and time, they aspire to be 'leaven in the dough', a 'light on the hill', a 'blessing to the nations', making real God's mission of love to all, particularly those who are poor or oppressed in any way.

'Recontextualisation' is an enduring process of reinterpretation and renewal, whereby the 'Good News' can be received afresh, relevant and life-giving in each changing 'context'. There will always be the imperative to, 'Make all things new', by returning to the source and drinking again from the well of God's transformative wisdom.

In their latest book in the Mission and Education series, *The New and the Old: Christian Communities Recontextualise Faith in a Change of Era*, Jim and Therese D'Orsa offer an accessible resource, grounded in scripture, tradition and contemporary scholarly disciplines. They explore with authority the importance and relevance of 'recontextualisation' for those twenty-first century leaders who seek to take seriously the call to share in God's 'ever ancient, ever new' mission of love for an evolving world. This book is an excellent companion for schools and parishes participating in or sharing the aims of the Enhancing Catholic Identity Project.

— **Most Reverent Vincent Long Van Nguyen OFM Conv STL DD**
Bishop of Parramatta

Vatican II's recovery and endorsement of Christian Tradition as both historically mediated and organically dynamic calls for a method of theological enquiry and of religious learning that responds to this living, Spirit-impelled Tradition.

Debates around the time of the Council focused on the 'reformulation' of doctrine; the greater global and intercultural awareness of recent decades has highlighted the constitutive role that contexts, and transitions between contexts, play in the unfolding of Tradition.

How do we come to experience and know the God who 'interruptedly converses' (DV 8) with humanity through Word and Spirit?

Jim and Therese D'Orsa's work draws together scriptural, missiological, anthropological and educational insights to describe the necessary contextualisation and recontextualisation of Christian faith and theology in the interplay of contexts and worldviews throughout history.

Their book will enrich our quest for effective approaches and pedagogies in religious learning and faith formation in today's contexts.

– **Very Rev Dr Kevin Lenehan**
Master, Catholic Theological College
University of Divinity, Melbourne

Recontextualisation is a word that is used variously and widely but rarely with any rigour. Teachers in some systems know that recontextualisation is a preferred stance for their pedagogy and so it is not surprising that they claim that label for their own teaching practice. In other quarters, recontextualisation is seen as a recipe for relativism and is denigrated accordingly.

Therese and Jim D'Orsa make a valuable contribution as they unpack the term in a rigorous way and explore its implications for Catholic schools. Their scholarship is timely and much needed as they provide an antidote to the confusion and ideology that unfortunately surrounds the challenge of inviting students to appreciate the significance of Catholic faith for their lives.

– **Dr Paul Sharkey**
Senior Catholic Educator and Educational Consultant
Coordinator Postgraduate Programs
Catholic Theological College Melbourne University of Divinity

CONTENTS

INTRODUCTION

Chapter 1 Scope of the Study   1

PART A
RECONTEXTUALISATION IN THE BIBLE

Introduction to Part A   15

Chapter 2 Contextualisation and Recontextualisation:
            Indwelling the Old Testament Journey in Faith   17

Chapter 3 The Gospel Writers Recontextualise the Good News:
            Indwelling the New Testament Journey in Faith   33

PART B
CONTEXTUALISATION AND RECONTEXTUALISATION FROM A MISSIOLOGICAL PERSPECTIVE

Introduction to Part B   49

Chapter 4 Contextualisation and Recontextualisation:
            Cross-cultural Mission Experience   53

Chapter 5 Culture: The Framework within which We Make Meaning   63

Chapter 6 Culture: The Dead Hand of Classicism   75

Chapter 7 Worldview as an Interpretive Category in Meaning-making   85

Chapter 8 The Worldview of Culture as an Interpretive Category   97

PART C
RECONTEXTUALISATION IN A HERMENEUTICAL PERSPECTIVE

Introduction to Part C 109

Chapter 9   How People Construct Meaning: And Why
This Matters in the Recontextualisation of Faith 111

Chapter 10   The Worldview of Faith as an Interpretive Category 121

PART D
RECONTEXTUALISATION FROM A THEOLOGICAL PERSPECTIVE

Introduction to Part D 133

Chapter 11   Recontextualisation: From Schillebeeckx to Boeve 135

PART E
RECONTEXTUALISATION FROM AN EDUCATIONAL PERSPECTIVE

Introduction to Part E 145

Chapter 12   Recontextualisation from an Educational Perspective: Transforming Worldviews 147

Chapter 13   The ECSI Project: Reflections on an Australian Experience 159

Chapter 14   Recontextualisation in Practice: Victoria – a Case Study 175

CONCLUSION

Chapter 15   The New and the Old: Christian Community Leadership
in a Change of Era 189

SELECT BIBLIOGRAPHY 201

INDEX 209

INTRODUCTION

1
SCOPE OF THE STUDY

Every book has a starting point. Often it is the need to clarify some issue or practice. In this case both the issue and the practice are the recontextualisation of faith in a time of deep change.

The questions we pursue in the pages that follow are:

- What does the term 'recontextualisation' mean?
- Where did it come from?
- Why is it important?
- How do we recontextualise faith in a change of era?

In this introduction and the exploration that follows we seek to situate current work on recontextualisation within recent Catholic experience, both cross-cultural mission experience, and the experience of the entire Church worldwide in undertaking the immense project of implementing the Second Vatican Council, which took place between 1962 and 1965. There is much insight to be gained from this. However, it is important to note that the process known as the recontextualisation of faith is as old as the Judeo-Christian tradition itself, as we shall see.

GENESIS OF THE STUDY: ECSI

The genesis of our work lies in the introduction of the *Enhancing Catholic School Identity* (ECSI) project into Catholic schools across many Australian dioceses, and the use in parishes of an adapted form of the project known as *Engaging with the Hopes of Parishes* (EHP).[1] Both of these initiatives are responses to the challenge facing the whole Church to recontextualise our

---

1 Brendan Reed, a Catholic priest of the Melbourne archdiocese, prepared a doctoral thesis with the Catholic University Leuven that involved the development of a parish engagement scale to ascertain a preferred orientation for parish life, and hence to provide guidance in pastoral leadership. Brendan Reed *Engaging with the Hope of Parishes*. Hamburg: Lit Verlag, 2019.

Catholic faith in a change of era, so that it is possible for people of our current age to understand and appreciate the great gift that we share.

While ECSI and the challenges it poses provided the immediate impetus for this study, ECSI is not the focus of the study. It remains a broader one – the recontextualisation of faith in a change of era. For an explanation of this phrase see below.

The ECSI project was initially developed in Belgium at the Catholic University Leuven (Katholieke Universiteit Leuven – KUL) as a means of affirming both the 'Catholic' identity of Catholic schools and the religious identity of their students.[2] The project was initially limited by a lack of funds, a problem that was alleviated somewhat when the Catholic Education Commission of Victoria agreed to co-sponsor its development.

In Australia, the ECSI project now involves Catholic schools, primary and secondary, in Victoria, South Australia, New South Wales, and Queensland. The project runs in other countries as well. It focuses on establishing a 'preferred future' for Catholic schools, and the 'recontextualisation of Catholic faith' is central to its conceptual framework. Recontextualisation holds a similar place in EHP.

While our topic has long been important within the Catholic theological tradition, it would be no exaggeration to say that most teachers in Catholic schools had not heard of recontextualisation prior to the introduction of ECSI. While recontextualisation has also been an important concept in mission theology, it has suffered from relative neglect in the wider Church. Its rediscovery is part of the story of theology since Vatican II. We wish to address aspects of this story, its background and significance, in order to help readers to situate recontextualisation within the faith journey of Catholics. We include reference to the extraordinary journeys made by Christian missionaries working to contextualise faith in cultures other than their own, and the hard lessons learned on those journeys.

We explore this topic because of our conviction that, whether schools or school systems engage in the ECSI project, or whether they attempt to meet the challenge of recontextualising faith through some other means, it is essential that, in this time of deep change, leaders come to grips in one way or another with the Biblical imperative to recontextualise faith.

Recontextualisation is not a specifically religious term, having provenance in several academic disciplines, each of which helps expand its meaning

---

2   As of 2021, ECSI incorporates over 500,000 subjects (students, parents, teachers, principals, priests, and members of schools' offices and boards) in some 1500 educational institutions worldwide. Didier Pollefeyt 'Teaching the Unteachable or Why Too Much Good is Bad Religious Education in Catholic Schools Today.' https://doi.org/10.3390/rel12100810,1

and practice. The disciplines include missiology, anthropology, theology, education, hermeneutics, and biblical studies.

From a missiological perspective, to clarify the meaning of 'recontextualisation', it is first necessary to address 'contextualisation'. At a semantic level also, something must be 'contextualised' before it can be 'recontextualised'.

CONTEXTUALISATION IN CHRISTIAN MISSIONARY EXPERIENCE PRIOR TO THE 1970S

The term 'contextualisation' was initially formulated by Protestant and Catholic missiologists independently of one another and reflected the complex cross-cultural mission situation that was emerging in the 1970s.[3] The concept developed in two stages. Initially, contextualisation was understood to mean the way in which missionaries, raised in European understandings and practices of the Christian faith, conveyed that faith to peoples living in totally different cultural settings.[4] 'Contextualisation' understood in this sense was substantially *a one-way process*. It was also termed 'translation' or 'adaptation'. 'Contextualisation' described the meaningful transmission of Christian faith in the cross-cultural settings in which missionaries operated. To appreciate the significance of the developments in how contextualisation was understood in recent Christian history, it is necessary to briefly consider some of the assumptions underpinning cross-cultural mission prior to the 1970s.

As modern mission history unfolded during the first and second expansions of Europe into South America, Asia, Africa, and Oceania, it was generally assumed that the way in which Europeans understood and practised their faith was *normative* for all other peoples.[5] There were of course well-known exceptions, but these were very much in the minority.

---

3   The term was first coined, in reference to theology, in 1972 by a Taiwan-born Presbyterian minister, Shoki Coe, working for the World Council of Churches' Theological Education Fund. He thus named and highlighted one of the major and most fruitful areas of Christian theology historically. While far from new – contextualisation having been at the heart of theology from the beginning of the Christian story – its nature and importance became recognised once again. It began again to flourish within many societies including Australia. For an introduction to Shoki Coe see Daniel H. Beeby, 'Coe, Shoki (C.H. Hwang)' In *Biographical Dictionary of Christian Mission*. Editor Gerald H. Andersen. Grand Rapids: Eerdmans, 1998.
4   Catholic missiologists are divided on the use of this term. The equivalent in Catholic theology is 'inculturation' which first appeared in theological texts in the 1970s and in official Catholic teaching in 1979 in Pope John Paul II's apostolic exhortation *Catechesi Tradendae* (#53). For the purpose of clarity, and because it is important to our discussion to note that context is more wide-ranging than culture, we follow respected Catholic theologian and missiologist Stephen Bevans in using the term 'contextualisation' rather than 'inculturation' in this book.
5   The notion that one culture can be taken as normative for all other cultures is known as classicism. The classicist mindset equates 'culture' with the notion of 'civilisation', in this case civilisation as it had emerged in Europe.

Missionaries invited local peoples into Christian faith *as they themselves understood and practised it* without realising the influence that European or North American cultures and history (context) had on their own understanding and expression of faith. A prevailing assumption was that Church unity was best preserved by *uniformity of belief and practice.* Prior to the 1970s leaders of the Catholic Church operated largely according to the 'one size fits all' principle.

Against this background, it is unsurprising that the concept of mission up until the post-Vatican II period (post 1965) – a period which coincided with what we are terming the 'postmodern' period in contemporary Western cultures – was a simple one, namely helping people living in non-European cultures to 'translate' or 'adapt' a European understanding of Christian faith and practice. To become Catholic was to become a pseudo-European. Missing in this experience was any understanding that *meaning-making is a culturally determined process and that not all peoples make meaning in the same way, because a person's culture provides that person with a primary frame of reference in meaning-making.* Furthermore, this culture is the product of a local history. We will explore each of these key ideas in the chapters that follow.

RECONTEXTUALISATION

Recontextualisation, like contextualisation, is a hermeneutical process; it is concerned with how we make sense of things, understand them, interpret them, and give them meaning.

As we have noted, we construct meaning within the frame of reference offered us by our culture which provides us with a language, symbols, concepts, images, beliefs, values, and other points of reference such as stories and a worldview. Since we generally take our culture for granted, much of our meaning-making goes on outside of our immediate awareness. If our cultural frame of reference undergoes a major change, then meanings that we once took for granted must be re-negotiated to remain intelligible. The process by which this occurs is called 'recontextualisation'. Put another way, *recontextualisation is the process by which meaning is sustained when the framework and context in which meaning was initially created undergo major changes.*

For instance, the Christian faith began with Jesus in a cultural world that had, due to the fall of Jerusalem and the destruction of the temple, ceased to exist by the time the gospels were written. The gospels were written in Greek for audiences often unfamiliar with Jesus' cultural world and its points of reference.

The gospels, each in a different way, post the fall of Jerusalem, represent a recontextualisation of understandings about the significance of Jesus' life, teaching, death, and resurrection in what was for both Christians and Jews at the time, a change of era. As Christianity spread, Christian leaders also provided a contextualisation of these traditions for people living in various parts of the Greco-Roman cultural world. So, in the life of early Christianity, recontextualisation and contextualisation were processes that were both features of the life of the Church. This remains the situation today.

When, in the 6th and 7th centuries CE, Christianity was taken to what would become the Europe we know today by missionaries such as St Columban, these had to contend with new cultures and the meaning systems that existed within those cultures. They had to *contextualise* the gospel for it to be meaningful. They were very successful, and Christianity subsequently became deeply embedded in most European cultures. As the Medieval period gave way to the modern period, the situation changed; European cultures became more secular, and science, rather than faith, eventually became the generally accepted criteria of what constituted both knowledge and truth. The emerging modern worldview became the dominant frame of reference within which people in Europe made sense of their lives. This was a dramatic change of era, and many Church leaders of the time rejected the development outright.

The modern worldview lost its position of dominance but remained very influential into the late 20th century when the emergence of postmodern thought confronted it. The new and complex cultural situation that resulted has presented *major challenges* to a faith that had been successfully contextualised within pre-modern societies. To remain relevant and meaningful, the Christian message needed to be *recontextualised*. This did not happen until late in the modern period when Catholic bishops at Vatican II (1962-65) began this long-overdue task, one that has continued ever since, gaining renewed momentum under the leadership of Pope Francis, just as the impact of postmodern thought was undermining assumptions on which the culture of modernity was constructed.

While Boeve following Schillebeeckx uses 'recontextualisation' (see Chapter 11), missiologists tend to use the term 're-contextualisation' (hyphenated). Both groups are referring to the fact that recontextualisation is the dynamic by which faith remains meaningful within a culture when the dominant framework used in meaning-making undergoes significant change. Apart from missiological discussion, as in Chapter 4, we will simplify matters by using 'recontextualisation' throughout this study.

CONTEXTUALISATION AND RECONTEXTUALISATION: A NEVER-ENDING STORY

In this introduction, and in Chapter 4, we have endeavoured to identify important elements in the backstory to 'recontextualisation'. The bigger story is that of God's divine purpose (mission) within history. It includes the churches' efforts to respond by making God's offer of faith and salvation meaningful to people as their cultures undergo deep change. As already noted, it is a labour for which there are significant insights accessible through the medium of the Biblical witness. At the same time, it is a story that continues to unfold; we do not know where history is taking us, and cannot know the form of mission challenges that lie ahead.

In the decades since Vatican II and as the insights of this major turning-point in Catholicism have played out in the Church's life globally, the Church's life and mission are being reshaped by an understanding of mission as God's mission made accessible to us in the life, death, and resurrection of Jesus.

There are major efforts under way to delve into the roots of our mission tradition, and to re-appropriate this foundation of Christian life for our times, allowing it to shape theologies and practical projects. Mission is slowly being re-understood in a Church-constituting way. Put in simple terms, the Church exists because of God's mission incarnated in Jesus of Nazareth, and now mandated to the Church. This means that mission is more than a list of activities to be done; it is now understood as a *dynamic life-giving force creating community and identity,* and with a very practical edge demanding that the global community put the marginalised at the centre of its consideration. The many writings of Pope Francis on the subject remind us of this central Biblical imperative.

Faith communities are called to discern how the various forms of mission find their place on communities' agendas, be they agendas about social justice, reconciliation, care for the earth, inter-religious dialogue, or recontextualisation of faith. Theologians inevitably struggle with the questions these newer forms of mission draw to the surface of Church life in the new environment that is both postmodern and now postsecular. It is becoming increasingly clear that the implementation of the post-Vatican II mission project requires the efforts of every baptised Christian, and so to some extent, formation and education are the responsibility of every leader.

Finally, the post-Vatican II story of mission is a story with implications for the encounter that teachers and leaders have with young people who are native to the current era characterised by deep globalisation and consequent pluralisation of societies, an era that is now well advanced. For them, any ambiguities inherent in religious belief are amplified by living in an unstable Western culture. The situation demands a re-orientation of the teaching-learning processes in Catholic schools. Additionally, this re-orientation also needs to be repeated in parish settings so that parishioners are enabled, rather than disabled, in their understanding and practice of faith. If this can be achieved, then parishes and schools can move together for the good of all God's people.

There have been relatively few times in human history when both culture and faith have undergone simultaneous transformation as rapidly as they have in our time. In other words, the challenges facing the present generation of teachers and parish leaders *seem unique in human history.* We hope that our contribution to achieving some clarity about the historical and cultural processes presently underway may lead to insight, and provide teachers with encouragement in the grand project of Catholic education. These are our goals in the chapters that follow.

IMPORTANT TERMINOLOGY

Living in a 'Change of Era'

The global dynamics – globalisation, pluralisation, and secularisation – with their attendant consequences such as detraditionalisation, are the defining features of the current age,[6] one that demands of us what Pope Francis identifies as 'a new humanism' in response to deepening divisions. In his writings, such as *Evangelii Gaudium* (2013), *Laudato si'* (2015), and *Fratelli Tutti* (2020), Pope Francis has spelled out at some length the features of our context that need to be addressed. These features define what Pope Francis, in a landmark address delivered at Florence cathedral early in his pontificate, referred to as constituting a 'change of era' in contradistinction to 'an era of change'.[7] It is an era in which the increasingly perilous state of the earth, and its inhabitants, is becoming more centre-stage in human consciousness spurred on by climate change and global rivalries fought out in proxy wars. The current age is one characterised by the deep changes noted above and, in the view of Pope Francis, has reached, the gone beyond, the tipping point that is moving the human family and its 'common home'[8] into a new era – a change of era has occurred.

---

6 Jim and Therese D'Orsa. *Explorers, Guides and Meaning-makers: Mission Theology for Catholic Educators.* Mulgrave: Garratt Publishing, 2010, chapters 7-9, 95-133. The situation presented in these chapters not only persists but has only deepened in the last decade.

7 Pope Francis' address to the Members of the Fifth Convention of the Italian Church gathered at Santa Maria Della Fiori Cathedral, Florence, 10 November, 2015. s\https://www.vatican.va/content/francesco/en/speeches/2015/november/documents/papa-francesco_20151110_firenze-convegno-chiesa-italiana.html

8 Note full title of *Laudato si'* https://www.vatican.va/content/francesco/en/encyclicals/documents/papa-francesco_20150524_enciclica-laudato-si.html

In this 'change of era', our view of what constitutes 'the world' is no longer shaped by geography as in Roman, Medieval, and early Modern times, but by a realisation of our interconnectedness to others who are 'different' and to the earth itself in ways that previously would have been considered inconceivable. The framework within which people now make sense of their lives has to be re-negotiated in the context of cultural and religious pluralism and threats to life on this planet. For most people, matters that they once took for granted as 'how the world is' must be re-examined and assessed.

In a 'change of era' it is no longer possible for members of the older generation to pass on either faith or culture in the same way that they themselves received it, since members of the younger generation are native to the new context and its worldview which they take for granted as 'how things are'. There are now forces at work that challenge traditional understandings of family, school, and parish. In a change of era the taken-for-granted assumptions that underpinned these three basic forms of social existence, whether drawn from faith or culture, are open to critique and challenge. With this comes both confusion and opportunity.

Pope Francis made it clear in his address in Florence cathedral that this new era cannot be dealt with by 'putting our hope in structures, organizations, in perfect plans…' Of course, he was not discouraging prudent planning or good organisation, but publicly warning against *'putting hope in'* such arrangements (a practical heresy that he calls modern-day Pelagianism).[9] Speaking of the self-emptying Jesus in the presence of the giant fresco of the Last Judgement on the ceiling of Florence's famous Duomo, Francis spoke of Jesus' face on the cross becoming like that of our 'humiliated brothers and sisters, slaves, emptied…'. He made it very clear that a 'new humanism' that places Christians alongside and among the victims of past and present dehumanising forces, must shape our Christian response. Indeed, in a change of era the self-emptying of Jesus Christ's humanism is to be the hallmark of a new Christian humanism.

Modern and Modernity

The term 'modern' has multiple meanings. As used in ordinary speech it means 'contemporary' or 'current'. As used in history, 'modern' refers to a specific era in which a new worldview, the modern worldview, emerged in Europe. Other historical eras are named with respect to 'modernity', another name for the modern period. Thus, the era immediately prior to modernity it called the 'pre-modern' or 'pre-critical' era. Distinctions

---

[9] A heresy which denies original sin, and which promotes the conviction that we humans can manage our affairs without the help of God.

are made within modernity such as early modernity, high modernity, and late modernity. While there is some disagreement about exactly when the modern era started, there seems consensus that it ended around the 1970s with the advent of postmodern thought.[10]

Modernity has its roots in what is known as the 'Age of Enlightenment' and extends from the 17th through to the early 19th century, when it reached its peak. It was a period of vigorous philosophical and political debate with new directions and rationales proposed for public life. Modernity inherited ideas generated during the 'Scientific Revolution' that created optimism about the future of humanity and gave rise in the modern period to public debate about political policies. These ideas about human life and the meaning of history led to assumptions about the inevitability of human progress, and the right way to conduct public life, including the necessity to separate church and state. Unbounded faith was placed in human reason and scientific method, to the detriment of affectivity and other ways of constructing and validating knowledge. Modernity has affected us in the West profoundly, and through the colonial activities of Western nations and corporations, has impacted much of the world.

Modernity's optimism legitimated practices that have led to the current disastrous state of the earth. Whereas in the pre-modern period scientists like Newton saw themselves as using their talents in the service of God, with their inventions and works done in God's service, in the modern age such affirmations were rejected as religion was relegated to the realm of affectivity and private life.

Because religion was relegated to the private sphere, new academic disciplines developed in this period did not require the legitimation of religious authority as had been the case previously. Theology became separated from the mainstream academy and found its life in seminaries and universities that maintained departments of theology. In our time this situation is changing slowly, and a fruitful dialogue is beginning to take place between theology and other disciplines. It is not easy to generate spaces for this to occur. Dialogue of this kind is one of the mission imperatives of our time. At the Catholic school level, it occurs as teachers and leaders seek the integration of faith and culture within the curriculum.[11] In parish life it occurs as communities seek dialogue partners from beyond the

---

10 *Encyclopedia Britannica* 'Modernity' accessed at https://www.britannica.com/topic/modernity
11 See the exploratory study by Jim and Therese D'Orsa. *Catholic Curriculum: a Mission to the Heart of Young People*. Mulgrave: Garratt Publishing, 2011. An Educator's Guide to the subject has been prepared by Patricia Hindmarsh entitled *Catholic Curriculum: Learning for 'Fulness of Life* . Mulgrave: Garratt Publishing, 2017.

communities in order to enable projects such as social justice or care for the earth initiatives to occur.

Life in the modern period was envisaged as human life minus religion.[12] Charles Taylor refers to this as a 'subtraction story', and points to the tendency of people today to interpret modernity in terms of what has been lost. He proposes that the secularity that is a legacy of modernity can also be interpreted as a positive thing, and that we should be thinking about our current age as providing the opportunity to create an 'addition story' that acknowledges our debt to modernity. But we are getting ahead of ourselves. Let it be said up front, however, that initiatives such as the ECSI project find their place among those that seek to respond strongly to the opportunities and challenges of our postmodern-postsecular age.

Secularity was a feature of modernity. It recognised that there are areas of human life in which faith legitimately plays little or no part.[13] This is different from *secularism* which interprets secularity as excluding faith from the public square. 'Secularisation' has multiple interpretations along a soft-hard continuum.

In the 1970s a group of French philosophers known as the Postmoderns, faced with the profound failures of the modern worldview during the 20th century, mounted a powerful critique to its philosophic underpinnings, challenging its narrative of endless human progress. Modernity was forced to give ground in the face of the postmodern critique, especially regarding its assumptions about the nature of history's unfolding. What we are experiencing today bears resemblance to what has occurred in human history whenever there has been a change of era. Powerful new ideas emerge that impact on the process of human meaning-making, but the old ideas persist for a time alongside them. Thus, modernity continues to shape our culture even as some of its key ideas are being reshaped – ideas about human progress, and what secularity means as contexts change.

Postmodern-postsecular

In this study, we describe the current era as postmodern-postsecular. Let us focus on the 'postmodern' element first. By this we mean that our era remains very much influenced by postmodern thought, particularly its

---

12   Charles Taylor *A Secular Age*. The Belknap Press of Harvard University Press, Cambridge MA: 2007, 26–29.
13   Secularity understood in this way is recognised in Catholic teaching. Science for instance has its own method of validating its own insights as true. This holds for other disciplines such as anthropology and psychology. What the Church does is enter into dialogue with academic disciplines to understand the conclusions reached and their implications for humankind. Similarly while the Church sets out moral principles by which government should act, but it does not propose specific solutions to complex political issues since the latter can be interpreted in different ways within different political systems.

critique of totalising narratives that seek to embrace all aspects of life and interpret it from a single perspective, especially in economic matters. The postmodern critique was aimed particularly at the shortcomings of Nazism and Soviet-era Communism and the horrific human tragedy these caused in Europe. These we agree are closed stories.

Some interpretations of the Christian story have also been critiqued as a closed story. However, as we have argued in our previous book (*Pedagogy for the Catholic Educator* 2021),[14] the theology of the kingdom or reign of God, as reclaimed by the Biblical renewal of recent years, has shown us that the Christian story is *intrinsically an open story*. This central image in Jesus' teaching about the mission God had entrusted to him, provides an approach to the future that is wonderfully open and challenges the Christian imagination.

Postsecular

Modernity saw an expansion in the notion of secularity in its various facets – separation of Church and state, democratic government, freedom of the press, freedom of assembly, creation of a market economy, and the secularisation of knowledge. With these lasting achievements also came other elements such as relegation of religion to the private sphere. In Australia, we know that this thinking was applied to public education in which there was to be no religion taught; such education was supposed to occur in the home or in the church acting as a Sunday school, but outside school hours.

Among those who rejected this view and wanting all areas of learning to form an integrated whole with faith strongly held and taught, was Australia's first canonised saint, Mary MacKillop, who founded her sisterhood to help make such an education possible and available, initially in primary schools and later in secondary. Other pioneering Catholic educators with a similar vision followed both here and in other countries.

An important consequence of postmodern thinking was appreciation of 'difference', and equally important, *a recognition of the right of people to be different*. This raised the question of how best to address religious difference while maintaining the secularity of public life? This is a defining issue for a postsecular society. The answer has been to open the public square to all.

We have begun to see the public space of our society as the domain wherein all, no matter their religion or ideology, may participate subject to goodwill and fairness. This is the postsecular environment. It certainly does not abandon the positive understanding of modern secularity, such as the separation of church and state, and the secularisation of knowledge,

---

14 Jim and Therese D'Orsa *Pedagogy and the Catholic Educator*. Mulgrave: Garratt Publishing, 2021.

but leaves the path open to new developments in our understanding of secularity and their implications for people of faith.

STRUCTURE OF THE TEXT

This exploratory study is set out in five main parts.

Following this introduction, **Part A** explores aspects of contextualisation and recontextualisation within the Old and New Testament traditions. (Chapters 2 and 3).

In **Part B** we examine the Catholic experience of contextualisation in recent cross-cultural mission history (Chapter 4) and discuss key understandings about how people make meaning in the context of a changing culture, (Chapters 5, 6, 7, and 8). In addressing meaning-making, we aim to secure two key terms – 'culture' and 'worldview'.

In **Part C** (Chapters 9 and 10) we address the process of recontextualisation by considering:

- the processes by which people construct meaning from the perspective of *hermeneutics*
- the *worldview of faith* and the part if plays in meaning-making.

In **Part D (**Chapter 11) we focus on recontextualisation from a theological perspective.

In **Part E** (Chapters 12, 13, and 14) we provide some reflections on recontextualisation from within the recent Australian educational experience, focusing particularly on the *Enhancing Catholic Identity* (ECSI) project.

In the **Concluding Section** (Chapter 15) we draw together a selection of themes explored in the book, and examine the kind of community that might encourage and strengthen current attempts to recontextualise faith seen as a pressing pastoral and missional imperative in today's schools and parishes.

The writer of Matthew's gospel provides us with a template for community leadership. In meeting the needs of his predominantly Jewish community for a recontextualised Christian faith in an utterly changed world, he brings out of his storeroom profoundly new understandings and perspectives, as well as the more familiar ones – 'the old' (Matt 13:52). In a creative synthesis, Matthew's gospel moved the early Christian experience forward, authentically recontextualising traditions of meaning originating in the Jewish faith, in the light of the life, passion, death, and resurrection of Jesus of Nazareth, and of the destruction of Jerusalem and all that this meant in the Jewish religious world. In doing so, Matthew produced a gospel that has played a central role in Christian education in faith from the first century CE to the present day.

Part A
RECONTEXTUALISATION IN THE BIBLE

In Part A we explore key Biblical understandings available to us as a people who accept God's invitation to enter the grand journey of faith to which the Bible provides witness. It is a journey undertaken *in this world* in which a people, having opted to join the Bible's hopeful forward movement of 'blessing to the nations', has an opportunity to involve itself, at each turn in the road, more deeply in God's creating and redeeming love for the universe.

A key phrase is that of *indwelling* the text, as opposed to dipping into, or even studying the text. If we truly indwell the text, we become deeply part of a story carried forward by a faith community in each passing era. This involves both the story as we inherit and interpret it, and the story to which we in our time and place contribute a chapter.

'Indwelling the text' involves relating, as Israel did throughout its history, with others beyond ourselves. 'The nations' – is the Biblical mantra for those others beyond the community with whom Israel was called to develop a fruitful relationship. Today 'the nations' inhabit most societies on earth, and certainly contemporary Australia. Much of this book raises the issue of how fruitfully we are able to encounter them.

The Bible itself was born out of processes of deep change which led leaders in Old and New Testament times to probe deeply into the fundamentals of their faith in God and to reinterpret those fundamentals faithfully in a different time and place. At such times, communities of faith were shepherded by leaders with the ability to steer them through the swirling waters of change till they emerged richer, wiser, and surer, in calmer waters. These leaders helped the people to articulate the fundamentals of their faith in a way that made sense as contexts changed.

This book is addressed to such leaders being called forth within the Church today.

It was, and remains, by means of the life of a faith community that God's unfolding designs (God's mission) for humankind was and is taken forward. Indeed, we would contend, along with a range of Biblical scholars and missiologists, that God's mission is the hermeneutical key with which to unlock the meaning of the Bible itself.

In exploring the Old and New Testaments in terms of recontextualisation, we become aware that mission studies and biblical studies – two foundational streams of Christian reflective consciousness – are beginning to flow together and to join forces as the times demand. In so doing, they are producing powerful insights for those seeking to experience and engender hope today, in a change of era.

Recontextualisation is more likely to be successful if faith has been soundly contextualised initially. In Chapter 2 we explore how the dynamics of contextualisation and recontextualisation play out in the Old Testament, while in Chapter 3 we examine aspects of how they function in that part of the New Testament we know as the four canonical gospels.

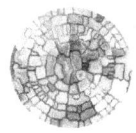

2

CONTEXTUALISATION AND RECONTEXTUALISATION:

INDWELLING THE OLD TESTAMENT JOURNEY IN FAITH

What can the Bible offer people of faith in an era of deep change? The commitment of so many seems to be ebbing, and the false gods of self-centredness, material success and domination of others seem to be in the ascendant. In attempting to answer that question, it is important first to lay down some fundamental understandings about that part of the Bible known as the Old Testament.

The initial context of Israel's faith as a community constituted by a covenant with God was the experience of liberation from Egypt. The fact that the Jewish people existed at that time as a people was due to their connection to common ancestors in Abraham, Isaac, Jacob, and Joseph. When they were formed definitively as a people at Sinai, however, others were grafted onto this rootstock. This occurred because, when Israel left Egypt, a 'mixed multitude' went with them (Exod 12:38). As the book of Exodus records (Exod 19-24), these people, probably other enslaved groups who, like the children of Israel, broke away from the Egyptian yoke and moved out into the desert, stood with the descendants of Abraham at Sinai and became included in God's chosen people. 'Already the point was being made that Israel was more a covenant community than heredity linked by blood'.[1]

As we ponder the privilege of being a community of faith, one that is profoundly plural in both culture and the range of understandings it encompasses, existing in a pluralist society in a globalised world, it is salutary to remember the nature of our community's beginnings. We also note that as the people journeyed forward, they struggled in their relationship with

---

1 James Okoye *Israel and the Nations*. Maryknoll, N.Y: Orbis, 2006, 3.

those in whom their existence was embedded – 'the nations'. As we shall see, there was to be no fundamental resolution of this relationship till it occurred in the life, death, and resurrection of Jesus.[2]

THE BIBLE IS BORN OUT OF EXPERIENCES OF DEEP CHANGE

The Jewish faith after the liberation from Egypt underwent several recontextualisations as a result of times of severe trial, and in consequence, understanding of faith grew. With the help of good leadership, the people would come to learn that:

- God is the God of all peoples.
- God is the God of all creation.
- God was involved in the events of Israel's history, both the good and the bad.
- God loves God's people.
- God is capable of compassion and forgiveness.
- God makes new beginnings possible.
- Human life finds its destiny in God.
- There is more to human life than simply our experience within time.

These understandings grew out of the way Israel's prophets and leaders interpreted, in the light of faith, their experience of actual historical events (all of which were capable of other explanations). Together they came to underpin a culture of faith that was unique – an example to the nations and a source of hope to all humankind.

Events over which Israel had limited control became the impetus for the recontextualisation of faith. Sometimes this renewed understanding occurred as they moved from nomadic to a more settled life. At other times it occurred due to their status as vassal state, and it occurred dramatically when Israel came under a conqueror who exiled its elites, leaving the rest of the people behind to fend for themselves, as occurred in the Babylonian exile of the 6th century BCE. The return from exile some decades later (538 BCE) thanks to the decision of the enlightened Persian leader, Cyrus, was also a time of deep change and renewal. At these times traditions were reshaped and took life, sometimes recorded in written form.

Thus we can say that the Bible as we have it today was actually born out of experiences of dramatic changes in context resulting in confusion,

---

[2] This issue is especially important for the Gospel of Matthew. See the chapter with which this study closes (chapter 15).

emergent leadership, re-understanding, re-expression of traditions, re-grouping, and then a renewed journeying forth in faith.

An example of this process at work occurs in the shaping of the book of Deuteronomy. As James Sanders, American Old Testament scholar well known for his work on the process of canon formation in the Bible explains it, the canon of scripture that we accept as the bedrock of our Christian faith came into being through a process of creating and re-creating the story of God's relationship with a people who experienced themselves as chosen to share God's creating and redeeming mission in the world, that is, to be a blessing to the nations.[3]

> I will make you a great nation, and I will bless you, and make your name great, so that you will be a blessing...and in you all the nations of the earth will be blessed. (Gen 12:2-3).

In Galatians 3:8, Paul refers to this passage as the 'Gospel in advance'.

> And the scripture, foreseeing that God would justify the Gentiles by faith, declared the Gospel beforehand to Abraham saying 'All the Gentiles shall be blessed in you.'

In his work on the origins and function of the canon of scripture, Sanders speaks of Israel's crucifixion-resurrection experience that occurred with the exile in Babylon and its aftermath in the sixth and fifth centuries BCE. Out of this devastation, the religious community of Judaism was born. At this time the ancient traditions of the Law and the Prophets received the shape that we have inherited.

In his opening section of 'Torah and History', Sanders traces the originating Jahwist (J) and Elohist (E) traditions of the Northern Kingdom, and the disastrous fate of the northern communities at the hands of the Assyrians in the 8th century BCE when many thousands were taken into exile, never to return. He points to the survival of their traditions through their grafting onto those of the Southern Kingdom, and the reshaping of all of this material by the scholars we have come to know as P (Priestly tradition) during the Babylonian exile, giving us the books of the Torah. *Leviticus* deals with holiness and ritual, *Numbers* with case law, and *Deuteronomy* urges recognition of Israel's unique God and the necessity for loyalty to that God. The amalgam of various legal codes and historical material constituting the canon of the Torah as we have it today constituted an essential element in the formation of post-exilic Israel as a nation.

---

3   James A. Sanders *Torah and Canon*. Second Edition. Eugene OR: Cascade Books, 2005.

The development of a legal code in Israel is a classic example of recontextualisation occurring across Israel's history as contexts changed, enabling the faith community to survive. It was a community-building process. We should not be surprised to find ourselves caught up in a similarly demanding, and creative exercise as, guided by the magisterial documents of the Church, and the work of widely respected mainline biblical and theological scholars, we make our way forward into an open future.

The invitation of this chapter is to enter this grand and forward-moving Biblical story of blessing to the nations via a faith community who knew God was at work in the world. We seek to attune ourselves – albeit by means of a very limited selection of the possible examples – to our ancestors in the faith who, like us, at certain times, experienced deep change. Through the ministry of excellent leaders – kings, prophets and others sent by God – they came again and again to embrace a recontextualised faith and to enjoy renewed insight and commitment to their mission to be a blessing and a hope to the nations. So too can we learn not only to discern where genuine leadership can be found, but also begin ourselves to exercise such leadership towards one another.

If we are to enter this narrative and successfully take it forward, we must also acknowledge the value of gaining further insight into the composition of the Bible utilising the various strands of what is known as the historical-critical method of Biblical study.[4] These shed light on aspects of the history of the composition of the text as we now have it (which is not to be confused with the history of events). Although many elements of modern Biblical scholarship are broadly agreed – for example, it is generally accepted that there are many traditions that were reworked across time[5] – there are still areas of scholarly disagreement. These do not, however, affect the clear evidence of *a plurality of traditions* emanating from various communities amid the circumstances in which they found themselves at different times. A plurality of traditions is embedded in the nature of the Bible itself.

---

[4] The historical critical method is a composite of such streams as source criticism, form criticism, tradition criticism, and redaction criticism. For a helpful introduction to these elements of Biblical study see Donald Senior. 'Interpreting the Scriptures: The Church and the Modern Biblical Renewal' in John J. Collins, Gina Hens-Piazza, Barbara Reid, OP. and Donald Senior, CP (eds.) *The Jerome Biblical Commentary for the Twenty-first Century.* London: Bloomsbury, 2022, 1923-1949.

[5] Scholars delving into the sources of the books of the canon have long identified many traditions within the Biblical text. Scholarly constructs known as J (Yahwist – from the German Jahwe), E (Elohist), D (Deuteronomist) and P (Priestly) refer to discernible sources that at various times recorded and reshaped ancient traditions. Ibid, 42-43.

BECOMING A BLESSING TO THE NATIONS MEANS JOURNEYING INTO THE UNKNOWN

Given that God's promise to Abraham was that his descendants would be a blessing to the nations, it must be noted that initially, and for a long period thereafter, how this would be realised was not at all clear. In fact, God's call to Israel's founding family and their successors proved to be an invitation to journey into the unknown. As God's missional[6] intentions unfolded, Abraham's descendants were to learn that the blessing would flow via the life of a people, a distinctive community that would be founded definitively through a salvific experience of liberation from social, economic, and religious oppression in Egypt. In this process God revealed Godself as liberator, and required those so liberated to act similarly towards others.

In a sense, and paradoxically, the blessing would also come through Israel's infidelity and failure. This is because, through these failures, the redeeming love of the God of creation – God's willingness to breathe into the failures and brokenness of the people a new creation – was evident for those who had eyes to see.

From their founding experience, the core values of Israel's culture would be distilled including their understandings about God, and the relationships with God and each other into which they were called. These core values shaped them as a *contrast people* and were of such significance as to subsequently shape the faith of millions and provide a basis for shared responsibility for creation and for personal and communal salvation up to the present day.

The community formed out of the founding experience would be re-formed many times during what we call Old Testament times, as circumstances in their geo-political context changed and impacted their communal life of faith in various ways. Both elements – *community and faith* – are important to our exploration. However, Israel's capacity to be a blessing to the nations ebbed and flowed across history as the cycles of disintegration, re-grouping, and renewal proceeded. Today we too are called to re-group as a Church community, adhering to a faithfully recontextualised faith, so that we too may be a blessing and a hope to the nations.

When we re-examine the sacred text, and ponder on our contemporary situation, we learn that within the Judeo-Christian tradition there have always

---

6 We are using 'missional' in relation to God to emphasise that God has revealed Godself as purposefully at work within the universe and within human history. However, the events of human history need to be interpreted for this revelation to be meaningful to us. God has a purpose in which humans are invited to participate. For people sharing Biblical faith, the nature and direction of this unfolds within human history beginning with God's choosing Abraham to be a blessing to the nations.

been times of dramatic change in context impacting faith communities and calling forth processes of renewal. Some obvious and important examples of these have been noted above. The scale of these experiences parallels that of Christian communities today in terms of changes to both faith and culture, and the hope that we cling to for a better, fairer world.

At such dramatic times, things that had been taken for granted – core values and understandings about identity and mission – became confused at first, but under the guidance of the Holy Spirit, were re-understood and re-expressed and once again able to nourish the faith life and hope of the people. The good news of God's creating and redeeming love could be heard anew and received as good news. Never was this to be experienced more dramatically within Israel's history than in the return from the Babylonian exile and the re-founding of community and faith that accompanied it under the leadership of Nehemiah the Persian prince and Ezra the Jewish scribe.[7]

ISRAEL AS A MISSIONAL COMMUNITY

Mission, in the sense of God's purpose in the world, acts as hermeneutical key both to the Bible's content, and to the process by which the Bible came into being.

The recognition of mission as hermeneutical key to the Biblical text is a relatively new development within Christian theology, but it is now becoming widely accepted as the corpus of literature emerging on the subject attests.[8] When we say that mission is the hermeneutical key to Biblical understanding, we are not claiming that mission is the only theme. That would be nonsensical. The claim is simply that God's mission and human response to it comprise the central interest and goal of the story

---

7 This partnership of a 'secular' state – in the person of Nehemiah the Persian prince, and faith leadership in the person of Ezra the Jewish scribe – provides us with an important model for contemporary Church renewal. We might reflect, for example, on how the agencies of the state have worked together with faith leaders in dealing with the crisis arising from the sexual abuse of minors by Church personnel. This has been an effective partnership, certainly in this country, allowing for a renewal of faith within the Church with leadership emerging from among well-credentialed lay people alongside the more traditional leadership provided by clerics.

8 Pertinent to our discussion on the Old Testament, examples include classic texts such as Donald Senior and Carroll Stuhlmueller. *The Biblical Foundations of Mission*. Maryknoll New York: 1984, and a growing corpus from both Catholic, Protestant and Evangelical sources e.g. James Okoye *Israel and the Nations: A Mission Theology of the Old Testament*. Maryknoll New York: Orbis, 2006.; Michael W. Goheen. *A Light to the Nations: The Missional Church and the Biblical Story*. Grand Rapids: Baker Academic, 2011; Michael W. Goheen, Editor. *Reading the Bible Missionally*. Grand Rapids: Eerdmans, 2016; Christopher J.H. Wright. *The Mission of God: Unlocking the Bible's Grand Narrative*. Downers Grove: IVP Academic, 2006.

we enter when we faithfully engage with scripture.⁹ In that sense, mission brings unity and cohesion to Biblical study.

An extraordinary aspect of Israel's faith was the capacity to discern God's creating and redeeming action (God's mission) through contextual changes with all their accompanying angst and suffering. This discernment crystallised into traditions that were passed down orally, later recorded in writing, and later again collected and re-formed as situations changed. For example in the Torah, foundation of Israel's faith, the Exodus from Egypt is depicted as a liberating act of God who confronted and defeated Pharaoh as both political power and rival deity.¹⁰ Although originally recorded out of the experience of liberation from Pharaoh, the Exodus would later be reinterpreted in the light of the Babylonian exile and the liberation offered by Cyrus of Persia who in 539 BCE, having conquered the Babylonians, issued a decree allowing the return of the exiled Jews to their homeland.¹¹

In establishing a covenantal relationship with ancient Israel, God called the people to be a contrast society within the world of their time, that is, a community of people *who did life differently from their neighbours*, worshipping one God who ruled over their lives, and living by God's requirements – a people with a unique culture. A central element of Israel's mission was to proclaim that the one God is the God not just of Israel, but of all the nations, the earth itself, and the history of the earth and its peoples.¹² This proclamation was to be by way of the concrete witness of their fidelity to God demonstrated in the way they lived together.

In the words of Michael Goheen, American professor of missional theology and prolific contributor to both mission studies and biblical studies, the people of Israel were called to be a 'display people' for the nations, demonstrating how being in a covenantal relationship with God changes a people ¹³ and so shapes their culture. Most notable among these requirements was that Israel should do what is right and just by placing the most vulnerable – described often in the Bible as the widows, the orphans, and the aliens – at the centre of their social consideration and obligation, thus modelling 'a genuine human existence'.¹⁴ They were to be carriers of God's intention to bring such liberating salvation to the whole world. Their

---

9   Richard Bauckham 'Mission as Hermeneutic for Scriptural Interpretation in Goheen, ed., 2016, 28.
10 Christopher J. H. Wright 'Reading the Old Testament Missionally' in Michael W. Goheen (ed) 2016, 110.
11 See for example Psalm 126.
12 Michael Goheen 'Scripture as Narrative Record of God's Mission' in *Introducing Christian Mission Today*. Downers Grove: Illinois. IVP academic, 2014, 40.
13 Ibid, 42.
14 ibid, 44.

creating, healing, reconciling mission was to be revelatory of the very nature and purpose of God at work in the world.

In consequence of the covenant made with God after the liberation from Egypt, the Israelites were expected to be a contrast community in two distinct ways. The first flowed from their central belief in and allegiance to the one God who reigns over all of creation (monotheism) in contrast with the polytheistic beliefs of their neighbors and conquerors, and secondly, as a people who placed the most vulnerable at the centre of their social consideration – the opposite dynamic to the all-too-common human tendency to cast such people aside.

Located in the context of polytheistic cultures, Israel's core belief in the one and only God who reigns over heaven and earth was the fundamental proclamation of the God they acknowledged, and of their own identity and mission. It was a proclamation that occurred by witness rather than by word. They lived, or were covenanted to live, in a way that came to be interpreted as a proclamation in itself.

Israel's historical experiences, interpreted within its faith understanding, gave rise to a set of symbols that became important to how its leaders constructed and re-constructed its culture, and within that its religion, as contexts changed. God as creator, and as liberator of the oppressed, the notion of living in a covenant with God, the concepts of commandments and law derived from God, the temple as centre of worship, the prophet as God's messenger, the king as the focus of political and economic power, the widows, orphans and aliens as subject of God's particular concern – all became symbols in Israel's story. These arose in particular historical circumstances, but then across time took on a hermeneutical value that transcended those circumstances and helped create a language of faith that not only expanded, but also has endured even into the present.

INDWELLING THE TEXT

Clearly, in engaging Old Testament texts, we are involved in more than personal academic study; such experience must ultimately have an ecclesial outcome leading to commitment to God's salvific mission and the hope that it offers. Because bringing about a new creation and a liberating salvation for others is a most challenging commission, it requires dialogue partners, as we have noted often in our treatment of mission. [15] Especially effective are those opting to live in the way that Israel was called to live, in contrast to the lifestyle of those who worship the false gods of self and material

---

15   For example, Jim and Therese D'Orsa, *Pedagogy and the Catholic Educator*, Mulgrave: Garratt Publishing, 2020, 212, 311, 328, 345.

success, not only failing to care for the marginalised, but even oppressing them. Becoming a blessing to the nations demands a way of life that runs counter-culturally to the value system of much of the society that is our milieu today. It means offering hope to those who are marginalised and actualising such hope by the way we construct our culture.

Like Israel we will have to reconnect with our identity as a people whom God calls into a re-creating, salvific mission in the world. 'Reconnecting' implies recognising that we too are called to re-create the Biblical story repeatedly as the context shifts 'from the old to the new, reconstructing the past in memory and constructing the future in expectation.'[16] We thus begin to 'indwell' the text.

The work of recontextualising faith is a challenging process, not least because for us as for the original Biblical communities, it occurs under the impetus of confusing events. When it is pursued faithfully, as occurred under Ezra and Nehemiah following the return from exile in the 6th century BCE, or the Gospel writers in the later decades of the first century CE, the faith community is re-created. If it does not occur, there is a danger of the community being seriously weakened, or facing terminal decline, as is occurring in some Western countries at present. Both possibilities confronted Israel at various intervals during its history. For example, some Israelites became so enamoured with the glittering culture of Babylon that they wished to remain there and enjoy its comforts rather than face the unknown and the hardships of re-founding a covenanted community in the land of their ancestors. Their response echoed that of those Israelites who, generations earlier, as they wandered in the desert after their escape from Egypt, began to see their previous life of slavery through 'rose-tinted glasses':

> *The whole congregation of the Israelites complained against Moses and Aaron in the wilderness. The Israelites said to them, 'If only we had died by the hand of the Lord in the land of Egypt, when we sat by the fleshpots and ate our fill of bread; for you have brought us out into the wilderness to kill the whole assembly with hunger'.* (Exod 16:3).

THE IMPORTANCE OF LOCATION TO ISRAEL'S IDENTITY AND MISSION

Within the world of the Old Testament, Israel was geographically located at a major crossroads of the known world. In this, the society experienced something of what most societies today experience as the result of deep globalisation – the flow of life and ideas from other societies and cultures deeply impacting their own life.

---

16 ibid, 30.

Particularly well known for his work on the missional nature of the Old Testament, Anglican scholar Christopher Wright notes: 'They could not have lived on a more crowded international stage … a veritable concourse of nations'. Thus, as with the life of today's faith communities, the nations were the spectators of Israel's life and history.[17] In Exodus 15:14-16, for example, the Song of Moses envisions how the smaller neighbouring nations would have been affected by Israel's victory over Egypt, the great power of the day.

> *The peoples heard, they trembled;*
>   *pangs seized the inhabitants of Philistia.*
> *Then the chiefs of Edom were dismayed;*
>   *trembling seized the leaders of Moab;*
>   *all the inhabitants of Canaan melted away;*
> *Terror and dread fell upon them;*
> *by the might of your arm, they became still as a stone*
>   *until your people, O Lord, passed by,*
>   *until the people whom you acquired passed by.*

Going beyond Israel's smaller neighbours, the rise and fall of the great powers across successive ages provided the major impact on Israel's life depending on the power in the ascendancy at any one time, be it Egyptian, Assyrian, Babylonian, Persian, Greek, or Roman. Across the generations, the people of Israel would find themselves subject to a change in the dominant international power. At those times some of Israel's most talented leaders, particularly the prophets, did their work in bringing Israel's core values and understandings to bear on the new disorienting circumstances, and in so doing recontextualised age-old traditions, and offered the people new hope in difficult times.

SOUND CONTEXTUALISATION ENABLES SUCCESSFUL RECONTEXTUALISATION

Successful recontextualisation depended in Old Testament times as it does now, on the original contextualisation of faith having drawn meaningfully on the people's experience and their culture. We can see this at work in the development of Israel's theology.

Due to its pivotal geographical location, Israel was inevitably impacted by the surrounding cultures in terms both of key *theological ideas,* and in terms of *source material* used in creating the theologies that found their way into its

---

17   Christopher Wright. *The Mission of God: Unlocking the Bible's Grand Narrative.* Downers Grove: IVP Academic, 2006, 467-8.

sacred texts. A well-known example is that of the prophet Hosea who in the 8th century BCE used Canaanite marriage rituals as imagery in developing his theology of Yahweh's love for the people of Israel even as he confronted them for their apostasy in giving allegiance to other gods (see *Hosea* chapters 1-3).

We might ponder, for example, on the fact that we ourselves rightfully use many of the insights and practices of secular society in Church life. For example, educational and health agencies incorporate legally to provide sound governance structures. They can do so without giving fundamental allegiance to society or the state but always to God. Hosea led people in his time and place towards God, even while drawing on elements of the worldview of non-Israelite peoples. In *Hosea* chapter 2, for example, we see the prophet referring to the Canaanite god Baal whom the people credited as the source of fertility. The word 'baal' was also used in general parlance among the Israelites for lord or husband, but through the prophet God says this term is not to be used because of its connotations with the Canaanite god and all that surrounded his cult. The whole thrust of Hosea's prophetic leadership in this instance indicates that Israel's allegiance was not with God. The people had taken on more than vocabulary from their Canaanite neighbors; they had embraced their worldview!

In weaving its theologies together, Israel's leaders also borrowed from neighboring cultures elements not only of practices, but also of stories with which the people were familiar. At the same time these leaders transformed key aspects of their source material.

An example well known to us is the Mesopotamian cosmogony (account of the origin of the world as held by the Babylonian overlords) known as *Enuma Elish* that deals with battles between gods and provides an account of the formation of the world and of human beings as slaves for the gods. While echoes of the *Enuma Elish* are readily discernible in the first Genesis account of the creation of the world and of human beings (Gen 1:1-2:3) , the contrasts with the biblical text are striking. For example, in *Enuma Elish*, human beings are created out of the blood of the slain god Kingu and are created to be slaves of the gods. In Genesis the creation is very different. Humans are God's vice-regents on earth.

> *Let us make humankind in our image, according to our likeness; and let them have dominion over the fish of the sea, and over the birds of the air, and over the cattle, and over all the wild animals of the earth, and over every creeping thing that creeps upon the earth.* (Gen 1:26).[18]

---

[18] See Mark S. Smith 'Genesis' in John J. Collins, Gina Hens-Piazza, Barbara Reid, OP, and Donald Senior CP (eds). *The Jerome Biblical Commentary for the Twenty-First Century*. London: Bloomsbury, 2022, 205-211.

Mankind, far from being a remnant of dead divinity as in *Enuma Elish*, is in Genesis a creature, an adopted child of God, vice-regent of God on earth.[19]

A second contrast is that the God of the Israelites is clearly depicted as the one and only god. The Babylonians on the other hand, worshipped many gods.

Like faith communities today, the people of Israel shared common experiences with those around them, but endowed these with a different meaning in the light of their founding experience of God as creator and liberator. We know for example from the Genesis account,[20] that the community understood themselves to be invited into the very creative purposes of God in the world, looking after the earth, tilling it and keeping it. In the book of Exodus they are depicted as experiencing redemption from slavery and from sin and, as parties to a covenant with God, they were to act similarly towards their fellow humans. Thus we see that in the Biblical witness contextualisation and then recontextualisation, are not about abstract ideas or disembodied beliefs. Our faith is, and always has been, carried and given life in real communities, and has a definite this-worldly aspect included in its nature and agenda.

Also borrowed from Israel's neighbors was the theological understanding of God as king – the only king Israel acknowledged up until the time its leaders decided in the 11th century BC that, rather than being a contrast society in terms of leadership and governance, they might do better if they were more like their neighbors and had an earthly king. Such a change in governance, a move away from the model of a confederation of tribes, could provide a visible source of unity among the various tribes as they grew in numbers and influence. Such consolidation seemed necessary given the tribes' vulnerability compared with their more powerful neighbours.

Yet they were running a great risk. Far from being counter-cultural in the matter of governance as they had been, Israel found itself in danger of being submerged into the worldview and value system of its neighbours. Inevitably there was turmoil and anguish. 1 Samuel 8 graphically describes the situation as Samuel grew old and the elders came to him and asked that he appoint a king. Having prayed to God, Samuel described to them the likely outcome of taking on this form of governance, namely, slavery and oppression, yet they persisted.

---

19 ibid
20 The Genesis account was redacted at various times in Israel's history, attaining its final form as late as 400 BCE, but it contains narrative traditions that reach back to the 9th and 8th centuries BCE.

But the people refused to listen to the voice of Samuel; they said, "No! But we are determined to have a king over us so that we may be like other nations and that our king may govern us and go before us and fight our battles." When Samuel had heard all the words of the people, he repeated them in the ears of the Lord. The Lord said to Samuel, "Listen to their voice and set a king over them." Samuel then said to the people of Israel, "Each of you return home."

As the subsequent history of Israel attests, God was able to work with the ambiguities and limitations of the situation and, despite a few outstanding kings and many poor ones featuring in that history, began to open new possibilities regarding God's own reign as king. We see evidence of this in so many of the psalms, for example psalm 93 used in Catholic liturgy on the feast of Christ the King:

> The Lord is king, he is robed in majesty;
>   the Lord is robed, he is girded with strength.
> He has established the world, it shall never be moved;
> your throne is established from of old,
> you are from everlasting.
>
> The floods have lifted up O Lord,
>   The floods lift up their voice;
> The floods lift up their roaring.
>
> More majestic than the thunders of mighty waters,
> more majestic than the waves of the sea,
> majestic on high is the Lord!
>
> Your decrees are very sure;
>   holiness befits your house;
> O Lord, forevermore.

There is food for thought here for those of us who find it necessary to take on some of the practices of the broader society in matters such as governance, risk management, and other elements that may be regarded as essential for institutional survival. Can God remain 'king' (that is, reign and be seen to reign) over our lives and institutions? If this is to be the case, do we need to pursue these practices in a counter-cultural way? Where is the evidence that, as we take on what are necessary 'secular' agendas, we wrestle with questions such as these?

God as the mighty king ruling over all the earth features throughout much of Israel's worship and life, and the usage clearly contains elements borrowed from the idea of kingship that they knew from their neighbours' experiences of kingship – but Israel's God was clearly a very different kind of king, one characterised by forgiveness and compassion, one who could bring good out of evil.

If, in recording the community's witness to their relationship with God at work in their lives, Israel's leaders borrowed from surrounding cultures, so in a sense did God 'borrow' certain elements from these cultures. For example, when God's self-revelation was expressed in the form of an agreement with Israel, it was cast in the form of a covenant,[21] the practice of covenant-making of the neighbouring Hittites being borrowed and transformed into a pact with a difference.

Christopher Wright makes the point that these ancient covenants required witnesses for their validity. Located as it was at the crossroads of the known world, Israel's covenantal relationship with God was likewise witnessed by the nations. What over time would the nations actually see? Unfortunately, not enduring fidelity, but more often rebellion and even apostasy.[22]

INTERPRETATION: IDENTIFYING HERMENEUTICAL METHOD

In pursuing the theme of faithful recontextualisation in the Bible, scholars and practitioners need an adequate theory of interpretation to guide their practice. This is because recontextualisation itself is a form of interpretation. Despite pitfalls, recontextualisation of core understandings of Israel's faith continued faithfully throughout Old Testament times and into New Testament times.

For example, in the first third of the first century CE, Jesus critiqued his fellow Jews, particularly the power-holders and the rich who looked down on and oppressed the poor. When new Christians in fledgling Christian communities in the final third of that century encountered these sayings of Jesus from the sources available at the time, these same words may have sounded like a denial of Jewish claims to be the people of God. Of course this is not what Jesus said, nor was it his intention. Faithful recontextualisation of Jesus' teaching required discernment and leadership then as it does now. Under the guidance of the Holy Spirit, this occurred initially in the recontextualisation processes that gave us the Old Testament. Late in the first century CE leaders were called forth who, under the guidance of

---

21　Covenant is one of the most constitutive features of Israel's faith. Several covenants between God and the children of Israel feature in the Old Testament, the central one being that made through Moses on Mount Sinai and recorded in the Book of Exodus.

22　Wright, 2006, 469. Wright cites Micah 1:2 when the prophet calls on the earth and its peoples as witnesses in his 'lawsuit' against Samaria and Jerusalem. Also Jeremiah 6: 18-19 and Amos 3:9. In the latter the nations called upon as witnesses are actually the two great world powers of the time – Assyria and Egypt.

the Holy Spirit, interpreted Jesus' life and death for their communities in times and places removed from their origins. New Testament examples of recontextualisation will be the subject of our next exploration.

3

THE GOSPEL WRITERS RECONTEXTUALISE THE GOOD NEWS:

INDWELLING THE NEW TESTAMENT JOURNEY IN FAITH

The gospels offer an interpretation of events that happened within history. They interpret these events from the perspective of both faith in a God who saves and faith in the risen Christ as integral to 'salvation history'. The gospel writers all believed that Jesus had been raised from the dead, even as they struggled to appreciate the significance of an 'event' that projected Jesus' narrative beyond the bounds of human history.

BACKGROUND TO THE EVANGELISTS' TASK OF RECONTEXTUALISATION

At the time the gospels were written, Jewish culture was in the process of transformation. The Jewish rebellion against the Romans that ran from 67-70 CE had been put down, or was in the process of being put down. In the aftermath Jerusalem, as the centre of the rebellion, was sacked. With that the major symbols of 'Jewishness' in Jesus' time – the temple, temple worship, and the temple priesthood – were all either destroyed or abolished. The economy of the country was effectively ruined. Thus, in writing about events in Jesus' life, the gospel writers were constructing a narrative about an era radically different from the one in which their readers now lived – an era in which for a time it had been possible to be both Jewish and Christian.

In the period after 70 CE, the Pharisees led a movement that would re-establish Jewish identity and cultural practices on a new basis. This came to be known as rabbinical Judaism, a lay led religious movement centred on the synagogue. Judaism, now without land and temple, focused intently upon Torah, while the Christians, facing the same losses, turned to Jesus Christ as the crucified Messiah. This necessarily led to a 'parting of the ways', and it seems that eventually Christians were expelled from the synagogues (see John 9:22;12:42: 16:2). The split amplified major tensions between Jews and Christians, as well as within the Christian communities themselves. The division is particularly evident in the Gospel of John and to some degree in the Gospel of Matthew. For example, Matthew seems anxious that Christian communities do not organise themselves along the lines of the new Jewish communities. In John, 'the Jews', meaning the Jewish leaders, are the enemies of Jesus. None of the gospels say anything good about the Pharisees. This seems more of a reflection of what was happening at the time of writing than a reflection of the actual situation during Jesus' lifetime.

The collapse of the Jewish world as it had been known for centuries had a profound impact on both Jews and Christians alike. The former found the resources to rebuild their culture within the rural communities of Israel and in the Jewish diaspora. The Christian communities created an identity by interpreting Jesus' story within the older Jewish tradition of salvation history.

The leaders of early Christian communities who captured the traditions carried in the communities since the death and resurrection of Jesus, under the guidance of the Holy Spirit, 'changed the narrative' of salvation history recontextualising it and including the Jesus' story, and in Acts, their own story. The gospel writers had the difficult task of contextualising the story of Jesus for gentiles unfamiliar with the context in which it occurred, and recontextualising it for Jewish Christians familiar with the Jewish cultural world and its hopes, but at the same time coming to grips with the significance of Jesus' life death and resurrection as these fitted into the story they had taken for granted. For both groups the leap of faith in Jesus had cultural as well as religious significance. These stories were combined and interpreted from the perspective of God acting in history to offer the gifts of revelation and salvation to all humankind. This recontextualisation took the salvation narrative, and the hope it offered, beyond a particular people, 'to the nations'.

FACING THE TASK OF RECONTEXTUALISATION TODAY

Inspired and assisted by the four canonical Gospel writers, today's Christian leaders can face the task of recontextualising the narrative of the crucified and risen Jesus and his Gospel with a degree of confidence. This is because the Gospel writers have been there before us telling the story of Jesus effectively for their readers and hearers at a time already removed from that in which Jesus lived, died, and was raised from the dead. Can we learn from their leadership? Given that the Gospel is a 'rich and compelling song' that, throughout our Christian tradition has been sung in many keys and with many variations,[1] are we also able to recontextualise that 'song' in a key that captures hearts in our contemporary cultures experiencing the impact of a change of era?

As we have noted in Chapter 1, the contextualising of faith so that it may be understood and rendered meaningful is an essential of God's mission in every culture and every era. It becomes especially challenging in a time of major change when leaders are called upon to help Christians recontextualise their shared faith, because with a change in culture the way in which key understandings are expressed no longer assists the meaning-making processes that nurture Christian life. These must be recast so that the good news of God's creating and redeeming love, as revealed in the life, death and resurrection of Jesus, may continue to capture minds and hearts.

Ours is a time when we are drawn again to awareness of the incarnational nature of Christian faith. Jesus became human in a particular time, place, and culture. Christians believe that his life, death and resurrection, have significance for people in every place, culture and historical circumstance and that its very particularity is essential to its ongoing significance. The reality of this presupposes that people can understand and appreciate the incarnational nature of Christian faith. God's salvation occurs, as was the case for Israel, within history, and very much within particular places and communities.

TOWARDS AN OUTWARD DYNAMIC AND ITS IMPLICATIONS

In delving into the faith history of Jesus' own forebears as depicted in the Old Testament, we see that the relationship between the Israelites and other peoples – often referred to as 'the nations' – was an ambiguous one historically. Across time the weight of understanding tended strongly towards the idea that all would or should be drawn towards God's dwelling place on earth, Jerusalem (see for example Isaiah Chapter 60, a poetic vision in which Jerusalem is the focus of all the nations who bring rich gifts to enhance the physical fabric of Jerusalem and who offer allegiance to Jerusalem's king, who is God of all). The dynamic envisaged was obviously centripetal and carried the implication that, in being drawn to Jerusalem, 'the nations' would be blessed.

---

1 Dean Flemming *Contextualization in the New Testament: Patterns for theology and mission.* Downers Grove: Intervarsity Press, 2005, 296. Dean Flemming is professor of New Testament studies at European Nazarene College, Buesingen, Switzerland.

After Pentecost, the Holy Spirit led the early Christians step by step into a deeper understanding of God's intentions, and to a broader understanding of the Christian community's mission within those intentions. It eventually became clear to them that faith in Jesus Christ also involved a centrifugal, that is an outwards movement to encounter 'the nations' *in situ* with the good news of God's love manifested in Jesus, and with the significance of his death and resurrection.² Clearly, therefore, 'the nations' needed to understand the message in their own language and thought patterns, that is in and through their own culture, which is the only way we humans can truly understand anything. The message had to be contextualised so that it was meaningful in their culture. In this sense the commissioning of the disciples to be bearers of the good news (see Matt 28:16-20) implied a commissioning to employ every effort to contextualise the good news effectively.

As the Christian faith spread across Europe in the Middle Ages and as power in the Catholic Church became centralised in Rome, beginning at the time of Gregory VII (1028-1085) and reaching a high point with the First Vatican Council in the 19th century (1869-1870), this important insight became lost and had to be reclaimed in the 20th century.³

RECONTEXTUALISATION OF FAITH AS THEOLOGICAL PROCESS

If the contextualisation of faith is a theological process, then so too is the recontextualisation of faith within a particular cultural world. In the widely accepted understanding of theology's nature and goal provided by St Anselm of Canterbury (1033-1109), contextualisation and recontextualisation are each truly an exercise in faith seeking understanding, that is in theologising.⁴ In this sense, each of the gospels develops a theology of Jesus and his mission. What can we glean from the text of each gospel about the evangelist's theology of mission? What issues arise for us as we then bring our own lives

---

2 Drawing on the work of Richard Bauckham in *The Bible and Mission*, Michael Goheen provides some useful points on how the centripetal dynamic and the centrifugal dynamic are each important in Christian life and mission. We form community not as an end in itself, but in order to go beyond the community. In moving outwards in mission we encounter people and invite them to become part of the community in order to be enabled, in their turn, to go forth into the world to help its peoples and their societies and cultures to draw closer to the Kingdom of God. Michael Goheen, *Introducing Christian Mission Today*. Illinois: Downers Grove, 2014, 64. We would argue that each dynamic – the outward and the inward – is essential to the other, that each must serve the other, and that both must be kept in tension and balance in the life of healthy Christian communities.
3 See Francis Moloney. 'Scripture Since Vatican II' in Neil Ormerod, Ormond Rush, David Pascoe, Claire Johnson, Joel Hodge (eds). *Vatican II. Reception and Implementation in the Australian Church*. Mulgrave: Garratt Publishing, 2012, 48-49.
4 St. Anselm. *Stanford Encyclopedia of Philosophy* May 2000. Revised 2020.
https://plato.stanford.edu/entries/anselm/#FaiSeeUndChaPurAnsThePro
St. Anselm was treating of faith as the love and trust that seeks deeper knowledge of God.

and cultures into the ambience of each of the gospels?

In what follows, we will briefly sample some key elements of each of the evangelists' presentations of Jesus' mission and note the agenda this provides for the theological task of recontextualisation today.

THE GOSPEL OF MARK – CROSSING BOUNDARIES FOR THE KINGDOM OF GOD

There are differences of opinion among scholars as to the date of Mark's gospel. Francis Moloney offers a convincing argument that the Gospel of Mark was completed shortly after the destruction of the temple in 70 AD.[5] Whatever the historical date, it is important to note that, like the other gospels, that of Mark was finalised several decades after the death of Jesus. Thus it is a construction of the life death and resurrection of Jesus written for people removed in time, place, and culture, from the original events. As we have acknowledged in our introduction, during the interval from the life and death of Jesus to that of the gospels being written, catastrophic changes had occurred in Jewish life and faith. Jerusalem had been captured by the Romans and the temple destroyed. The process of the re-founding of Judaism had begun at Jamnia as we noted above, and as both renewed Judaism and Christianity became established, the split of the Jesus movement from its founding context became well advanced. Each gospel writer faced the task of recontextualising the narrative for people against that background, and did so in his own way, weaving a theology of Jesus and his mission designed to meet their situation and concerns.

How is the mission of Jesus presented in Mark? Very briefly, Jesus' mission is presented very much in terms of crossing boundaries – geographical, social, ethnic – in proclaiming and making present God's kingdom or reigning presence for those 'on the margins'.[6]

In this gospel a great deal of Jesus' teaching and healing ministry takes place in Galilee which, in contrast with the religious, cultural, and political centre of Judaism in Jerusalem, was regarded as somewhat uncivilised. Galilee was also an area at the crossroads of travel and trade and so was a social melting-pot where all sorts of people, both Jews and Gentiles met. Being located predominantly in this setting, Mark's Gospel presents Jesus'

---

5 Francis Moloney *Mark: Storyteller, Interpreter, Evangelist*. Peabody: Hendrickson, 2004.
6 In his work Francis Moloney uses 'the reigning presence of God' rather than 'Kingdom of God', arguing that in the passage of the term from the original Aramaic, into Greek, and then into English, the dynamism of Jesus' usage has been eliminated and what we are left with is more of a static territorial image emphasising the authority of the king. Such limitations do not do justice to either Jesus' proclamation or to that of the Christian tradition that has grown from it. See Francis Moloney *Mark: Storyteller, Interpreter, Evangelist*. Peabody MA: Hendrickson, 2004, 126.

ministry as carried out very much within the geographical margins of Israel and to people on the social margins, that is to the humble folk of the land, the lake, and the villages. However, from the beginning it embraces both Jews and Gentiles. The latter are noted particularly in Mark's retelling of the Jesus' story, alerting the reader in advance to the great shift in understanding about God's mission in the life of the early Christian communities – the shift of focus from God's offer of salvation only to the Jewish people to that of salvation being clearly available to all the nations. See for example, Mark's commissioning of the disciples in Mk 16:15-16:

> And he said to them, "Go into the whole world and proclaim the good news to the whole creation. The one who believes and is baptized will be saved; but the one who does not believe will be condemned.

While in Mark's gospel Jesus' ministry is situated in a limited area geographically, we see the evangelist deliberately depicting Jesus as crossing into the lands east of the Sea of Galilee, that body of water that acts as a kind of bridge between Jewish and Gentile territory, an area where Jews generally preferred not to venture.

> On that day, when evening had come, he said to them, 'Let us go across to the other side'. (Mk 4:35).

The depiction of the great storm and Jesus' calming of the waters should not draw our attention away from Jesus' destination, nor the bridging role played by the lake itself. In chapter 5 of the gospel we find a quite lengthy encounter with the demoniac (Mk 5:1-20) occurring in what was clearly gentile territory.

Mark turns explicitly to a mission among the gentiles in his careful telling of Jesus' two multiplications of the loaves and fishes, one in Israel and the second on the gentile side of the lake, and his healing of gentiles in Mark 6:31-8:10.[7]

From an examination of the gospel text, with gentiles purposefully featured again and again, there can be no doubt that the gentiles are an important component within Mark's target audience. In addition to the examples above, we see that later in the gospel, Jesus speaks of the temple as a 'house of prayer for all nations' (Mk 11:17). He also says that the good news must be proclaimed to all nations (Mark 13:10). The woman who anoints him in the house of Simon the leper at Bethany will, Jesus promises, always be linked to the great commission situated toward the end of the gospel, a commission to go to all nations.

---

[7] Francis Moloney *The Gospel of Mark*. Grand Rapids: BakerAcademic, 2002, 129-164.

Truly I say to you, wherever the good news is proclaimed in the whole world, what she has done will be told in remembrance of her. (Mk 14:9).⁸

Her act of loving service and the proclamation of the good news of Jesus will, in the words of the gospel, always be linked together.

The theme of the good news directed to the whole world is dramatically reinforced at the time of Jesus' death when the curtain of the temple is torn from top to bottom (Mk 15:39). This image of the torn curtain is a way of indicating that the temple is now open to all,⁹ and by extension that God's salvation is available to all. And the first to proclaim Jesus after his death is not a Jewish disciple, but a Roman (gentile) centurion – 'Truly this man was God's Son!' (Mk 15:39).¹⁰

As we encounter the world in a change of era, what are we to make of Jesus' mission to the margins, a mission with a 'Galilean accent'¹¹, a mission with a strong cross-cultural motif? Reflection on Jesus' mission with a 'Galilean accent' reminds us of the often-quoted challenge presented by Pope Francis to those who minister to others as missionary disciples that they take on 'the smell of the sheep'. (*Evangelii Gaudium* #24)¹²

In considering the hermeneutical issues confronting us in reading Mark today, Johannes Nissen, a Danish New Testament scholar whose work bridges mission studies and biblical studies, makes the point that, in the spirit of Mark's presentation, today's disciples must root their mission in the margins of society.

When the gospel makes "somebody" out of the "nobodies" of society, when it restores the self-worth of the marginalized, then **it is truly good news of a new order of life**.¹³

Every society has its Galilee, its marginalised and voiceless.¹⁴ Rather than the centres of power, this 'Galilee' is the starting point for mission. Those

---

8   This passage provides the title and theme of a famous work of feminist biblical theology by Elisabeth Schüssler Fiorenza. *In Memory of Her: A Feminist Theological Reconstruction of Christian Origins*. London: SCM Press, 1983.
9   Moloney, 2006, 109.
10 Johannes Nissen *New Testament and Mission: Historical and Hermeneutical Perspectives*. Frankfurt am Main, Third Edition, 2004, 37-48.
11 Nissen is quoting from Orlando Costas *Liberating News: A Theology of Contextual Evangelism*. Grand Rapids: Eerdmans, 1989. pa-francesco_esortazione-ap_20131124_evangelii-gaudium.html
12 https://www.vatican.va/content/francesco/en/apost_exhortations/documents/papa-francesco_esortazione-ap_20131124_evangelii-gaudium.html
13 ibid, 45. Emphasis added. Despite their being close to 2000 years old, when we enter the gospels, we find ourselves in the company of other readers, and the quality of the narrative begins to affect us.
14 Reflecting on the voiceless, Francis Moloney points out that in Mk 16:8 the women are voiceless, and yet there is the promise of Jesus that they are to carry to Peter, that in Galilee 'there you will see me' (16:7). Jesus will be with those who are fearful, voiceless, and marginalised. This is the same promise made at the last supper in Mk 14:28. (Moloney. Personal communication).

who inhabit the centres of power will always try to co-opt the gospel to their cause, a perennial dynamic only too clear throughout history. Those at the centre of power must of course be confronted, and are likely to respond with oppressive consequences just as occurred in the case of Jesus in his rejection and death. Costas, an evangelical missiologist and theologian, has spoken forcefully of the temptation of gearing the gospel message 'to a select few instead of the harassed multitudes', and finding ourselves 'left with a historically harmless church, a private gospel and a plastic Jesus'. A prophetic, liberating, and holistic mission must ask: Where is our base, who is our target audience, and what is the scope of our evangelistic task?[15] These are central questions in authentic recontextualisation of the Gospel in our society.

THE GOSPEL OF MATTHEW – DISCIPLES ON A GLOBAL MISSION

We will focus further on Matthew's gospel in the final chapter as we draw our study to a close. Here we note briefly note the essence of Matthew's approach to Jesus' mission. It is significant that this is a Gospel addressed to Jewish Christians, probably located in Syria.[16] The themes of this gospel were particularly challenging for them, given their religious history as Jewish people.

In Matthew, disciple-making for the kingdom is the key missional motif. This discipleship is characterised by practical compassion for the suffering. As we see in the great scene of the last judgment in Matthew 25, a scene that features all nations, God's kingdom and his justice are described dramatically, not in abstract terms, but in terms of practical compassion for those most in need.

> *When the Son of Man comes in his glory, and all the angels with him, then he will sit on the throne of his glory. All the nations will be gathered before him, and he will separate people one from another as a shepherd separates the sheep from the goats. Then the king will say to those at his right hand, 'Come, you that are blessed by my Father, inherit the kingdom prepared for you from the foundation of the world; for I was hungry and you gave me food, I was thirsty and you gave me something to drink, I was a stranger and you welcomed me. I was naked and you gave me clothing. I was sick and you took care of me. I was in prison and you visited me . . . (Matt 25:31-46)*

---

15   Orlando Costas *Liberating News: A Theology of Contextual Evangelism*. Grand Rapids: Eerdmans, 1989, 69-70.
16   The Jewish nature of Matthew's Gospel is obvious in many ways not least in how the writer puts emphasis on Jesus as fulfilling the Old Testament scriptures. Jesus is a Jewish messiah, but a messiah for the whole world. Many scholars locate the original community out of which the Gospel came and to whom it was firstly directed as being in Syria.

Readers of the gospel should note that what is sometimes termed the 'great mission command' of Jesus (Matt 28:18-20)

> And Jesus said to then, "All authority is heaven and on earth has been given to me. Go therefore and make disciples of all nations..."

is both a recapitulation of Jesus's teaching ministry prior to his death, but goes beyond this; it is a key to understanding what the gospel is about in the light of Jesus' resurrection and his sending of the Holy Spirit.[17]

These final words of sending are not the only reference in the gospel to disciples being sent forth. For example, in Matt 10:5-16 there is a significant sending of the twelve. It was a sending not to the gentiles, not even to the Samaritans, but to the lost sheep of the house of Israel. By way of contrast, the post-resurrection sending expressed in a mandate to encounter all nations is an outflowing of the community's post-Pentecostal insight into the logic of Jesus' life, death, and resurrection. In the light of the Holy Spirit poured out on them, it became crystal clear that the good news they had been privileged to receive and to experience – Jesus the good news incarnate – must be taken to all nations, not only to the Jews. Thus, mission in Matthew ultimately has a universal, and therefore a multicultural, dimension. This tension between the local and the universal permeates the whole gospel of Matthew.

The centripetal dynamic referred to in Chapter 2 in regard to the relationship of Israel and the nations in Old Testament times, in this gospel, is balanced by a centrifugal dynamic. The great vision of Isaiah's chapter 60, with the multitudes of the world streaming to Mount Sion, has a counterpoint in the final words of Matthew's gospel with the community sent out beyond their comfortable geographical and social settings into the whole world. No longer is the dynamic one of accepting the homage and gifts of the nations; now those who claim Sion (Jerusalem) as their religious centre must go out to the whole world and bring the good news of God's creating and saving love manifested in Jesus to all nations. The poor and oppressed are to have priority, and to be gathered into the community, but the community into which they are gathered is of its nature an outwardly-focused one. Salvation history has taken on a global dimension.

Christian communities today face the challenge of achieving the right balance between gathering and sending. The authenticity of re-contextualised mission is related to this balance.

---

17 ibid, 31.

THE TWO-PART WORK OF LUKE-ACTS – A LIBERATING GOSPEL

In Luke-Acts the liberating, message of Jesus as proclaimed at Nazareth (Luke 4: 18-19) is a key motif with Jesus portrayed in the words of Isaiah as the prophetic one teaching, challenging on behalf of the marginalised, and providing insight into the truth of things:

> *The Spirit of the Lord is upon me,*
> *Because he has anointed me*
> > *to bring good news to the poor.*
> *He has sent me to proclaim release to the captives*
> > *and recovery of sight to the blind*
> > *to let the oppressed go free*
> *To proclaim the year of the Lord's favor.*

The Holy Spirit who figures prominently as a character in Luke's gospel, (for example Luke 1:15; 1:35; l:41; 2:25-26; 3:16; 3:22; 4:1; 4:14; 4:18; 10:21; 11:13,) becomes the principal actor in the Acts of the Apostles.[18] The time of Jesus and that of the Church is linked by the presence of the Spirit.[19]

Luke is unique in that in his work the good news, originally contextualised by Jesus the teacher for his original audiences, is subsequently spread and contextualized for gentiles again and again throughout the empire and to the 'ends of the earth' by Christian communities. In Luke's gospel, the good news to the poor is emphasised as it is in Mark and Matthew. In addition all, and especially the rich, are called to repentance and a profound change of outlook and way of living.

In Luke's gospel we have examples of the scriptures being re-interpreted by Jesus to guide the meaning-making of his disciples, for example in the Emmaus story (Lk 24:13-35).

> *Then beginning with Moses and all the prophets, he interpreted to them the things about himself in all the scriptures* (Luke 24:27).

And similarly to the frightened disciples gathered after Jesus' death.

> *Then he opened their minds to understand the scripture* (Luke 24:45).

This hermeneutical task would be repeated by the Christian leaders in Acts, for example Peter at Pentecost (Acts 2). It remains a key one for us

---

18　For an accessible treatment of the theme of the Holy Spirit as principal protagonist in Acts see Francis Moloney 'Mission in the Acts of the Apostles "The Protagonist is the Holy Spirit"', *The Australasian Catholic Record* Vol 96, No 4, October 2019, 400-410.

19　See for example Nissen, 56-57.

today as we seek to recontextualise the story of Jesus in our time and place in a time of deep change.

In contemplating our own hermeneutical and teaching responsibilities, it is important that as leaders we do not over-spiritualise Jesus' message. In Luke, the mission to the poor has a hard edge. Here it is worth noting that in quoting from Isaiah 61 Jesus omits one phrase dealing with the healing of the broken hearted, and inserts a sentence from Isaiah 58:6 ('to let the oppressed go free'). There are of course so many instances in the gospels when Jesus comforted the broken-hearted – his attention to all aspects of human suffering is not in doubt – but in this, Luke's programmatic passage setting the trajectory of Jesus' ministry, we are left in no doubt that the Lucan Jesus has real physical poverty and oppression in his sights.[20]

As we bring our own societies and cultures into an encounter with this gospel, we need to be well attuned to its demanding message. As we argue in this book, a recontextualisation of both faith and culture – a delving into the roots and a rebuilding of both – is needed in our societies at this time. It is both a privilege and a challenge to ensure that faith is re-contextualised in such a way that it *evangelises culture in the process*. In this process culture will change positively as a new era unfolds. At the same time, in what is effectively a reflexive process, our understanding and appreciation of our Christian faith will also be purified and strengthened.

THE GOSPEL OF JOHN – FAITH AND MISSION

Like each of the other gospels, the Gospel of John has its own importance and particular character, and like them is a profoundly missional document.[21] The theme of sending forth is clear: 'As you have sent me into the world, I have sent them into the world'. (Jn 17:18). It is a theme that will be repeated in the post-resurrection missional mandate: 'Peace be with you. As the Father has sent me, so I send you'. (Jn: 20:21).

As we recontextualise our Catholic faith tradition in a new era, we will need to accompany those within and beyond our communities who are struggling to come to the fullness of faith in difficult circumstances. John depicts people passing through stages of coming to faith – we see the whole gamut from no faith (Jewish leaders Jn 2:13-25); to partial faith (Nicodemus Jn 3:1-21); to full or perfect faith (Mary and the royal official – Jn 2:1-11 and Jn: 4:46-54). These presentations are encouraging as we edge forward

---

20 Nissen, 51.
21 For a treatment of John's gospel from a missional perspective see Therese D'Orsa 'Mission in the Gospel of John: Reflections on a unique spiritual tradition' in Jim and Therese D'Orsa (eds). *New Ways of Living the Gospel*. Mulgrave: Garratt Publishing, 2015.

in our own faith journey striving with the help of the Holy Spirit towards perfect faith in our lives and helping those whom we lead in their own faith journeys.

John's gospel has dimensions of both universality and incarnationality. It does, therefore, offer much to a faith that is incarnated in faith communities, but has a universal dimension. With its echoes of Genesis – 'In the beginning was the Word,' (Jn 1:1) – the gospel's prologue invites its readers into a story with cosmic dimensions, but also one which is encapsulated in a particular place – 'and the Word became flesh and lived among us.' (Jn 1:14).[22]

By the time John's Gospel came to be written[23], the traumatic events of the destruction of the temple were years, even decades in the past, and faith communities were coming to terms with life in a dramatically changed world. As we bring our own lives and context into an encounter with this gospel, we note how the Johannine community dealt with the terminal split from Judaism and the challenge of having to make their own way, given that they had become unwelcome in certain synagogues.[24] As faith communities today, we too are exploring very different ways of being on mission in a situation which has seen the collapse of ways we have known throughout much of our lives. We are exploring the unthinkable in terms of cultural and ecclesial change, practising faith in a digital age, and at the time of writing, in the midst of a global pandemic and a brutal war in Europe (Ukraine), and ongoing similarly disastrous conflicts in Africa and Asia.

John's is a gospel that provides us with insight into the cross-cultural and inter-faith encounters so typical of our own age. We note especially John's depiction of Jesus' encounter with a Samaritan woman – a woman regarded as holding a hybrid faith, and of being of inferior race. She is very clearly portrayed as a truth-seeker, and becomes a missional leader – a forerunner of those who in changing times are emerging in unexpected places and situations. (See John 4:4-42).

THE GOSPEL WRITERS AS MEANING-MAKERS – LITERARY FORM

How were the gospel writers so successful in creating meaning for and with those to whom their gospels were directed? One of the most obvious

---

22 Mary Coloe *John 1-10* Wisdom Commentary Volume 44A. Collegeville, Minnesota: Liturgical Press, 2021, 6.
23 It is generally agreed by scholars that John's Gospel was written between 90 and 100 AD.
24 The fact that Christians had become unwelcome in some synagogues is attested to in John's gospel, e.g. Jn 16:2 'They will put you out of the synagogues…' However, there is evidence from archaeological sites that Christians met in Jewish synagogues in parts of the empire well into the Christian era.
See Judith M. Lieu. *Image and Reality. The Jews in the World of the Christians in the Second Century*. Edinburgh. T & T Clark, 1996.

contributors to the gospel writers' success in recontextualising the story of Jesus lies in their choice of a familiar literary form. Thus, those to whom the Gospel was directed were not distracted by the medium of communication; rather, they found themselves on familiar ground.

The literary form chosen for all the gospel accounts of the life of Jesus, that of the Greco-Roman *bioi* (biography), is particularly significant to our discussion. This was a literary form that differed in certain important respects from what people today expect from biographies.

The *bioi* had the following features:

i. It did not aim to cover the entire life of the subject, but treated that life according to the points the writer wished to make. Hence Mark's Gospel, where there is no account of Jesus' origins or early life – he appears on the scene as an adult – is not ruled out as an example of *bioi*. It takes its place alongside the gospels of Matthew, Luke, and John, each of which includes various imaginative and also profound treatments of Jesus' origins.
ii. Strict chronology was not called for in this literary form, but rather the use of *selected themes* allowed the life and teachings of the subject to have maximum impact. We see that the gospel writers each pursued their chosen themes regarding their theological treatment of Jesus' identity and mission.
iii. Authors of ancient *bioi* often had a target audience in mind and worked their biographical material towards a specific purpose (e.g. in the case of the gospels to instruct readers/hearers about Jesus). Two readily recognisable statements of purpose are as follows:

I too decided, after investigating everything carefully from the very first to write an orderly account for you, most excellent Theophilus, so that you may know the truth concerning the things about which you have been instructed. (Luke: 1:3-4).

Now Jesus did many other signs in the presence of his disciples, which are not written in this book, but these are written so that you may come to believe that Jesus is the Messiah the Son of God, and through believing you may have life in his name. (John 20:30-31).

Is it very clear to ourselves and to those whom we are teaching and leading that we are introducing our hearers to Jesus the life-giver? Are we clear that institutional agendas must not be allowed to hijack, but rather to serve, that purpose?

Luke-Acts also has striking affinities with historical writings of the Hellenistic world. Luke's two-part magnum opus known as Luke-Acts shows characteristics of both biographical and historiographical genres. [25]

The Gospel writers drew on rhetorical conventions of the day to appeal to and persuade their audiences. If the Gospels were read in assemblies, as is believed to be the case,[26] the accounts of events were likely to be lively and compelling. More than a story was being told – as with good storytellers of every era, listeners were encouraged to enter deeply into the action.

Few people at the time could read classical Hebrew and so the use of a simple form of Greek served to make the gospels accessible both in Israel and beyond. The evangelists used common (*koine*) Greek, which it seems safe to assume they felt comfortable with, and so did their audiences. In a change of era we must ask: is the language we use suited to our target audience? Do we ever seek feedback to help us with this?

The gospels were clearly well-inculturated in the world in which they first came to life. However, as Flemming reminds us, these works are not simply biography or historiography, *they are gospels*. Their origin lies in the need of the early Christian communities to present to others God's good news incarnated in Jesus of Nazareth. They are biographies with a higher purpose.

THE GOSPEL WRITERS AS MEANING-MAKERS – TARGET AUDIENCE

As with contemporary Christian leaders, the gospel writers had their own roots in specific communities with their particular questions and needs in regard to education and meaning-making. In terms of wider target audience, however, they probably set their sights beyond one particular community.[27] In this the gospel writers differ from Paul whose letters in the first instance were obviously addressed only to a specific community.

It seems for example that Mark's work was directed to gentiles. It includes latinised terms and Mark puts himself out to explain Jewish terms

---

25 Dean Flemming *Contextualisation in the New Testament*. Downers Grove: InterVarsity Press, 2005, 238.
26 Ibid, 239. Flemming is drawing on the work of Whitney Shiner *Proclaiming the Gospel: First Century Performance of Mark*. Harrisburg: Trinity Press International, 2003.
27 For example the Gospel of Mark is generally believed to have been written for Christians in Rome who had suffered the persecution of Nero. Matthew is believed to have been directed to Jewish Christians in Syria. Similarity in the circumstances of these communities to others across the Mediterranean world would probably, at least to some extent, have been known to the authors. Some of the first recipients of these gospels would also have connections in other places. It seems safe to assume that in terms of target audience there were both an immediate community as well as wider elements in the writers' sights.

and customs which would have been unnecessary for a Jewish audience. Matthew's work, on the other hand, was directed to communities of Jewish converts across the Mediterranean world, communities to which gentiles were also attracted, while Luke targeted small gentile communities of converts similarly spread across the Mediterranean world. John's Gospel was addressed to both Jewish and Gentile converts. As we have noted, there is no inkling of a 'one size fits all' approach taken by the Gospel writers. Have we really learned the lesson of tailoring our proclamation or teaching to the audience with whom we work?

The gospels are, for contemporary readers, quite challenging documents, whose authors sought to re-contextualise the story of Jesus for their immediate audiences as the world in which they lived underwent major changes. Having achieved this aim at least in part, the story then had to be contextualised again and again for people living in the cultures that Christian missionaries encountered in Europe, Asia, Africa, the Pacific, and eventually in Australia!

Part B
CONTEXTUALISATION AND RECONTEXTUALISATION FROM A MISSIOLOGICAL PERSPECTIVE

The missionary thrust of Christian communities continued beyond New Testament times but initiatives proved problematic in both political and theological terms. Politically Christian communities became aligned with administrative forms adapted from the Roman empire resulting in the overlap of Christian religion, politics, and church governance. With the collapse of the Roman Empire in the 5th century CE, the Christian Church, by default, became the major stable influence in civil life and continued to organise itself according to patterns set by the empire.

Theologically, the Christian community was divided as members sought to clarify the meaning of sacraments, the Trinity, and how Jesus could be both God and man. Despite these divisions, the Christian missionary impulse continued both through the agency of groups who were mainstream Christians, and of groups whom the former regarded as heretical. It was these who spread the Gospel east into Asia and south into Africa, while the former spread it north and west into Europe.[1] The missionary strategy in

---

[1] Recent discoveries in Pakistan providing evidence of Christian presence in the 11th century further enlarge existing knowledge of the work of groups such as the Nestorians who left their mark in China as early as the 9th century CE. See Robert McCulloch 'The Kovado Cross: Christian Presence in Pakistan before 1000AD'. *The Far East*. May 2022, 4–5.

this period was generally to convert to Christianity leaders who would then sponsor the conversion of their people.[2]

In Europe the association between leaders of the Catholic community and civic powers often led to problematic levels of evangelisation of ordinary people, with Church rituals inheriting the magical quality that had been part of their previous public religion. Some Church leaders co-opted this understanding to establish their position in society and in the Church. Corruption came to a head with the sale of indulgences sponsored by the pope to fund the building of St Peter's in Rome. In the early 16th century, Luther's call for reform (1517) was not out of place, but it unleashed pent-up political forces that took on a life of their own, both political and theological.

With the Christian Church, split between various Protestant Christian communities and Catholic Christian communities, at loggerheads with each other, the search for peace was not easy. The decisive Catholic event in this period was the Council of Trent (1545-1563) called to resolve theological differences. While the Council failed in this aim, it did identify the need to state Catholic doctrine more clearly and to reform the clergy particularly by standardising their training leading to the establishment of seminaries. This eventually resulted in the clergy being better educated than most Catholics. The unintended consequence of this reform was the creation of a clerical elite within the Christian community. Theologies of priesthood soon emerged that entrenched this position so that ordination and leadership of a faith community became conflated, opening the pathway to clericalism as a dominant feature of Catholic culture as we experience it even today.

The 'discovery' of the New World in the 15th century re-invigorated the Catholic missionary impulse among the major religious congregations whose members were assigned to 'convert the pagans' found initially in the Americas and Asia. To these in the 19th century were added the 'pagans' of Africa and Oceania.[3] The assumption at the time was that if these people had any religion, it must be false.

The missionary experience of the churches in dealing with peoples from other cultures unfolded mainly in the context of colonial expansion from Europe and was based on the mistaken belief on the part of Europeans that indigenous peoples needed to be 'civilised', which meant 'Christianising' them as well, since in the European imagination both went together.

---

2   This chapter in the story of Christian mission is well told in Stephen Bevans and Roger Schroeder's *Constants in Context*. Maryknoll NY: Orbis, 2006.

3   These endeavours became possible with technological improvements in navigation and ship building.

By the 1960s the colonial dynamic had run its course and colonisation was viewed by the powerful European nations as a form of exploitation that had to be resisted. The close association of the churches with colonial administrations became increasingly problematic.

The Catholic missionary experience from the early 20th century onwards had emphasised the need to create an indigenous clergy with indigenous bishops who became important players in building up local Catholic communities across the 20th and into the 21st century.

Those involved in the missionary expansion of the Church into the Americas, Asia, Africa and Oceania learned a good deal about anthropology, not so much by studying it formally as by encountering local peoples, learning their language and customs and coming to slowly understand how local peoples construct meaning and create their individual and collective identities.

These experiences led many missionaries to think the unthinkable – that their way of understanding Christian faith was not the only way, and certainly not the best way for people without a European background to understand and deeply appropriate it. They began to see that indigenous peoples did not share the European 'story' nor the taken-for-granted symbols it contained. They created meaning and identity using other stories and symbols that were as meaningful to them as European ones were to Europeans.

It was experiences such as the above that, by the 1970s, placed the issue of contextualisation centre stage in mission theology. When missionaries returned to Europe and the USA, the state of the Catholic Church they encountered there, given the cultural changes that had occurred while they were away, convinced them of the need to 're-contextualise' faith for Western Christians. They could see clearly that a change of era was occurring. It was also clear that for so many, Christian faith and practice had lost their meaning and no longer engaged people, especially the young.

This is the part of the Catholic story we seek to take up in what follows. We employ the terms 'culture' and 'worldview' in telling the story and so offer a working definition of both that will be further developed and clarified in later chapters. For the present 'culture' can be taken as meaning 'how things are done around here', or 'our way of life' and 'worldview' can be equated with the frame of reference a people or an individual uses in making sense of their culture.

4
CONTEXTUALISATION AND RECONTEXTUALISATION:

CROSS-CULTURAL MISSION EXPERIENCE

In Chapter One we made the point that much has been learnt from the churches' missionary experience, particularly their engagement with non-European cultures. In this chapter we expand on this topic to identify the difference between 'contextualisation' and 'recontextualisation' as this emerged in recent cross-cultural missionary experience. From a logical point on view something must be 'contextualised' before it can be 're-contextualised'.

CONTEXTUALISATION

The term 'contextualisation' coined originally in Protestant missiological circles refers to the fact that, when a person goes from one country to another to work on behalf of the Gospel, that person has to negotiate a change of culture. How they do this has a significant impact on whether or not they are effective as cross-cultural missionaries. An essential goal of cross-cultural mission work is to render Christian faith meaningful for people. Mission personnel have to come to terms with the fact that the people who host the missionaries relate to the world within a different frame of reference from their own. What the locals take as 'normal' and 'right' is very likely to differ, at least to some degree, from the constructions of 'normal' and 'right' brought by the outsiders, because each party operates out of a different language and interpretive schema. The result has often been confusion, suspicion and unnecessary conflict.

Many of the missionaries who participated in the great Catholic missionary movement into South America from the 16th century onwards, and in the second Christian missionary movement, Protestant and Catholic, of the 19th and 20th centuries into Asia, Africa, and Oceania, failed to understand that they did not bring a 'pure' understanding of Christian faith to their cross-cultural missionary encounters. They took for granted that their own culture, which defined what was 'normal' and 'right' for them, should also define what was 'normal' and 'right' for others. Their understanding of Christian faith also reflected the assumptions of their own culture as to *how people learn, how they develop as moral beings*, and *how they ought to organise themselves as a society*.

Given the limits of theological understanding at the time, missionaries from the 15th to the late 19th and early 20th centuries generally believed their fundamental purpose was saving the souls of peoples who would otherwise be lost, that is, fail to achieve their eternal salvation. Missionaries saw themselves as bringing to these people salvation of a particularly 'spiritual' kind. To access salvation, understood as 'getting to heaven', people had to be baptised and brought into the Christian community, because the firm belief was that outside this community of faith there was no 'salvation'. In summary, the Catholic Church's mission was understood as proclaiming the Gospel, saving 'souls', and planting and nurturing church communities to sustain and continue this work. Of course, acting out of a deep sense of Christian charity, they also brought substantial material assistance where possible, but the saving of souls remained the over-arching priority.

The biblical and theological renewal of the 20th century would provide helpful insight into the nature of the Church's mission. Catholics would be reminded once again that the two dimensions of human life – the physical, that is life in the world as we know it, and the spiritual, that is life beyond this world – should not be separated, because their intrinsic connection reflects their relationship in the creating and redeeming work (mission) of God as revealed to human beings. Any sense of hierarchy between these two elements betrays the balance on which the whole Judeo-Christian tradition rests.

Returning to the wisdom available from the experience of the missionary movement of recent centuries, we see that, although there were some outstanding examples to the contrary, many missionaries during these centuries lacked an understanding of what today we call 'culture'. This is not surprising given that the social science of cultural anthropology did not emerge until the late 19th century, and therefore was not included in their preparation for what we term today as 'cross-cultural mission'.[1] European peoples tended to think of human difference in terms of

---

[1] Even in such recent times, in the experience of the writers of this volume, some personnel have made their way into cross-cultural mission service – without sufficient or indeed any cultural preparation – on the mistaken assumption that their professional knowledge could be fruitfully

'civilisation' or the perceived lack thereof. In this perspective they saw themselves as the means by which not only Christian faith came to colonial peoples, but also 'civilisation' arrived as well. Their commitment to the introduction of Western medicine, Western-style schooling, and Western-style administration was often comparable to their commitment to bringing Christian faith. One was seen as the complement to the other.

All this is tantamount to saying that the history of Christian mission often overlapped the history of European colonisation, so closely were the two processes integrated within European colonies. In Europe, governments sometimes funded education for 'foreign missionaries'.[2] Even in the secular sphere, mission and colonialism were seen as two sides of the one project – bringing 'civilisation' to peoples who were judged from the perspective of the European worldview to be 'pagan' and 'primitive'.

The European Enlightenment of the 17th and 18th centuries succeeded in embedding into the Western worldview what is known as the 'secularisation principle', the separation of Church and state in the public domain and the relegation of religion to the personal and private domain. Ironically, however, the very public connection between mission and colonisation tended to continue in the colonies, a fact that demonstrates just how close the connection between the two was taken for granted in those locations.

In the colonial world, local peoples often decided, or were forced, to abandon or repress their culture and religion on becoming Christian. In seeking advancement within a colonial regime this seemed to many locals to be a sensible move. However, the pragmatic nature of such commitment to Catholicism or Protestantism was clearly problematic. In such circumstances, the understanding and practice of faith was not deeply contextualised. It is extraordinary that, despite this, many of the colonised who embraced Christianity developed deep faith in far from optimal circumstances. In the case of others, however, the faith held remained superficial or syncretic.

MODERN CONCEPT OF CULTURE

As we have noted, what many Christian missionaries lacked was a deep understanding of the way of life (using modern terminology we would call this 'culture') of the peoples they served and how and in what way this gave them an identity different from Europeans. Towards the end of the 19th century, the discipline of anthropology began to take shape and with this

---

transferred without knowledge of the culture and worldview of those to whom they were seeking to minister.

2   For instance, the Prussian government funded the first department of missiology. Hans-Werner Gensiche, 'Warneck Gustav', in *Biographical Dictionary of Christian Missions*, ed. Gerald H. Anderson. New York: Macmillan Reference USA, 1998, 718.

came an emerging understanding of 'culture' as 'the way of life of a people', a 'way of life' shaped by the environment in which they live. This 'way of life' includes the framework they use to construct meaning.

Cultures were recognised as 'successful' to the extent that they enabled a people to meet their human needs and to live together somewhat peacefully in a particular environment. In trying to understand a culture, pioneer anthropologists sought to explore these issues by systematic observation. They were 'outsiders' to a culture trying to come to an understanding of the way 'insiders' made sense of things.

Explorations were carried out with *isolated peoples* in such places as the USA, Canada, the Pacific, New Guinea, and Australia. The anthropologists' initial assumption was that in dealing with these groups they were exploring earlier stages in the emergence of 'civilisation'. At the time, scholarly thinking in the academy was in the thrall of Darwin's theory of biological evolution and applied it to human ways of life, assuming them also to be subject to evolution. The belief was that cultures could be measured against the yardstick of what was considered to be 'civilisation'. In this perspective Western culture represented the zenith in cultural evolution and that by comparison all other cultures were inferior. This belief made no sense at all to the Chinese, Korean, or Japanese, for example, whose complex and sophisticated cultures predated those of Europe and who remained convinced that their cultures were superior to those of Europe.

The emerging perspective in anthropology was that European cultures were 'successful' because they enabled European peoples to live together relatively peacefully within their national borders. However, history also demonstrates that Europeans found it difficult to survive in the less benign (for them) physical and social environments encountered in Asia, Africa, Central and South America, or even parts of Australia. In such places, the indigenous peoples often had a successful history of survival reaching back thousands of years. Judged by indigenous standards, European culture was a 'failure' because it did not prepare Europeans to survive in these environments.

The conclusion reached quite early in the development of modern anthropology was that 'culture' is a relative concept and that the notion of 'civilisation', as then being used as a synonym of culture, was meaningless. 'Success', in anthropological terms, is measured by the capacity of a society to survive changes in its environment. Those that do not adapt to such changes simply fail or are absorbed by those societies that do.

MISSIOLOGY AND ANTHROPOLOGY

Anthropology presented significant challenges to missionary work in the late 19th and early 20th centuries. Anthropologists were interested in the cultures of the same peoples to whom missionaries were sent. The former were of the view that the latter often acted as destroyers of culture through their lack of understanding of local peoples. More positively, however, missionaries were often scrupulous in recording the customs and languages of the peoples they served. They did this so that those who followed them could build on their work. Today many indigenous languages survive because of these efforts.

The endeavours of missionaries to record local customs and languages provided something of a treasure trove of data for anthropological research once it was discovered in the libraries of Catholic universities such as KU Leuven, or in the those of missionary religious congregations. In due course, missionaries began to take the findings of anthropologists seriously, and the anthropologists came to appreciate the work being done by missionaries in recording elements of the cultures of many peoples. A process of mutual learning began to take place once both groups realised that they shared a common project, namely, *to understand the worldview* that underpins a people's way of life, and how this worldview influenced that way of life. Understanding the worldview that underpinned a culture was central not only to understanding how the culture functioned, but also to how the Christian gospel could be meaningfully offered to its members.

Anthropology provided missionaries with insights into the ways in which their work with indigenous peoples had been flawed by lack of understanding of their culture and worldview. Missionaries came to recognise that to contextualise faith in a way that was meaningful to people living in a culture different from their own, they had to recognise areas of legitimate difference in ideas about what was 'normal' and what was 'right'. They also had to realise that their understanding of the Gospel and of Christian tradition was strongly shaped by their European culture. Thus, while they could challenge local conceptions of what was 'normal' and 'right', local leaders could question the European assumptions implicit in their presentation of the Gospel. The concept of mission began to move from monological engagement with the person or group who was 'other', to a dialogical engagement with cultures and the meaning frameworks that underpinned them. The shift gained pace with the collapse of colonialism in the 20th century.

Armed with such insights, Christian missiologists began to re-explore the biblical texts. There they discovered that Paul and the Gospel writers were experts in contextualising and recontextualising Christian faith for the various audiences they sought to influence. They also discovered that recontextualisation was integral to understanding the Old Testament as noted in Chapter 2. A consequence of all this work was that anthropology became an integral part of training for professional cross-cultural missionaries.

CONTEXTUALISATION IS DIALOGICAL

What Western missionaries learned from their study of anthropology was that, when they encounter peoples of other cultures, their presentation of the Gospel necessarily comes within a Western wrapping. Unless the Western assumptions and expressions constituting this wrapping are addressed, it is often hard for other peoples to make sense of the gospel or the Christian beliefs and practices that have developed within the Western Christian tradition. In terms of Christian faith, as we noted in our introductory chapter:

> Contextualisation is the process of working with the Gospel received and appropriated in one cultural context and rendering it meaningful for people living in another cultural context. Contextualisation involves the transfer of meaning **across cultural boundaries.**

Missionaries have discovered that the first step in contextualisation is learning the language of the people being evangelised so that it is possible to communicate with them directly. Mastering the language is the principal gateway into another culture.

Contextualisation is a dialogical process. A Christian missionary can put questions to the local peoples about how their culture functions, based on his or her understanding of the Christian message. But equally, the local people can put questions to the missionary about his or her particular understanding of the gospel. In this way, new insights arise into the meanings central to a culture as well as into the meanings central to the gospel. In the process of contextualisation the links between a culture and faith are revealed, the meaning of both expands for those involved in the encounter, and both parties to the dialogue are enlightened.

CONTEXTUALISATION OF FAITH: SOME OUTSTANDING EXAMPLARS

An example of the contextualisation process at work in Church history is found in what is known as 'the rites controversy'. This occurred in the 17th century as a result of the work of Jesuit missionaries in China. The Jesuit approach to mission was often different from that of other missionary groups such as the Franciscans and Dominicans who followed the 'saving souls' and 'church planting' models, often without attention to the way of life shaping the humanity of those whom they were addressing. While some Jesuits such as Francis Xavier followed the model of maximising converts and baptising them in great numbers with little attention to their culture, others took a different approach.

Matteo Ricci (1552-1610) made the decision to evangelise Chinese people from within Chinese culture, rather than as a missionary standing outside it. This was no mean feat because, up to that time, no Westerner had been welcomed into the Chinese court. Ricci trained as a Chinese scholar and became fluent in the language, literature and art. Through his European training he was already a skilled astronomer and cartographer. This combination of skills saw him win patronage from the Chinese emperor and enabled him to enter the imperial court. Having established himself in this way, he began a ministry to spread the Christian faith among members of the court. Ricci learned what was taken as 'normal' and 'right' within Chinese culture and sought to make the gospel meaningful for people living according to this worldview.

A problem for the growth of Christianity in China at the time was the Confucian custom of venerating the dead. While most missionaries saw this as a form of idolatry, Ricci interpreted it as a cultural custom, an expression of Confucian philosophy and worldview with no particular religious significance. His stance drew opposition from other missionary groups working in China who appealed to Rome for a ruling on the matter. This came some three centuries later, affirming Ricci's stance! Ricci's interpretation of Chinese rites viewed them in terms of the worldview of their culture, rather than as a stand-alone practice interpreted from a European perspective.

Ricci was not the only early missionary to evangelise from within a culture. His fellow Jesuit, Roberto de Nobili (1577-1656) followed his example in India as did Alexandre de Rhodes (1593-1660) in Vietnam.[3]

CONTEXTUALISING FAITH IN AUSTRALIA

Contextualisation as described above raises some important questions for the transmission of Christian faith in the Australian cultural context today:

---

[3] Building on the work of others, the very talented de Rhodes became so integrated into Vietnamese culture that he was able to produce a Vietnamese-Portuguese-Latin dictionary and the first catechism in the Romanised script. See Peter C. Phan. *Mission and Catechesis: Alexandre de Rhodes and Inculturation in Seventeenth-Century Vietnam.* Maryknoll, N.Y: Orbis, 2005.

What are the points of connection between Christian faith and Australian culture and how have these evolved over time?

Put another way:

How effectively has Christian faith been contextualised in Australian culture up to the present time?

In terms of the dialogical process of mission described above:

What questions does Australian culture put to Christian faith?

In the previous chapter we noted that the Holy Spirit is present and at work in all cultures. That is, there are elements in all cultures that serve as the 'seeds of the Word' in the phrase attributed to Justin Martyr, an early father of the Church (c100-c165 AD). What are these elements – these seeds of the Word – in our culture?

In convoking the recent Plenary Council 2020 the bishops of Australia made much of the need to 'listen to what the Spirit is saying' at this time. While always timely, this invitation seems somewhat ironic in the circumstances given the lack of attention paid so far to uncovering how the Spirit has been at work in Australian culture(s) for thousands of years, and up to the present. Indeed, it is hard to find many theological works that treat this matter seriously.[4]

The issue is also a lacuna in the Religious Education curricula used in Australian Catholic schools. Limitations in how Christian faith has been contextualised in Australia alerts us to problems that are likely to arise in exploring what 'recontextualising Christian faith' might mean in the emergent Australian cultural context.

In conclusion, we note again the difference between contextualisation and recontextualisation.

Contextualisation involves *the transfer of meaning across a cultural boundary* through a process of dialogue among parties that stand on each side of the boundary.

---

[4] An exception is the exploratory work focused on the then contemporary Australian culture of Australian theologian John Thornhill SM in his book *Making Australia: Exploring Our National Conversation*. Newtown: Millennium Books, 1992, and Houston, Jim editor. *The Cultured Pearl: Australian Readings in Cross-cultural Theology and Mission*. Melbourne: Victorian Council of Churches, 1986.
Following the bicentenary of European settlement in this country (1988) there was, particularly across the subsequent two decades, a considerable output of work attempting to theologise in the Australian context, e.g. Gideon Goosen. *Australian Theologies: Themes and Methodologies into the Third Millennium*. Strathfield: St Pauls's Publications, 2000.
Journals such as *Australasian Catholic Record*, *Compass Theology Review*, (till 2016) and *Pacifica* (till 2017) are also fruitful sources for Australians doing theology in the post-Vatican period. Articles vary in the degree of their engagement with Australian Culture.

The dialogue negotiates the difference in worldview of the parties involved. This is the classic cross-cultural missionary situation.

Recontextualisation involves the transfer of meaning within a cultural boundary when the worldview underpinning the culture undergoes a major change.

It also involves a process of dialogue, but in this case it is *a dialogue among people of the same culture* as they grapple with the implications of this change.

In Europe, a particular understanding of Christian faith was contextualised in Medieval times, and some version of this contextualisation was transported across the world in the various missionary movements. But the meaning-system that underpinned this contextualisation has since undergone major changes – during the long modern period (from the 17th to the early 20th century) and during the shorter postmodern period that began in the late 1970s. Although Australians continue to be very much influenced culturally by the secularity which is a major characteristic of modernity, a new cultural factor generally termed 'postsecular' is emerging. This is the result of the fact that, although formal religious affiliation has fallen in the West, dramatically in some places, religion continues to be an important factor in the lives of many, and under the impact of globalisation, this influence is growing. However, what people interpret as religion is also changing!

Postsecularity recognises the importance of religious people making their voices heard in the public square. In Australia we are living under the impact of the cultural manifestations of all three periods simultaneously – modern, postmodern, and postsecular – which makes life complex. As noted in our introduction, it is not a matter of one period effectively replacing another; it is more a matter of the cultural expressions of one period sitting alongside those of the previous periods.

Today we live in a postsecular culture influenced by insights that emerged *in all three periods*. These changes have resulted in many people struggling to make sense of faith or its place in their lives. Recontextualisation in our present context must take into account the multiple interpretations of what is 'normal' and 'right' that have resulted from these shifts in the framework that Western people employ in making sense of their lives.

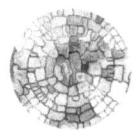

5

CULTURE: THE FRAMEWORK WITHIN WHICH WE MAKE MEANING

As discussed in the previous chapter, in the light of recent cross-cultural mission experience, the concept of culture emerges as central in addressing both contextualisation and recontextualisation. In cross-cultural encounter the issue of meaning-making is thrown into sharp relief because the culture being encountered is not the visitor's original frame of reference.

In this chapter the aim is to develop some clarity around the concept of 'culture' as this term is used in anthropology. We proceed bearing in mind that 'culture' is acknowledged by many scholars and commentators as a notoriously 'slippery' concept. However, it is a key element in our exploration of recontextualisation because culture is central in enabling faith to remain meaningful when the context in which it is constructed undergoes deep change. Hence, we take time to come to grips with this vital area. However, we also need to note that context cannot be equated fully with culture since context also includes the history of a society that leads to the construction and development of the culture.

TWO PERSPECTIVES ON CULTURE – SYNCHRONIC AND DIACHRONIC

'Culture' provides us with a conceptual way of explaining *human difference*. The experience of cultural difference is as old as human society, stretching back at least to the point when people began to tell stories about themselves and thus to distinguish 'our way' from 'your way'. Since 'our way' depends on 'our story', the story of any social group is an important facet of its culture. In fact, culture, society, and history are concepts corresponding to human realities that intertwine.

A culture can be examined from two perspectives: synchronic (how things stand at the present time) or diachronic (how things have changed across time). If we view culture from a synchronic perspective, we are interested in how the culture functions *now*. Early anthropologists adopted this perspective which, while valuable, produced a rather limited, because static, understanding of culture.

When examined from a *diachronic* perspective, the focus is on how the culture came to have the particular configuration that it has today. This involves studying *the mechanisms by which a culture changes and develops*.

In making sense of any culture, it is necessary to keep both the synchronic and the diachronic perspectives in balance.

Highly regarded Catholic theologian, Robert Schreiter, points out that there is no general agreement, even among anthropologists, about the meaning of culture.[1] The reason for this is because across history this meaning has evolved, with the result that it has multiple formulations depending on the place and stage in its evolution in which a particular author is embedded.

In the next chapter we trace four broad stages through which the formulation of the concept of culture has passed:

1. Classicist understanding (ancient times until the late 19th century).
2. Modern understanding (late 19th century until 1960s).
3. Postmodern critique (1970s until the 2000s).
4. Postsecular-postmodern (2000s until now).

In accounting for collective human differences, the meaning of 'culture' has expanded as we have moved from one stage to another. This movement is from a purely synchronic to a more diachronic understanding as discussed above. For the moment, we will place the spotlight on the synchronic understanding of culture.

CULTURE – A PRACTICAL REALITY

People were intuitively aware of the existence of 'culture' long before it became the subject matter of the discipline of cultural anthropology and was systematically studied and analysed at the academic level. For example, the quotation below from Benjamin Franklin was written in 1785, over a

---

[1] Robert Schreiter 'Inculturation of Faith or Identification with Culture?' in Norbert Greinacher and Norbert Mette eds. *Christianity and Cultures. Concilium* 94/2. London: SCM Press, 1994, 17. Robert Schreiter died in 2021. He was an esteemed professor of theology working for over forty years at Catholic Theological Union Chicago. He was especially well known and appreciated for his work on reconciliation within societies. In the above article (p 17), Schreiter argues that there is no general agreement among theologians not only about 'culture' but also about 'faith' as well, so discussions about the relationship between faith and culture are bound to be problematic unless clear understandings are agreed upon.

century before anthropology was established as an academic discipline.

Cultural anthropology is the modern discipline that has 'culture', and the human being within culture, as its principal subject matter. Many other disciplines also study 'culture', but as a topic of secondary interest. These include history, the social sciences, the human sciences, hermeneutics, political science, and theology.

As we noted in the previous chapter, Christian missionaries travelled to faraway places and studied isolated peoples long before cultural anthropologists began to do the same thing at the end of the 19th century. A great deal of anthropological data was collected by missionaries resulting in 'mission anthropology' becoming a branch of the discipline in the mid 20th century, and assuming central importance for those being prepared for mission work in cross-cultural settings. Their experience in these settings was instrumental in the notion of contextualisation gaining validity in theological education in the West.

In the chapters that follow we draw on the work of two foundational figures in the development of mission anthropology, Catholic mission anthropologist Professor Louis Luzbetak SVD (1918-2005), and Mennonite Professor Paul Hiebert (1932-2007).

CULTURE AND HUMAN DIFFERENCE: CASE STUDY

That culture is a real phenomenon employed in accounting for human difference is made clear in the following incident recounted humorously by Benjamin Franklin, one of the founding fathers of the United States of America.[2]

Savages, we call them

Savages we call them, because their manners differ from ours, which we think the perfection of civility; they think the same of theirs.

Perhaps, if we could examine the manners of different nations with impartiality, we should find no people as to be without rules of politeness; nor any so polite as not to have some remains of rudeness.

The Indian men, when young, are hunters and warriors; when old, counsellors; for all, their government is by the counsel or advice of the sages; there is no force, there are no prisons, no officers to compel obedience, or inflict punishment. Hence, they generally

---

[2] Benjamin Franklin was writing almost a century before the founding of cultural anthropology as an academic discipline, that is before the time when 'culture' became formulated as 'the way of life' of a people.

study oratory; the best speaker having the most influence. The Indian women till the ground, dress the food, nurse and bring up the children, and preserve and hand down to posterity the memory of public transactions. These employments of men and women are accounted natural and honourable. Having few artificial wants, they have abundance of leisure for improvement in conversation.

Our laborious manner of life, compared with theirs, they esteem slavish and base; and the learning on which we value ourselves, they regard as frivolous and useless. An instance of this occurred at the treaty of Lancaster, in Pennsylvania, anno 1774, between the government of Virginia and the Six Nations. After the principal business was settled the commissioners from Virginia acquainted the Indians in a speech that there was at Williamsburgh a college, with a fund, for educating Indian youth; and that if the chiefs of the Six Nations would send down half a dozen of their sons to that college, the government would take care that they should be well provided for, and instructed in all the learning of the white people.

It is one of the Indian rules of politeness not to answer a public proposition on the day that it is made: they think that it would be treating it as a light matter, and they show it respect by taking time to consider it, as of a matter important. They therefore deferred their answer till the day following when their speaker began by expressing their deep sense of the kindness of the Virginia government, in making them that offer.

'For we know' says he 'that you highly esteem the kind of learning taught in those colleges, and that the maintenance of our young men, while with you, would be very expensive to you. We are convinced, therefore, that you mean to do us good by your proposal; and we thank you heartily. But you who are wise must know that different nations have different conceptions of things; and you will therefore not take it amiss, if our ideas of this kind of education happen not to be the same with yours. We have had some experience of it; several of our young people were formerly brought up at the colleges of the northern provinces; they were instructed in all your sciences; but when they came back to us they were bad runners; ignorant of every means of living in the woods; unable to bear either cold or hunger; knew neither how to build a cabin, take a deer, or kill an enemy; spoke our language imperfectly; were therefore unfit as hunters, warriors or counsellors; they were totally good for nothing. We are not, however, the less obliged for your kind offer, though we decline accepting it; and to show our grateful sense of it, if the gentlemen of Virginia will send us a dozen of their sons, we will take great care of their education, instruct them in all we know, and make men of them.'[3]

This incident would have been explained in the 18th century not in terms of 'culture', but in terms of 'civilisation'. The commissioners from Virginia would have seen themselves as 'civilised', thanks to their 'education'. They would have judged the representatives of the Six Nations to be 'savages' because they lacked 'education'.

The commissioners' attitude highlights the *classicist understanding* of culture which holds that 'our way of life' should be normative for all other peoples. This means that 'our way' of understanding things, our norms, our beliefs, our way of organising society, and our approach to learning etc, provides the template by which all other peoples can be judged. 'Civilisation' implies a *normative* understanding of human difference.

Classicism provided the dominant model in accounting for human differences in the Western colonial period (15th to the mid 20th centuries). Overcoming its negative legacy and reclaiming local cultures, including their religious dimension, has become a major project in the post-colonial era.

Societies in many developing countries, and indigenous societies in developed countries, are presently recovering from a period in their history when they were victims of cultural domination by various Western powers and suffered under the tyranny of classicism.

MODERN UNDERSTANDING OF CULTURE

If we look at the case study above from the perspective of cultural anthropology, we can identify some important features of 'culture'.

- In the modern understanding, 'culture' equates to 'a people's way of life'.[4]

In the example above, we are dealing with two quite different cultures, rather than with 'civilisation' or the lack of it. Because each group has its own 'way of life', each has its own way of understanding what is 'normal'

---

[3] Benjamin Franklin in Paul Hiebert *Cultural Anthropology*. Philadelphia: J.B. Lippincott Company, 1976, 13-14.
[4] In the example above, we are dealing with two quite different cultures, rather than with 'civilisation' or the lack of it. Because each group has its own 'way of life', each has its own way of understanding what is 'normal' and what is 'right' for the education of its young people.

and what is 'right' for the education of its young people. This example makes it clearer that:

- 'Culture' provides each group with a unique, though not exclusive, perspective on life.
- 'Culture' is a function of the environment in which each group lives. The men of Virginia lived in towns where goods and services were provided via the local economy. The people of the Six Nations lived off the land and had to create their own economy.
- The skills needed to survive in these different environments have to be learned, and they are quite different. The skill set needed to survive in the wild is deemed quite useless for surviving in towns (and vice versa).
- 'Culture' is related to what people in a society come to value and pass on to the next generation. The values deemed important by the Six Nations people are quite different to the values of the commissioners from Virginia. Each group lives according to its own particular norms.
- Despite obvious cultural differences, the two groups hold some values in common. Therefore, they shared some norms, such as the need for civility, and the education of the young. They agreed on the form civility should take, but not on the form education of the young should take.

The above interpretations highlight important aspects of the modern understanding of culture.

GIVING SHAPE TO THE MODERN UNDERSTANDING OF CULTURE: LUZBETAK

Louis Luzbetak SVD provides a sound working definition embracing the principal features of the modern or empirical understanding of culture. It also provides us with a useful basis for addressing later developments in the understanding of culture.

Luzbetak's approach can be paraphrased as follows. Culture is:

> ... the plan, or design for living, that a society develops over time allowing its members to meet their basic human needs, to co-exist peacefully, and to collaborate in meeting challenges posed by living in their particular environment.

The components of this definition can be explained further as follows:[5]

---

5   Cf. Louis Luzbetak SVD *The Church and Cultures: New Perspectives on Missiological Anthropology.* Maryknoll NY: Orbis Books; 1988,156ff.

1. A plan for living together peacefully

- A society's 'plan' is *more or less comprehensive* in that it covers most aspects of life within that society. When it comes to culture, the whole is greater than the sum of its parts because the parts are interconnected in creating webs of meaning.
- The 'plan' is *more or less successful*. If it were not, then the society would collapse and there would be no culture, only chaos. Since culture represents 'success', for members of the society, cultural change at first seems counterintuitive. Why make changes when things are succeeding? Culture thus becomes a conservative force in many societies.
- The 'plan' is *a thing of the mind*. Once developed, a culture is learned and passed on from generation to generation. In this process it evolves to deal with new contingencies. How this occurs tends to be a characteristic of particular cultures.
- The 'plan' finds expression in *various cultural forms* (language, images, concepts, patterns of relationship, rituals, etc). An outside observer can infer the meaning that these forms have for members of the society and so identify important cultural values and norms. This interpretation might be right or wrong and needs to be validated by cultural insiders.
- The 'plan' *operates at multiple levels* and is shaped by elements that are largely taken for granted and so operate below the level of public awareness. As a result, the culture is often opaque to the members of a society. Values and worldview, the 'depth' elements in a culture, are not easily accessible to those outside the culture and are invisible, that is taken for granted, by those within the culture. When different groups interact, this factor often results in unintended misunderstandings.
- The 'plan' underpins the *'way of life of a people'*.
- The 'plan' is *passed from generation to generation* in the form of 'stories' that carry the narrative of a people. Among these cultural narratives the most important are the genesis stories, the stories of how the group formed into a society in the first place. (The Old Testament, for instance, tells the genesis stories of Israel, just as the New Testament carries the genesis stories of the Christian faith community).

2. Culture is Environment Specific

For Luzbetak, the 'environment' in which a culture develops has three important dimensions: physical, social, and ideational.

- The *physical* environment is the setting in which people live, are fed, and survive. A culture comes under pressure when this changes (as we see with climate change today). The 'plan' for living together peacefully has to adapt to meet the challenges posed by changes in the physical environment or in security – conditions such as food or housing for example.
- The **social** environment refers to the social arrangements, within which a society functions for example those pertaining to the law, education, government etc.
- The **ideational** environment – values, norms and ideas, myths, symbols and meanings – about how things should be. These underpin the various norms and practices associated with a particular people.

A major change in any one of these three dimensions creates a pressure to adapt the society's 'plan for living' and so for the culture to evolve.

As a thing of the mind 'the plan' inherent in any culture is meaningful for people living in that particular society. Culture provides members of a society with the framework within which meanings are created, transmitted, and sustained. Since cultures that survive are by that fact demonstrably 'successful' in adapting to their environment, culture understood in the modern sense, *is a relative concept, not a normative concept.*

Considering a particular culture to be normative is the mistake made by all forms of classicism. Classsicism takes one culture (e.g. European, Chinese, Japanese, or North American) as normative for other peoples.

FAITH AND CULTURE

Faith, if it is to be meaningful, needs to make sense to people living within a particular cultural framework. There are three possible situations where this is important:

1. Where Christian faith is being introduced into an existing cultural framework in which it has not previously been present. This is the situation calling for *contextualisation*.
2. Where Christian faith is already present in a culture and major changes occur in the existing cultural framework. This is the situation for *recontextualisation* and calls for serious pedagogical rethinking on the part of educators. This is the situation educators face today in Western societies.
3. Where the understanding of Christian faith evolves and creates new understandings of the Church's mission in history.

As we have noted above, the meaningfulness of a particular cultural framework is challenged whenever there are major changes in its environment – physical, social or ideational. Such changes create the need to recontextualise the culture, that is, to re-establish it as a reliable frame of reference in the creation of meaning.[6] The difficulties posed in adopting changes occurring at Vatican II often related to how faith was contextualised in a particular culture.

We see cultural dynamics at work currently with the rise of social media as a means of communication. While initially appearing harmless, social media have quickly evolved, resulting in consequences that may be very harmful, such as facilitating extreme online bullying, creating political and social disruption, or supporting human trafficking, to name but a few. Such impacts on a society's plan for living together more or less peacefully, are creating the need for governments to enact legislation that counters social media's negative effects. In this case, developments in technology lead to significant changes in the society's 'plan for living', that is in its culture.

When 'the plan' implicit in a culture does not adapt to major changes in the environment, then people become anxious. Likewise when changes occur in a people's understanding of Christian faith the same thing happens. They slowly lose confidence in a frame of reference that they have long taken for granted in making sense of their experiences. As a consequence their capacity to identify with other members of their society or church diminishes, as does their willingness to contribute to the common good. Important aspects of their personal identity become blurred, resulting in alienation from their culture. For instance, when Catholics lose confidence in the worldview of faith as it has been handed down and begin to regard it as, for example, supporting patriarchal and misogynist practices that are in direct contrast to the values of the culture which they value, they become alienated from their faith community and less willing to contribute to its wellbeing.

Catholic religious leaders have a history of resisting major cultural changes in their societies, but the risk they take in doing so is the alienation of their followers. This is because a religious tradition can easily cease to be meaningful for people living in a particular culture, particularly in the face of major cultural change. This occurred tragically during what respected Church historian John O'Malley SJ calls (borrowing from Hobsbawm)[7] 'the

---

6   Louis Luzbetak *The Church and Cultures: New Perspectives in Missiological Anthropology*. Maryknoll NY: Orbis Books; 1988, 156-222.
7   Eric Hobsbawm (1917-2012) was an influential British historian who wrote many works on factors influencing the development of the modern world. These works included his famous trilogy on what he called 'the long nineteenth century'.

long 19th century,'[8] when popes rejected out of hand the cultural changes that accompanied the rise of modernity.[9]

More recently, John Sivalon MM points to a similar response happening in the Catholic Church in the early part of the 21st century. He highlights the negative and often uncomprehending stance certain senior Church leaders took to postmodern culture.[10] Sivalon is a former superior-general of the Maryknoll fathers and brothers, a large religious congregation devoted to cross-cultural mission. Reflecting on his experience in Tanzania, he came to see that God is at work in all cultures, including the postmodern. The uncertainty that comes with a change of era can be interpreted as a gift that gives those committed to God's mission, encouragement and illumination on a journey that has cosmic dimensions. If God is at work in all cultures, so must Christians be.

Since faith is always understood, articulated, and practised within the context of a particular culture, recontextualising the culture has implications for how faith is understood and practised. In fact, cultural change often results in the emergence of new insights into the meanings central to a religious tradition, and so to the development of that tradition.

In highlighting the need for theological recontextualisation, The *Enhancing Catholic School Identity* (ECSI) project, to which reference was made in Chapter 1, tends to analyse the present context of Catholic schooling as if our culture were relatively stable. However, the reality is that a major shift has occurred in our culture *and continues to occur*. Our culture is not stable; it is caught up *in a process of transition*. In our view this renders the context even more complex and dynamic than seems to be envisaged by promoters of the ECSI project because *Australian culture is in the process of being recontextualised as we move from a culture shaped by the modern worldview to a culture shaped by a postmodern, postsecular worldview*. We will examine this shift in more detail in a later chapter.

---

8   The long nineteenth century' was the phrase used by Hobsbawm to refer to the time from the French revolution to the outbreak of World War 1. In regard to Catholic Church history, the period has been extended to the death of Pius XII in 1958 which ushered in the pontificate of John XXIII and the beginning of the Second Vatican Council (1962-5).

9   John O'Malley SJ *What Happened at Vatican II*. London: Harvard University Press, 2010, 4. O'Malley contends that Vatican II sought to address a range of issues posed by the French revolution that had so traumatised Church leaders that they remained largely unresolved at the end of Pius XII's pontificate in 1958. This reactionary period in Church history ran from the end of the 18th century through to the middle of the 20th century. In this period, particularly as an outcome of the First Vatican Council (1869-70) power within the Church became centralised in Rome.

10 John Sivalon *God's Mission and Postmodern Culture: The Gift of Uncertainty*. Maryknoll N.Y: 2012, 32.

With the basic understandings outlined above in place, we can now look both backwards and forwards in dealing with the notion of culture and the roles it has played and continues to play in accounting for human difference.

The modern anthropological understanding of culture which we have explored in this chapter is open to the critique that it presents a rather static conception of culture because it offers a synchronic perspective (culture as it exists now). Later developments in anthropology have addressed this limitation by adding a diachronic perspective (culture as it has evolved, and continues to evolve over time), and so help us to understand the dynamic nature of contemporary cultures. We will address this matter in the next chapter.

6

CULTURE: THE DEAD HAND OF CLASSICISM

In our previous chapter we discussed the emergence within the academy of the discipline of cultural anthropology and with it the modern, or as it is sometimes termed empirical, understanding of culture. This chapter addresses the classicist approach to culture, and so takes the discussion of culture as a key element in recontextualisation further by dealing with its historical evolution.

What we have termed the 'classicist' approach has, and continues to be, enormously influential. While not as directly identifiable today as previously, it still holds a significant place in the worldviews of many within societies such as our own.

CLASSICIST CONCEPTIONS OF CULTURE

- The experience of culture is much older than the usage of the term. For example, the notion was important to the Romans in trying to understand the diverse range of peoples who came under their sway within the empire. They formulated human difference in terms of 'civilisation', or the lack of it. For them, culture, that is being cultured, was a by-product of 'being civilised' which meant 'being like us'.

The etymology of the word 'culture' can be traced back to the Latin verb *cultivare* originally coined in the context of agriculture and referred to the nurturing of plants. It was later applied metaphorically to the nurturing of the human mind and the human sensibility deemed to be characteristic of a Roman citizen. In this understanding Roman citizens were 'civilised', and individual citizens 'cultured'.

Roman Classicism. For the Romans, peoples comprising the empire were divided into two camps: the civilised and the barbarians, that is those lacking the refinement of Roman civilisation. The Romans saw it as necessary to 'civilise' principally the leaders of the peoples they conquered and brought many of them to Rome to experience the Roman 'way of life' at firsthand. Over time, the Roman 'way of life' became the norm by which other societies were judged. Thus, a normative concept of culture (being cultured) emerged to account for the differences found among peoples within the empire. The proliferation of Roman ruins scattered around Europe, the Middle East, and northern Africa, stands as testimony to the fact that the 'Roman way of life' came to be taken as normative in the empire in ancient times.

Classicism in Medieval Europe. The fall of the Roman Empire in the 5th century CE and the gradual emergence of feudal Europe and the religio-political system known as Christendom saw the conception of 'civilisation' transferred to this new context.

Now to be 'civilised' meant to be part of an elite who were both educated and Christian. These two characteristics provided the norms defining a 'cultured' person. During Christendom nearly everyone in the known world was Christian, so such norms were unproblematic at a time when travel outside Europe was quite limited and most Europeans thought of themselves as comprising the known world.

When, in the 15th century, the 'New World' of the Americas was 'discovered' and explorers like Marco Polo made contact with Asia, Europeans became aware that there was a world beyond Europe, a world in which people were not Christian, and in which the elites had a different conception of what constituted 'civilisation'.

The civilisations discovered in Asia and Africa often pre-dated those of Europe. Such discoveries challenged a worldview which held that the European way of life should be taken as normative for all peoples.

From the European perspective held by the conquerors, the peoples discovered in the new territories were not human, because they were not Christian. Therefore, they could be exploited in much the same way as beasts of burden. European colonists in the New World effectively enslaved indigenous peoples, particularly in what today is known as Central and South America. Such exploitation contributed to the devastation of the indigenous populations, as did introduced diseases against which they latter had no immunity.

Principal among the defenders of indigenous peoples were the members of Catholic religious orders, particularly the Jesuits. Pope Paul III, under pressure from these missionaries, eventually declared that the peoples of the New World were human and were not to be enslaved:

> We, who, though unworthy, exercise on earth the power of our Lord and seek with all our might to bring those sheep of His flock who are outside into the fold committed to our charge, consider, however, that the Indians are truly men and that they are not only capable of understanding the Catholic Faith but, according to our information, they desire exceedingly to receive it. Desiring to provide ample remedy for these evils, We define and declare by these Our letters, or by any translation thereof signed by any notary public and sealed with the seal of any ecclesiastical dignitary, to which the same credit shall be given as to the originals, that, notwithstanding whatever may have been or may be said to the contrary, the said Indians and all other people who may later be discovered by Christians, are by no means to be deprived of their liberty or the possession of their property, even though they be outside the faith of Jesus Christ; and that they may and should, freely and legitimately, enjoy their liberty and the possession of their property; nor should they be in any way enslaved; should the contrary happen, it shall be null and have no effect.[1]

CONSOLIDATION OF CLASSICISM IN EUROPE

The normative notion of culture as civilisation evolved further in the 17th century with the emergence and development of Enlightenment thinking[2], and in the 18th century with the advent of the Industrial Revolution and the migration of labourers from rural areas to rapidly developing cities.

Enlightenment philosophers placed emphasis on the power of reason to advance the human condition. Successes here led to growing confidence in the power of human rationality leading eventually to science being seen as the sole means by which reliable human knowledge could be constructed. With the development of scientific method, science replaced 'appeal to authority' as a way of validating human insights.

As the Industrial Revolution progressed, driven by technological advances, the elites of Europe feared the potential of the new working classes to cause chaos because the latter were perceived to be 'uncivilised'.

---

1 Pope Paul III, papal bull *Sublimus Deus*, 1537. https://www.papalencyclicals.net/paul03/p3subli.htm
2 Enlightenment thinking placed a strong emphasis on rational thought in both its inductive and deductive modes. It disregarded theology as a form of rational thought since it depended on faith.

The need to 'civilise' these classes, and particularly their children, before the situation got out of hand, eventually became accepted by authorities and leading citizens committed to the common good. It was in this atmosphere that the 'gratuitous' education movements were born, forerunners to the public education we know today.[3]

Public education was eventually accepted as the means needed to 'civilise' the children of the working classes and to bring some discipline based on Christian moral principles into their lives. The initial aim was to teach the young to read and write and so to put them in touch with the high ideals and morals found in what was deemed 'the best' that European cultures had to offer, 'the best' including the Bible. The assumption still existed in Europe that to be civilised was to be Christian, understood as being either 'Catholic' or 'Protestant', depending on which country one lived in.

The nexus between 'being civilised' and 'being Christian' was challenged as the European Enlightenment unfolded. During this period, the humanist ideal that had first featured so strongly in the Renaissance of the 15th and 16th centuries became equated with reliance on human reason and its application in scientific and political endeavours and human progress. The humanist ideal largely replaced the Christian ideal as the Enlightenment progressed. 'Being Christian' was slowly excluded from the normative standard used to determine whether a society was 'civilised' or an individual was 'cultured'.

CLASSICISM EXPORTED TO EUROPEAN COLONIES

In Enlightenment Europe, civilisation became equated with education. That on offer was generally public and secular in order to avoid the divisive denominationalism that had come to characterise European societies. Public education sought to introduce the young to the classics in literature, poetry, arts, and law under the rubric of a 'liberal arts' curriculum. This form of education became the norm not only in Europe but also in the European colonies, where as a result of the work of Christian missionaries, to be 'civilised' still meant both being educated in the liberal arts tradition, and

---

3 The 'gratuitous' education movement as developed in France was a ministry of the Church, and became influential across the globe. Church leaders saw it as necessary to provide children whose parents worked in the factories with a basic education. This was not an easy task given that the parents had little or no education and did not necessarily value its attainment. Circumstances meant that the children were unsupervised and often indolent. Education offered these young people the chance to improve their situation and gave the Church the chance to implement a religious education program for them. Many of the religious congregations that specialise in Catholic education today were formed about this time. John Baptist de La Salle (1651-1719), founder of the De La Salle Brothers, was a prime mover in his home country France, and was succeeded by many other famous founders of religious congregations so that his influence quickly spread across the world. See Jim and Therese D'Orsa *Pedagogy and the Catholic Educator: Nurturing Hearts, Transforming Possibilities.* Mulgrave: Garratt Publishing, 2020, 65-75.

also being Christian. European culture and European faith set the norms against which the many cultures of Africa, Asia and the Pacific were judged.

CLASSICISM IN ACADEMIA

The notion that Europe set the standard for other societies became incorporated into the academy at a time when new disciplines were taking shape. This classicist assumption was uncritically accepted not only in academic circles in Europe and the USA, but also in the Catholic Church until well into the 20th century. Thus, a normative, classicist understanding of 'civilisation' became part of the implicit, taken-for-granted intellectual milieu in European societies and the Catholic Church.

The work of the many pioneering anthropologists who formulated the modern concept of culture as 'the way of life of a people' was compromised because they often interpreted the culture of the peoples whom they studied using the classicist assumptions implicit in their own culture. Instead of interpreting Aboriginal cultures, for instance, in terms of an Aboriginal framework, they interpreted them in terms of a European framework, so their findings made little sense to Aboriginal peoples.

CLASSICISM IN THE CATHOLIC CHURCH

Across thirteen centuries, classicism became embedded in the way Church leaders understood human difference. For them, being Christian in the European way was an integral part of being civilised. Classicism became embedded in the Church's theology, in its liturgy, in the construction of its social teaching, in its organisational structures, and in its legal system. These systems essentially still operate to greater or lesser degree according to the 'one size fits all' principle. This approach persisted until the 1960s when the modern concept of 'cultures' began to replace 'culture/civilisation', in official Catholic teaching.[4] However, changes in Catholic teaching have been slow to translate into changes in Catholic practice. This creates problems for teachers in Catholic schools dealing with students whose worldviews are shaped by the various understandings of culture at large in our society – classicist, modern, postmodern and now postmodern-postsecular.

---

4   Including in *Gaudium et Spes*, the key document of the Second Vatican Council (1962-5). It should be noted, however, that *Gaudium et Spes* is ambiguous in its usage of 'culture' – both the classicist and modern understandings feature in this document. The adoption of the modern (empirical) conception is especially obvious in Pope Paul VI's reflective summary of the work of the 1974 synod on evangelisation – *Evangelii Nuntiandi* 1975.
https://www.vatican.va/content/paul-vi/en/apost_exhortations/documents/hf_p-vi_exh_19751208_evangelii-nuntiandi.html

As we have noted in Chapter 4, major changes in Catholic teaching about the Church's mission flowed from the experiences of Catholic missionaries working in cultures other than their own. A number of these missionaries became involved in the development of the discipline of mission anthropology. They had witnessed at first-hand the unfortunate consequences of European classicism in mission situations, including the disparities that resulted when people living in non-European cultures were forced to live out their Christian commitment according to norms, expressions, and practices set in Europe. This experience led them to awareness of the bias that European classicism had introduced into Catholic theology, understandings of morality, Church law, liturgy, Church history, and even the interpretation of the Bible.[5]

When European colonies gained their independence in the decades following World War II, not surprisingly the leaders of the newly created nation states frequently disavowed the nexus between 'civilisation' and Christianity. Expatriate Christian missionaries in India, for instance, were sometimes expelled *en masse*. Those who were not expelled found themselves unable to return to their home country for renewal or to visit family because, if they did so, they would not be allowed to return to their mission bases in India. It was a very difficult situation that created a crisis for missionary congregations that Church leaders had to address.[6]

The Catholic Church as Global

Within the Catholic Church, classicism lived on more or less unquestioned, at least officially, until the Second Vatican Council (1962–65). During the Council's deliberations, many Church leaders realised that they now faced a major challenge – a global church could no longer function authentically within a mono-cultural understanding of either theology or philosophy.

Tracing the work of popes and episcopal synods since that time, we can find many attempts to rectify this situation. A particularly important passage in Pope Francis' *Evangelii Gaudium* (##115–118) summarises many aspects of that journey and should be carefully noted by those serious about contextualisation. The following is a sample of some of the points made. Study of these and their sources shows how Pope Francis draws on a range of official statements ranging from the Second Vatican Council to the time of writing (2013):

---

5   For a famous example see Vincent Donovan *Christianity Rediscovered*. Maryknoll N.Y: Orbis, 2003.
6   Pope Paul VI called a general synod on evangelisation in 1974 resulting in his summary, the apostolic exhortation *Evangelii Nuntiandi*, being issued in 1975. His successor Pope John Paul II addressed the issue of mission *ad gentes* in his encyclical *Redemptoris Missio* in 1990.

The People of God is incarnate in the peoples of the earth, each of which has its own culture. The concept of culture is valuable for grasping the various expressions of the Christian life present in God's people. It has to do with the lifestyle of a given society, the specific way in which its members relate to one another, to other creatures and to God. Understood in this way, culture embraces the totality of a people's life. Each people in the course of its history develops its culture with legitimate autonomy. This is due to the fact that the human person "by nature stands completely in need of life in society" and always exists in reference to society, finding there a concrete way of relating to reality ... (#115)

... The history of the Church shows that Christianity does not have simply one cultural expression, but rather, "remaining completely true to itself, with unswerving fidelity to the proclamation of the Gospel and the tradition of the Church, it will also reflect the different faces of the cultures and peoples in which it is received and takes root". In the diversity of its own culture, the Church expresses her genuine catholicity and shows forth the "beauty of her varied face" ... Through inculturation, the Church "introduces peoples, together with their cultures, into her own community", for "every culture offers positive values and forms which can enrich the way the Gospel is preached, understood and lived" ... (#116).

... It is he (the Holy Spirit) (sic) who brings forth a rich variety of gifts, while at the same time creating a unity which is never uniformity but a multifaceted and inviting unity which is never uniformity but a multifaceted and inviting harmony. Evangelization joyfully acknowledges these varied treasures which the Holy Spirit pours out upon the Church. We would not do justice to the logic of the incarnation if we thought of Christianity as monocultural and monotonous. While it is true that some cultures have been closely associated with the preaching of the Gospel and the development of Christian thought, the revealed message is not identified with any of them; its content is transcultural. Hence in the evangelization of new cultures, or cultures which have not received the Christian message, it is not essential to impose a specific cultural form, no matter how beautiful or ancient it may be, together with the Gospel. The message that we proclaim always has a certain cultural dress, but we in the Church can sometimes fall into a needless hallowing of our own culture, and thus show more fanaticism than true evangelizing zeal. (#117).

The bishops of Oceania asked that the Church "develop an understanding and a presentation of the truth of Christ working from the traditions and cultures of the region" and invited "all missionaries to work in harmony with indigenous Christians so as to ensure that the faith and the life of the Church be expressed in legitimate forms appropriate for each culture". We cannot demand that peoples of every continent, in which European nations developed at a particular moment of their history, because the faith cannot be constricted to the limits of understanding and expression of any one culture. It is an indisputable fact that no single culture can exhaust the mystery of our redemption in Christ.

We are all missionary disciples. (#118).

IMPLICATIONS: FROM A MONO-CULTURAL TO A MULTI-CULTURAL CHURCH

As the Church has become more global in its orientation, many of its leaders have, for some decades, realised that European classicism has become a major obstacle to understanding and carrying forward the mission of Jesus.[7]

Pope Francis, as the first non-European pope in recent centuries, has taken some important steps to re-contextualise the Christian message for a global Church, but has been hampered by a resistive central bureaucracy long accustomed to a 'Rome knows best' mentality when dealing with people from diverse cultural settings. The pope's notion of a 'synodal church' in which Church leaders engage with local peoples and their concerns is one attempt to overcome the legacy of European classicism.[8]

The problem with classicism within the Catholic Church has been the tendency of some of its leaders to view particular expressions of religious truth in absolute terms. However, truth must always be expressed in language, and language is the product of a culture. Expressions of truth therefore carry the contingency that accompanies all languages and cultures. They are provisional and therefore capable of further development.

---

[7] See, for instance, Aylward Shorter *Towards a Theology of Inculturation*. London: Geoffrey Chapman, 1988.

[8] In October 2021, Pope Francis inaugurated a two-year (October 2021-October 2023) process embracing all the dioceses (technically the local churches) of the world in listening to one another and to the Holy Spirit. The theme for the sixteenth synod of bishops is: *For a Synodal Church: Communion, Participation, and Mission.*

Classicism demonstrates that it is possible to mistake a given linguistic expression of truth for 'the truth'. It makes it possible to take a particular philosophic system as the only philosophic system compatible with Christian faith. It also makes it possible to construe Church history as fitting within a single trajectory, and to see salvation through a single lens. Clearly, this is highly problematic for the worldview of a global church.

As the post-Vatican II era has unfolded, there is growing realisation of the limitations that the mono-cultural understandings underpinning European classicism have had on the development of Christian faith and practice, particularly in countries that were formerly Europeans colonies. As a consequence, we have seen the emergence of 'local theologies'. These theologies begin with local situations and take Jesus' teaching about the kingdom or reign of God as a theological framework with which to work out what 'salvation' can mean for persons and communities in particular circumstances. These theologies emphasise the 'within history' dimension of Jesus' teaching while not in any way ignoring the 'beyond history' dimension.

The most well-known of these contextual theologies is liberation theology, which seeks to address the disparities between rich and poor in Latin America. Perhaps less well known but equally important, are the dialogue theologies, developed within Asian Christian faith communities. Dialogue is a key element in theology in all societies as each becomes drawn more deeply into a globalised world. This certainly includes Australian society.

A global church has to be able to deal with the degree of difference that is inherent in being global, if it is to remain unified. Working out how to find unity in diversity is a challenge facing the Catholic Church, in which the legacy of classicism remains unresolved. Classicism interprets difference in terms of uniformity; the cross-cultural missionary experience of the Church has taught us just how inadequate this is.

Cultures are rarely static entities because if they were so, given the rapid nature of change in today's world, they would quickly die out. In fact, cultures are dynamic in that they adapt to changes in the environment by re-configuring the worldview that lies at their heart and reformulating the stories through which this worldview is made available, thus enabling people to make sense of their lives in new circumstances. This is true for Church culture as it is for the culture of a society. The connections between culture and context are mediated by the operation of worldviews. This theme is explored in chapters 7 and 8.

The modern concept of culture presents a snapshot of culture at a point in time. The diachronic perspective highlights the limits of this approach. Studying artefacts, customs, and norms is important, but more important is understanding why these have significance for a people. Exploring this question is to examine what lies at the heart of a culture and the dynamics by which it adapts and changes as the context changes.

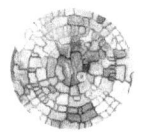

7
WORLDVIEW AS AN INTERPRETIVE CATEGORY IN MEANING-MAKING

Culture can be conceptualised as having a structure with three dimensions. The surface dimension is what can be *observed empirically*. This includes elements such as language, behavioural norms, social arrangements, rituals and so on. Underpinning this is the dimension of *cultural values* that provide the interpretive key for making sense of what can be observed. The third dimension – the deepest level of a culture – contains elements that determine *why* a particular selection of cultural values animates a culture. Anthropologists use words such as *'basic assumptions'*, *'myth'* and *'worldview'* when discussing this dimension.

In this chapter we explore the notion of *worldview* and its importance in meaning-making, particularly the meaning-making that occurs in the process of the recontextualisation of faith. Much of what passes for contextualisation occurs at the surface level of culture. *However, recontextualisation of faith needs to take account of cultural values and especially the cultural worldview, that is, it involves the depth dimension of culture.*

WORLDVIEW – PERSONAL AND PUBLIC

As tools in meaning-making, worldviews operate at two levels – *personal* and *public*.

A *personal worldview* is the interpretive framework that we, as individuals, use in making sense of our experiences. We acquire our personal worldview in the process of *enculturation* – that is the experience of growing up in a particular cultural milieu that we take for granted.

A *public worldview is* held by a group or a people. Thus, we can speak of 'the worldview of a culture', 'the worldview of Christian faith' or 'the worldview of an age'. Public worldviews have a sponsoring community. Within this community the elements that comprise its worldview are often contested. This is because, as interpretive schemas, worldviews function within boundaries that *allow for legitimate difference*.

The worldview of a culture provides individuals growing up in that culture with *a default frame of reference in making sense of life*. It helps define what an individual living in that culture can, without conscious reflection, take for granted as 'normal' and 'right'.

Our guide in exploring the important place of worldview in meaning-making is the influential mission anthropologist Paul Hiebert.[1]

In attempting to bring clarity to the worldview concept, Hiebert traces its historical development. He acknowledges the concept 'has its roots in several Western academic disciplines' and this produces a certain degree of confusion as to its meaning.[2]

HISTORICAL ROOTS OF WORLDVIEW AS A CONCEPT

The first root lies in the discipline of philosophy. German philosopher, Immanuel Kant, introduced the notion of Weltanschauung in the 18th century. By the mid-19th century it had become a standard German word meaning the perspective on the world adopted by individuals or even whole societies. *Weltsanschauung* referred to how people understood the world in which they lived. As used in philosophy, it is primarily a cognitive category. 'Weltanschauung' is a synchronic concept referring to how people see the world at a particular point in time.

The second root lies in the discipline of history. In the 19th century historians began to explore history from the perspective of ordinary people. This led scholars such as Wilhelm Dilthey, a key figure in the development of hermeneutics, to account for different periods of history in terms of their *Zeitgeist*. By this he meant the spirit of the times. In this conception different ages in human history are each characterised by their own *Weltanschauung*. *Zeitgeist* is a diachronic concept referring to how worldviews can change across time.

The third root lies in the discipline of anthropology. Here the synchronic and diachronic dimensions are integrated. Early anthropologists explored cultures from a *synchronic perspective* (how a culture functions in the present). As we noted previously, once historians became interested in the evolution of cultures, they took a *diachronic perspective* focusing on how some cultural

---

1 Paul Hiebert (1933-2007) held the position of Professor of Mission and Anthropology at a number of Protestant seminaries in the USA. He also served as a pastor and missionary in India prior to his return to academic life. He is the author of many books and articles in the fields of anthropology and mission anthropology. His work is highly regarded by Catholic missiologists.
2 A comprehensive account of this history is found in David Naugle's *Worldview: The History of a Concept*. Grand Rapids: William. B. Eerdmans Publishing Company, 2002.

elements emerge and endure, while others fade as history unfolds. The enduring nature of some cultural elements such as democratic government means that they are able to spread from society to society, so creating the phenomenon of acculturation, one of the major mechanisms by which cultural change occurs.

In the late 19th and early 20th century, anthropologists suggested that all cultures are structured in such a way that what is observed gains its meaning from underlying beliefs and values. However this is not the end of the story, as Hiebert notes:

> (Anthropologists) became aware of still deeper levels of a culture that shaped how beliefs are formed – the assumptions that people make about the nature of things, the categories in which they think, and the logic that organised these categories into a coherent understanding of reality. It became clear that people live, not in the same world with different labels attached to it, but in radically different conceptual worlds.[3]

The word 'worldview' was adopted by anthropologists as the best one available to account for such phenomena.

DEFINITION OF WORLDVIEW

Building on the work of earlier anthropologists, Hiebert suggests that the term 'worldview' refers to:

> ... the fundamental cognitive, affective and evaluative presuppositions a group of people make about the nature of things, and which they use to order their lives. Worldviews are what people in a community take as given realities, the maps they have of reality that they use for living.[4]

Anthropologists endeavoured to identify the worldview of the peoples they studied in order to understand how one society compared with another. This form of analysis helped them identify a number of *worldview themes* – deep assumptions that are found in a limited number in every culture and that help structure the nature of reality for its members.

Worldview themes emerge within a culture in the process of negotiating the 'plan for living together'. These themes usually arise as pairs of competing

---

[3] Paul Hiebert *Transforming worldviews: An anthropological understanding of how people change*. Grand Rapids: Baker Academic, 2009, 15.
[4] ibid.

values, that is, as *theme and counter-theme*. A group then has to negotiate the relative value of each.

Understanding the themes and counter-themes alive within a culture, and the relative value given to them, provides an important key for unlocking the underlying worldview. For example, two competing values in almost all cultures are *group-orientation* and *individual-orientation*. While no society is characterised totally by one or the other, these two categories highlight tensions that have to be negotiated in the formation of most cultures.

The table below sets out one categorisation of cultural sub-themes and counter themes that have to be negotiated in constructing a culture.[5]

TABLE 7.1

Group-oriented societies	Individual-oriented societies
• People are born into extended families in which they live all their lives	• Everyone grows up to look after himself/herself in nuclear families
• Identity is based on birth and the place a person occupies in the group	• Identity is based on individual achievement
• Children learn to think in terms of 'we'	• Children learn to think in terms of 'I'.
• Harmony should always be maintained and conflict avoided	• Speaking one's mind is the characteristic of an honest person.
• Violating the norms leads to a sense of shame and loss of face for self and the group	• Violating the norms leads to a sense of guilt and loss of self-respect
• Relationships between the boss and worker are seen in moral family terms The boss is responsible for the overall well-being of his worker	• Relationships between boss and worker are governed by contract based on voluntary exchange and mutual advantage
• Hiring and promotion must take kinship and friendships into account	• Hiring and promotion should be based purely on skills and rules of selection
• The relationship is more important than the task. People should not be fired.	• The task is more important than the relationship. People can readily be fired.

Western societies tend to be characterised by sub-themes on the right of the table. Asian societies tend to be characterised by themes on its left. However, there will be groups within each society that see the world differently from the majority of their peers. Cultures differ in how they negotiate the boundaries of legitimate difference in their worldview. Some allow much greater scope for pluralism than others.

The decisions taken by governments in dealing with the COVID pandemic, as well as the responses of their people to those decisions, has highlighted the important role cultural values and worldview play in how

---

5   Geert H. Hofstede, Gert Jan Hofstede, Michael Minkov *Cultures and Organisations: Software of the Mind*. London: Harper Collins, 1994, 67.

people see the world, and their place in it. It has also highlighted the limits of power in shaping such understandings.

HIEBERT'S MODEL OF WORLDVIEW

Hiebert, drawing on the insights of anthropology, proposes the following schematic model of worldview.[6]

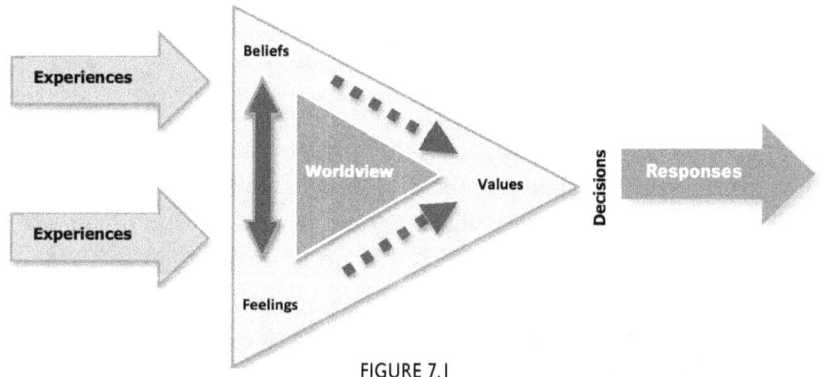

FIGURE 7.1

The model suggests that personal and collective worldviews determine what we attend to in the data of our experience as this presents itself to the senses. A worldview acts as a lens letting some data through to conscious awareness, while filtering out the rest. The process is selective and is shaped by cognitive, affective and evaluative criteria that an individual acquires in the process of growing up in a particular culture (enculturation).

Since we learn our culture in a process that goes on largely outside our awareness, we are often not aware of the criteria that are implicitly at work shaping our worldview. This is true at the group level as well as at the personal level.

The three sets of criteria – cognitive, evaluative and affective – do not operate in isolation from one another, but *interdependently*. For this reason, the themes and counterthemes alive in a culture overlap and so defy precise categorisation.

Cognitive themes include elements such as the mental categories people use; the types of logic they employ; their sense of time and space; the root metaphors they employ to explain how their world works; their sense of self; their ways of distinguishing between 'us' and 'them'; and their sense of 'this world' versus 'other worlds'.

In the West we tend to employ linear logic as opposed to the relational logic used in certain other societies. Our sense of time is predominantly

---
6 Hiebert, 28.

'clock time' that unfolds in regular increments. Some other cultures see time as cyclical. However, as Hiebert observes: 'no culture is controlled by one concept of time. One may be dominant in the culture, but other conceptions of time operate in different spheres of life.'[7] As a consequence, the concept of being 'on time' means different things is different societies!

Root metaphors also play a role in how people see the world. Two have proved very important in the development of Western thought: the world understood as mechanism (machine), and the world understood as organism. The first notion was introduced by Descartes who saw the world (universe) operating as a giant clock, with God as the clockmaker. The second metaphor emerged with Darwin's understanding of evolution. In the mechanistic view of the world, when a part breaks down it is replaced. In an organic view all parts are interdependent and must be nurtured into life in relation to one another. Root metaphors play an important role in how societies are organised and how leadership is construed. As applied to employment, the mechanistic model sees underperforming staff replaced; the organic metaphor suggests they be mentored!

Affective themes deal with how people experience the world and react to it emotionally. Our feelings shape how we understand the world and react to one another. People can adopt an optimistic or pessimistic view of their world. As Hiebert observes 'powerful pervasive and long-lasting affective themes act as a wall protecting beliefs from attack from within and without by providing emotional support to their truthfulness.'[8]

Affective themes can be summed up in the notion of 'sensibility', the characteristic way in which people respond to a range of common experiences. Sensibility is developed through a combination of enculturation, conscious learning, and practice. It involves a sensitivity to others particularly an awareness about how they are feeling, a capacity to respond appropriately to them in a range of circumstances, as well as the capacity to gauge one's own emotional strengths and weaknesses.

Evaluative themes define the social and moral order in a society. They provide the standards people use to make judgments about good and bad, right and wrong. In some societies moral and social order is thought of in legal terms; in other societies it is thought of in terms of *relationships*, while a third criterion often employed is *purity* or *cleanliness*. This criterion is seen as important in a number of Middle Eastern and African societies.

There is no definitive listing of the above sets of themes that can be appealed to in charting a cultural worldview Every culture has to work

---

[7] Hiebert ibid, 53.
[8] ibid, 59.

out their relative importance in coming to decisions. These will predictably change over time as human experience continues to unfold. Cultural worldviews either grow and develop, or remain in a state of stasis and eventually fade.

WORLDVIEW OF AN AGE

The worldview of an age refers to *worldview elements that are shared across several contemporaneous cultures.* For instance, in the modern period most European cultures shared the aspirations of the *worldview of modernity.* These were that:

- the impact of science and technology would be positive for all human beings
- the rise of modernity equated with the march of human progress
- science alone determines what is true; religious ideas reflect private opinions.

Furthermore:

- As the modern worldview took hold, Christianity in particular, and religion in general, would fade in importance in making sense of life.

As these aspirations became embedded implicitly or explicitly in education systems, they became part of the default frame of reference that people took for granted in making sense of life. The consequence was that society was understood and organised within a totally different framework from that which applied in the pre-modern world, leading to the emergence of the modern democratic state with its capitalist economy. As these developments unfolded, leaders of the Catholic Church, speaking out of a pre-modern worldview, found themselves progressively sidelined. With the European world having been organised for so long under the influence of the Church, and the Christian faith as then understood, rejecting this influence was seen as being 'modern'. While not everyone accepted this position, it became a dominant evaluative theme in European societies.[9]

The relationship between the worldview of the age and the worldview of culture can be represented as follows:

---

9 The spirit of the times is powerfully captured in Marcel Pagnol's films based on his books *My Mother's Castle* and *My Father's Glory,* (1990).

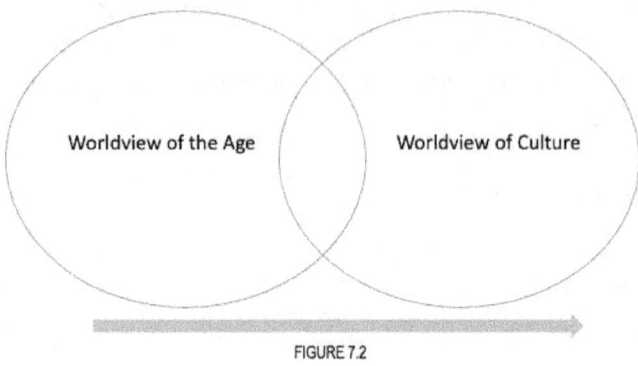

FIGURE 7.2

The worldview of a particular age can reshape the worldview of the culture across several societies. The process by which most young people acquire their culture today is quite different from the way in which this process happened for their parents.

The worldview dominant in the pre-modern era in Europe took the Christian faith for granted. In the modern period, this assumption came under challenge as people developed a secular understanding of the world. A split developed between Christian faith on the one hand and modern culture on the other. In consequence, the narratives by which cultures are transmitted from one generation to the next took on a new shape, one that emphasised the importance of science and human progress through the development of technology and downplayed the role of religion in society. Modern culture offered people 'salvation' of a 'this-worldly' type. Religion was seen as offering salvation of an 'other-worldly' type and judged to be irrelevant. The postmodern critics, in challenging the assumptions on which the modern world was based, made it possible to re-examine the place that faith plays in public life and the role of science in the creation of knowledge.

TRANSMISSION OF WORLDVIEWS: CULTURAL NARRATIVES

Worldviews have intersecting affective, evaluative and cognitive dimensions that contain embedded tensions. As a result, they are complex to both analyse and discuss. Their core elements tend to become more manageable when conveyed as cultural narratives. These illustrate how the tensions inherent in a particular cultural worldview are resolved at a concrete level, rendering the worldview more readily understood and more useful as a source in meaning-making.

In anthropology, important cultural narratives are given the special title of 'myth'. The title is 'special' because the word 'myth' is being used in a technical sense, and not as it is understood in common usage.[10] A cultural myth is a story that combines two things: elements of something that did happen, often in the long-distant past, and the aspirations of a people that give these elements special significance. Cultural myths interpret history from the perspective of a society's espoused values.

SOME AUSTRALIAN CULTURAL MYTHS

Australian culture has several sets of cultural myths. For instance, one set refers to the country's pioneers and the resilience they showed in taming what to them seemed a vast, uninhabited and wild land. The stories associated with this set of myths include those of the explorers Burke and Wills, Blaxland, Wentworth and Lawson, Sturt, Leichhardt, and so on.

Cultural myths tend to become romanticised over time so that their connections with actual history become weakened in the process of emphasising the characteristics that they are meant to exemplify. Classic examples here are the escape of the Israelites from Egypt as we have it from accounts written much later, and the struggles of early Australian settlers, including former convicts, in developing this country.

Cultural myths are usually celebrated in multiple art forms. For instance, the myth of the pioneers is represented in Frederick McCubbin's famous triptych painting *The Pioneers*, in the television series *Against the Wind,* and in the Patrick White's novel *Voss*.

Because cultural myths constitute important elements in the creation of public life, their appearance in multiple art forms helps reinforce public appreciation of the values they espouse. Whether a particular artistic representation of the myth is historically correct is irrelevant to its purpose. Cultural myths play an important role in the informal learning process by which an individual acquires his or her culture. Young children are introduced to cultural myths, often through performance, long before they become aware that these constitute part of their cultural heritage.

A second set of cultural myths are associated with the value of 'mateship' through association with the story of the ANZAC (Australian and New Zealand Army Corps) forces at the battle of Gallipoli in the First World War. This battle is remembered and celebrated every April 25th. Over time, ANZAC celebrations have evolved so that they now recall the spirit demonstrated by successive generations of members of the armed forces, both in war and in peace, serving to protect the interests of this country. The fact that our forces were soundly beaten at Gallipoli indicates the quite

---

10 In common usage 'myth' usually indicates a story that is not true or is an exaggeration of the truth. This is fundamentally different from the anthropological usage.

limited role history plays in the formation of cultural myths. The focus in this myth is not on the history, but on the bravery, and especially the solidarity with mates, demonstrated at Gallipoli in face of stiff opposition that eventually enabled many of the troops to escape and fight another day on other fronts.

A third set of stories concerns the *struggle for justice* in the formation of this country. This set includes stories of the attempts to rein in the Rum Corps, of squatters against small landowners, of the Eureka rebellion, of Ned Kelly and other bushrangers, etc. The underlying value in all these stories is that Australians hold as sacred the value that 'everyone deserves a fair go'.

It must be noted that this set of narratives stands in stark contrast to the way in which the Indigenous peoples of Australia were treated by those who colonised the country, including some members of churches who here, as in the USA and Canada, judged indigenous peoples as cultureless and ignorant. The policy in all these countries was to 'assimilate' native peoples. The policy of assimilation, a sad consequence of European classicism, saw families torn apart and lives destroyed with tragic consequences that contemporary Australians are still attempting to address.

Today the non-Indigenous population is more aware that aboriginal peoples do not constitute a single group, but represent many cultures that share common features – including especially the cultural importance of association with 'country'. 'Country' provides the foundation of Indigenous cultural myths and is central to Aboriginal cultural identity. Dispossession of land came close to destroying this identity and led to alienation from the non-Indigenous population. A Welcome to Country, conducted by traditional elders at major events, welcomes people onto the land of the custodians. An Acknowledgement of Country acknowledges the custodians of the land on which a meeting is held, and can be offered by a person of any descent.

While mainstream Australia recognises that 'everyone should have a fair go' is an important cultural value for them, this is not a cultural value experienced in practice by many Indigenous peoples. Their experience often runs as a counter theme and this is now part of their story. The consequence is often a certain negativity towards the mainstream culture, that people living within that culture often fail to understand.

Cultural myths explain why some values are held by society to be more important than others in determining the norms people are expected to live by, and around which the society is organised. Once the narrative that underpins these values fades from memory, then the values lose their currency, and the associated norms cease to direct life.

PERSONAL WORLDVIEW AND MEANING-MAKING

As we have noted above, when it comes to making sense of experience, the worldview of our culture provides us with the default frame of reference within which this happens. From what has been discussed in the sections above it is clear that the picture looks as follows:

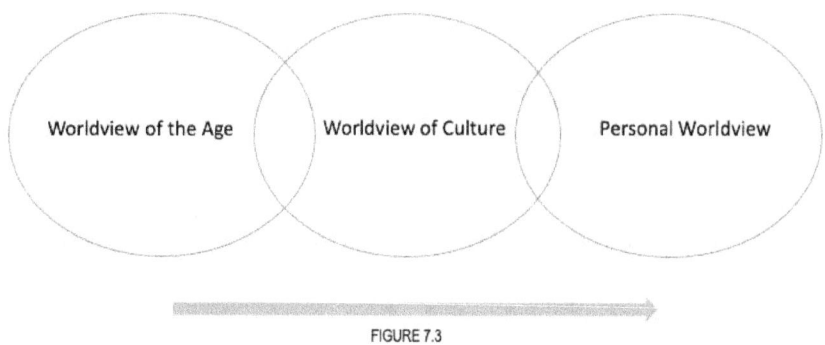

FIGURE 7.3

The framework within which we make sense of our experiences, draws on the worldview of our culture as this is shaped by the worldview of the age in which we live. Our personal worldview is fashioned by a whole range of cultural narratives, only some of which we know, but all of which influence the society in which we live, and so indirectly influence how we make sense of life, without our ever being aware of how this process actually works. This is the topic taken up in the next chapter.

The influence of the worldview of the age becomes important when there is a change of era such as we are experiencing at present. In this circumstance the worldview of the age becomes unstable and this instability affects the worldview of culture, and in turn the worldview of individuals. This is what happened in the postmodern era, with the consequence that in our own time people are no longer sure what can be taken as 'normal' or what is 'right'. In such circumstances it is understandable that there will be 'culture wars' as the divisions inherent in all cultures come to conscious awareness and have to be addressed. This is the challenge that recontextualisation seeks to address, both at the level of culture and that of faith.

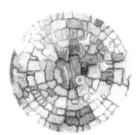

8

THE WORLDVIEW OF CULTURE AS AN INTERPRETIVE CATEGORY

The exploration of what it means to be human has a long history in both philosophy and theology.[1] A major change in direction occurred in the late 19th century when scholars of the newly emerging social science of anthropology began to adopt an empirical approach to studying the 'way of life' of those they termed 'primitive' peoples, focusing their efforts on groups living in relative isolation from 'civilisation'. It was in this context that what came to be termed a 'modern' understanding of culture emerged.

While we have noted this development previously, because of its pivotal importance to our work on the recontextualisation of both faith and culture, we will now focus on it in more detail.

ANTHROPOLOGY AS AN EMPIRICAL SCIENCE

Pioneers in the field of anthropology made accurate observations of the customs and behaviours of the peoples they studied. In this way they learned a good deal about their way of life. With the passage of time, they would also learn about the subtle ways in which their own culture influenced their attempts to make sense of another culture.

Since these pioneer scholars initially took their own cultural assumptions and norms for granted, they tended to impose them on the observations they made. Their studies were later severely critiqued as telling us more about the anthropologists' own cultural world than they did about the cultural world of the people whom they studied. In order to establish anthropology as a credible academic discipline, anthropologists had to do more than make extensive observations of behaviour and customs; they had

---

1 Anthropology understood in the philosophic sense as a study of what it means to be human dates to the ancient Greeks.

to develop models and methods for both describing and analysing cultures. This proved to be a slow process.

A BRIEF HISTORY OF EARLY MODERN ANTHROPOLOGY

It is commonplace to admit that culture is a 'slippery' concept, one that is difficult to secure in any definitive way. The main challenge in securing it lies in how the goals of cultural studies are construed. Is the purpose of modern anthropology simply to describe cultures? Or is its purpose to arrive at an understanding of what culture means for those living within it? Can cultural 'outsiders' ever really understand the meanings a culture has for 'insiders'? These were some of the questions that had to be answered as the discipline of anthropology progressed. At heart, it required a decision as to whether modern anthropology was to be construed as an empirical or an interpretive (hermeneutical) endeavour. Confusion about its purpose hampered development of the discipline and prevented consensus about the meaning of culture so that by the 1940s there seemed to be as many definitions of 'culture' as there were anthropologists working in the discipline.[2]

In the academy, social scientists attempt to develop working models of complex phenomena that are then used to analyse field data. In the case of anthropology, this data was collected by both anthropologists and missionaries. In the early stage of the discipline's development, anthropologists thought of culture as 'the way of life of an *isolated* people', as if such peoples did not interact with, or 'borrow' from, other cultures. Furthermore, the prevailing understanding of culture was synchronic and did not admit that the process of acculturation[3] was occurring or had occurred across time.

The fact that pioneer anthropologists spent long periods away from their universities, often living among the peoples they were studying, meant they were perceived as eccentric by their mainstream scientific colleagues, and the data they collected about customs and 'ways of life' seemed esoteric, particularly as the peoples studied were regarded as 'primitive'. In consequence, at the beginning of the 20th century modern anthropology remained a small, highly specialised academic field.

The small number of anthropologists trained in Britain were interested in how a society shapes its culture, and so considered themselves 'social

---

2   In a review of the literature in the 1950s anthropologists Kroeber and Kluckholn identified 168 definitions of culture. Their classic work *Culture: A critical review of concepts and definitions*. Papers. Peabody Museum of Archaeology & Ethnology, Harvard University, 47(1), viii was republished in 2020. Alfred Louis Kroeber, and Clyde Kluckhohn. *Culture: a Critical Review of Concepts and Definitions*. Pantianos Classics, 2020.

3   'Acculturation' is the term given to the process by which one culture adopts or adapts elements from another culture. It is one of the key processes by which cultures change and develop.

anthropologists', while the much larger group trained in the USA placed the emphasis on how culture shapes a society and so identified themselves as 'cultural anthropologists'. Missionaries schooled in anthropology followed one or other of these models depending on where they were trained.

The Second World War proved a significant driver in the development of modern anthropology. Allied military personnel involved in the war in the Pacific sought to recruit the peoples of the Pacific to help them with the war effort, as a labour force, to provide them with intelligence on the movement of Japanese troops, and to guide Allied troops through unknown terrain.[4] The Allies soon discovered that local peoples were culturally very different from themselves and that this led to suspicion and serious misunderstandings.

American military personnel had grown up in a country that was largely isolationist and were at a loss to know how to relate to peoples of a different culture. They needed help to understand local peoples, and not to regard them as 'underdeveloped Americans'. In consequence, the few American anthropologists then available found themselves in high demand.

With peace came the challenge of reconstructing the many countries devastated by war. This included most of Europe, Japan and the islands of the Pacific. There was a great demand for people who were familiar with culture and the processes of cultural change then an integral part of the world-wide reconstruction effort.

Following the war, anthropology departments in both American and British universities expanded rapidly and the number of anthropologists trained in them grew exponentially. The credibility of anthropology as a discipline also grew because of the helpful, practical role that anthropologists had played during the war years and the subsequent assistance given in training members of the diplomatic corps and groups such as the Peace Corps. The emergence of global corporations and agencies also increased the demand for anthropologists to train people working in cross-cultural situations.

---

4 The East Timorese, for instance, enabled a small company of Australian troops to survive and harass a garrison of some 20,000+ Japanese troops for more than two years. The presence of these Australian troops was not known at Allied Army headquarters in Australia. The East Timorese also assisted with the disembarkation of the entire cohort of European expatriate Catholic clergy when the latter were threatened with reprisals for helping the Australian troops. When it came time for the Australian troops to withdraw, their East Timorese allies were left to their fate at the hands of the Japanese, because the White Australia policy in place at the time did not allow for their being settled in Australia. This is one aspect among others of the Australian-East Timor relationships which is a source of deep shame for Australian leaders and their people.

RESEARCH MODELS AND WORKING MODELS

As anthropology grew in popular appeal, it developed two types of models to synthesise and explain its data. The first were models that aimed to explain the internal structure of a culture (research models); the second type aimed to predict how a people might act in certain circumstances (working models). Both types of models simplified what proved to be much more complex phenomena. They enabled cultural 'outsiders' to predict how cultural 'insiders' would react in a range of situations, even if the outsiders did not always understand why 'insiders' behaved the way that they did.

The utility of a working model derives from the range of phenomena that it explains and from its accuracy in making predictions. The main interest of mission anthropology was to develop working models capable of guiding mission personnel in the field as they sought to facilitate an encounter with the Gospel of Jesus Christ in a way meaningful for the people to whom they had committed their lives.

As we have noted previously, early anthropologists studied the ways of 'isolated peoples', often living with them for extended periods of time, before returning home to write up their findings. However, few learned the language of the people they studied. Their reports consisted of book-length observations about such things as group behaviours, communication patterns, family relationship, work patterns, housing arrangements and so on. The mastery of language on the other hand was a priority for many missionaries not least because of the need to translate the Bible into the language of the people. Because missionaries tended to stay longer in the field than anthropologists, for them learning the local language became central to their missional commitment and to their understanding of cultures. In consequence, the study of language became central to their training as cross-cultural missionaries.

FROM THE WHAT TO THE WHY

In the first decades of the 20th century Christian missionaries were in the field in almost every corner of the earth. As we have noted, an increasingly important aspect of their responsibilities was to study the peoples and their way of life so that those coming after them would not have to 'begin from scratch' when relating to the people or learning their customs and their language.[5]

---

5   It would be a mistake to think that all missionaries were interested in the local languages or local customs, but from the beginning of the 20th century Catholic missionaries were officially encouraged to be so, and with the emergence of local clergy this became necessary. The records of

Given that everyone is born into a culture and sees life from a particular perspective determined by that culture, it is not surprising that by the mid-20th century, some anthropologists began to interpret their goal as piecing together what this perspective is. This represented an important shift in practice from the *observation* of cultural patterns to the *interpretation* of them, involving a discernment of the meanings these patterns had for members of the society being observed. The result was that modern anthropology moved from being a strictly empirical social science to an interpretive one. The focus moved from the 'What are people doing?' to 'Why are they doing it in this particular way'?

If we know how another group understands the world, then we are better placed to relate to its members in a meaningful way. This becomes particularly important in understanding how a group addresses the religious dimension of life.

A difficulty in making sense of cross-cultural situations is that cultural 'insiders' are often themselves unaware of the frame of reference they are using in making sense of life's events – culture defining what they take as 'normal' – and so they pay little conscious attention to it. It is only when the assumptions on which a culture is based are challenged that these begin to appear in consciousness. This situation created significant methodological problems for modern anthropologists and missionaries: how do you get to the underlying assumptions that hold a culture together, when even insiders seem unaware of what these are? As a Chinese proverb has it: 'If you want to learn about water, don't ask a fish'!

A DIFFERENT KIND OF LEARNING REQUIRED

It eventually became clear that understanding a culture required a different form of learning from that used in the physical sciences. Unlike the situation of the physical sciences, anthropology studies people who are *subjects* capable of exercising *agency*. They are not objects. This means that, faced with the same circumstances, they do not always behave in the same way because they are free to interpret their circumstances differently. Therefore, understanding a culture requires an *inter-subjective* form of learning in which 'outsiders' put questions that 'insiders' answer. Outsiders know the 'what' of a culture, whereas insiders have access to the 'why'.

Catholic educators face a similar dilemma today. They, their students, and their students' parents, have grown up in a secular culture that all three groups take for granted. In this cultural world religion is regarded

---

local languages kept by missionaries have become important resources in saving these languages, including Australian Aboriginal languages, from extinction.

as a private matter and our cultural norms discourage public discussion of religious matters. As a result, it is difficult to discuss religious ideas publicly. Under this cultural constraint the language required to discuss religious experiences falls into disuse, and soon becomes meaningless.

A result is that many teachers in Catholic schools find that they are unable to effectively articulate their faith. Parents often find themselves in the same situation. Even when this is possible, teachers find that they are speaking in a language that is foreign to students, so communication is ineffective. Religious language now has to be re-contextualised to render it meaningful for students. This is an important step in recontextualising faith.

DESCRIPTIVE MODELS

In dealing with culture, modern anthropologists often use visual models based on metaphors: 'Culture is like …'. For instance, cultural anthropologist ET Hall and mission anthropologist Richard Cote, employ the image of an *iceberg* to explain many aspects of culture.[6]

This visual model draws attention to the fact that the most important elements of a culture are held *outside of awareness*, rather like the base of an iceberg, in the form of a sensibility that defines who is 'us' and who is 'not us'. If you have ever had the experience of being based for a long time in a country where English is rarely spoken, and one day you hear people talking with an Australian accent on a local bus, then you quickly recognise your Australian sensibility at work. You sense 'us' before you have time to think about the matter.

The iceberg model emphasises that culture has a depth dimension to it. It is this dimension that underpins cultural values and the more observable aspects of the culture.

Another visual model applied to culture is the *onion* model.[7] The key idea here is that cultures are built up as a series of layers that can be successively stripped away to reveal what is at their heart – the centre that gives everything else significance.

Hiebert argues that such descriptive models understand culture as having a structure with three levels. The *surface level* includes what can be observed such as norms and behaviours that govern group life. Below this is *the level of cultural values* that underpin the society's norms. Below that again is the *depth level* of a culture which includes its basic assumptions and worldview.

---

6   E.T. Hall *Culture: The Silent Language*. New York Anchor Books, 1973. Richard Cote *Revisioning-Mission: The Catholic Church and the Culture of Postmodern America*. New York: Paulist Press, 1996.

7   Richard Cote *Revisioning Mission: The Catholic Church and Culture in Postmodern America*. New York: Paulist Press, 1996.

It is the latter that determines why some values have priority over others, and why some are rejected in group life.

This three-stage model provides a useful tool in describing and analysing cultures.[8] Its weakness is that it takes a synchronic view of culture and therefore provides limited understanding of what is involved in the processes by which, over a period of time, a culture adapts to changes in its environment.

SEMIOTIC APPROACH TO CULTURE

Descriptive models of culture take *observations of behaviour* as a starting point and attempt to discern the meanings that what is observed have for local peoples. An alternative approach observes how *'signs'* (linguistic and non-linguistic) meld together in the creation and communication of meaning for a particular group. Empirical observation of signs provides the basis for the *semiotic model* of culture developed by well-known American cultural anthropologist, Clifford Geertz.

In outlining the semiotic approach to culture, missiologist Robert Schreiter notes:

> Culture is a vast communications network whereby both verbal and non-verbal messages are circulated along elaborate, interconnected pathways, which together create the systems of meaning. Central to this process are the bearers of the message … They are called 'symbols', 'signs' or 'signifiers' … Perhaps the most generic term is 'sign', so that the bearer of the message is seen to stand for the message. The movement of the message through the pathways of the system is determined by a number of codes or rules which are important to the intelligibility of the message to the receivers of the message. The sharing of sets of rules makes it possible for the signs to be understood correctly, since the same sign in the same system may carry different meanings or, when translated into another system, the same sign may have radically different meanings.[9]

The complexities involved in interpreting cultural signs are captured well in the following example taken from Charles Kraft:

> Consider the problem that a single American girl continually encounters of where to place herself on the forty inches of front seat of an American car when a male is driving. Does she sit in the

---

8 Edgar Schein, for instance, uses the model in describing organisational cultures.
9 Robert Schreiter *Constructing Local Theologies.* New York: Orbis Books, 1985, 49.

middle? Close up? Against the door? Clearly there is a code here, and clearly it is based on communications and shared understandings about the girl's relationship to the driver. In long-standing American courtship ritual, she is supposed to begin somewhere in the middle; and as the relationship becomes more intimate, she acknowledges this by moving closer and closer to him. If she is angry, she moves against the door, expressing coolness and distance. If the driver is ineligible for courtship, she sits in a neutral position; to move against the door would communicate the wrong thing. How soon the girl moves over, and how far, clearly expresses something about what kind of girl she is, as well as what her relationship to the driver is. Such codes are learned but are not written; and constantly tested and compared, but seldom talked about. They are premises and rules and meanings we draw on to communicate and to understand one another, yet we are rarely conscious of them.[10]

The passage highlights the challenge for modern anthropologists in attempting to identify what the 'webs of significance' are that go into making up a culture. Culture is a human construct, and so is understandable, but not by everyone!

Geertz himself notes of culture:

> The concept of culture that I espouse ...is essentially a semiotic one. Believing, with Max Weber, that man is an animal suspended in webs of significance he himself has spun, I take culture to be those webs, and the analysis of it to be therefore **not an experimental science in search of law, but an interpretive one in search of meaning.**[11]

Geertz views anthropology from a hermeneutical perspective, rather than as a strictly empirical science. His dilemma is one faced by most modern anthropologists – how to make sense of a people's 'plan for living' on its own terms, without distorting it, because the observer has a biased view of what is 'normal' due to growing up in another culture.

Both Schreiter and Luzbetak note that the semiotic model is much more complex to use in practice than descriptive or visual models.

As modern anthropologists reflected on the cultural data that had been cumulating over nearly half a century, they began to see that the patterns they

---

10 Lessing and Lessing quoted in Charles H Kraft. *Christianity in Culture* New York: Orbis Books, 1991, 47.
11 Clifford Geertz *The Interpretation of Cultures.* New York: Basics Books: 1973, 5. Emphasis not in original.

observed (whether by descriptive, or semiotic analysis) were not random, but had an inner coherence. They recognised that cultures operate in a holistic manner and are comprehensive frameworks of meaning, covering most aspects of the life of a people. Cultures cannot easily be dismantled, as if they were made up of discrete parts, without doing damage to the whole. The worldview of a culture provides people with a source of coherence.

Early missionaries judged some elements of a local culture to be consistent with Christianity and sought to jettison the rest. This meant, in practice, that their Christian converts were expected to adopt a European way of life in a non-European context. The missionaries did not recognise that, like the people they wished to serve, they too had a culture and that *they often equated their culture with Christian faith*. The process of evangelisation slowly came to be understood as the *transformation* of the cultural worldview, rather than its obliteration or substitution, and that this occurred by the embedding of the 'worldview of faith' within the worldview of a people's culture. It came to be realised by those in the field that this could be successfully *achieved only in partnership with the people themselves*. This was a lesson hard-learned in Christian missionary experience, both Catholic and Protestant.

DEPTH DIMENSION OF CULTURE – MYTHS AND GENESIS STORIES

Culture is a group construct; it is the possession of a people. It is, therefore, meaningless to talk about the culture of an individual outside the context of the group or society to which he or she belongs.

Whenever a group of people come together over a period of time to achieve some purpose, patterns soon emerge in how the members of the group think, feel, imagine and behave. Across time, the story of the group emerges, and it becomes possible to distinguish 'our story' from 'their story' and so a basis is created for developing a collective identity.

Cultural narratives play an important role in transmitting the worldview of a culture. To understand people of a different culture it is necessary to understand their important cultural narratives and to identify the values these contain. To change a culture, it is often necessary to change or modify the narratives used to convey that culture.

Among the depth elements *narrative* and *myth* have special importance. Cultural myths[12] exist in the form of stories (narratives) that are handed down

---

12 'Myth' is used here in a technical sense. In common speech 'myth' means something that is not true. However, a cultural myth is a story that has roots in historical fact but rather than record what happened, it combines this with what the group have come to wish had happened. Cultural myths become the way in which a people conveys cultural aspirations, that is, seeks to convey 'this is what we are like at our best'. For example, for Australians the myth of the heroes of ANZAC (Australian and New Zealand Army Corps) combines the bitter defeat at Gallipoli,

from generation to generation. They become the means by which values, basic assumptions, and norms are handed on. Of particular significance here is a group's genesis story, the story of how 'our' group came to be. At present, Australians are renegotiating their nation's genesis story to include First Nations cultural history dating back 60,000 years.

In Australian Aboriginal cultures, genesis stories are called *dreamtime stories*. There seem to be as many versions of the Dreamtime as there are Aboriginal cultures because each story is anchored in the 'country' a group regards as its own.[13]

The Bible records the genesis story of Israel. This is not, as many people think, the Book of Genesis – a book that contains a genesis story of the whole of creation. The genesis story of Israel is the Exodus,[14] when Israel underwent the process of formation as a people. This story is told in the Book of Exodus and repeated elsewhere in the Bible, for example in such psalms as 77 and 78; 80 and 81; 105 and 106; 135 and 136. Psalm 136 with its invitations to communal response is familiar to Catholics from the Easter vigil liturgy:

> *O give thanks to the Lord, for he is good,*
> *for his steadfast love endures forever ...*
> *Who alone does great wonders,*
> *for his steadfast love endures forever ...*
> *Who struck Egypt through their firstborn,*
> *for his steadfast love endures forever; ...*

The power of genesis stories lies in *a people's capacity to recontextualise their story*, that is, to retell it in a new context, so that later generations are able to recognise aspects of their own personal and collective stories within the genesis story of their people. For instance, the resilience of the early pioneers is reflected in that of boat people arriving from Vietnam from the 1970s, or refugees arriving from the Middle East in the 2000s, demonstrating resilience comparable to that of the early settlers in setting up homes in this country, often from almost nothing. That Aboriginal people could survive and thrive culturally for 60,000 years, including the most recent and perilous chapter beginning with white settlement, is beginning to be

---

Turkey in 1915, with the mateship and valour of struggle in such a way as to produce something far greater and more enduring than the hoped-for glorious victory that did not occur.

13 Australian Aboriginal peoples hold a collective concept of ownership, each clan and nation owning 'their land', with group identity tied to it. This led to major confrontations with English settlers who saw Aboriginal land as 'empty', and so owned by no one. The Aborigines' cultural ties to the land were ignored until well into the late 20th century, when the High Court of Australia recognised them and the government of the day passed the Native Titles Act in 1993.

14 The *Book of Genesis* was written after the Babylonian captivity and provides a prequel to the main story of Israel's formation and journey as a people of faith.

appreciated as greatly enriching Australia's genesis story. It is the connection through story that enables people to feel that they belong. Those who are able to creatively and authentically weave together the various elements and tell a story, be it in literature or art, or music, that their hearers accept to be true, are an important asset in every society including ours.

In the realm of faith, are we able to recontextualise the genesis story of our faith tradition, that of God as creator and humans as partners with God in taking care of (husbanding) the land, as we deal with the situation of mother earth in a time of severe stress impacting the planet and its peoples? In terms of Christian faith, are we able to recontextualise the Gospel story of Jesus who lived, died, and overcame death, as we re-found our faith communities in contemporary Australia in a changed and changing era?

Genesis stories shape the expectations that members of a culture have of anyone who would consider herself or himself to be 'one of us'. They are the principal means by which the worldview of a culture is transmitted from generation to generation. The process by which this happens is far from simple.

Genesis stories celebrate national values that, in turn, provide the base on which attitudes and behavioural norms – Geertz's 'webs of significance' – are built. As we noted earlier, culture has a number of dimensions. However, it is the depth dimensions of worldview and myth that provide the key to making sense of life in changed circumstances. This implies finding points of connection with people whom we initially regard as 'other' because they see the world differently from us or our group. It is why dialogue becomes so important in the classroom. It breaks down barriers to acceptance and sets a platform for 'belonging', that is feeling part of the group. Many Catholic schools are exceptional in promoting a sense of cohesion among their students and staff. This is an important goal that takes effort to create and even more effort to sustain – a culture of acceptance that operates across cultural and religious boundaries that often tend to divide.

Pollefeyt and Bowens make the point that Christian values education in Europe, seen as a model of religious education has failed, and in fact contributes to secularisation.[15] In terms of the concepts presented in this chapter, it is not hard to understand why. The aim of religious education is to create a space for faith in the worldview of students, so the worldview of faith can become embedded in their personal worldview. This project seeks to produce change at *the deepest level of this worldview*, not at the values level. Christian values such as service, courage, faith, hope, and love, all have their secular counterparts. If the cultural worldview in our society is secular,

---

15 Didier Pollefeyt and Jan Bowens *Identity in Dialogue*. Zurich: Lit Verlag, 2014.

young people can espouse the secular version of these values without the worldview of faith ever becoming embedded in their personal worldview. This is an issue that the recontextualisation of faith seeks to address.

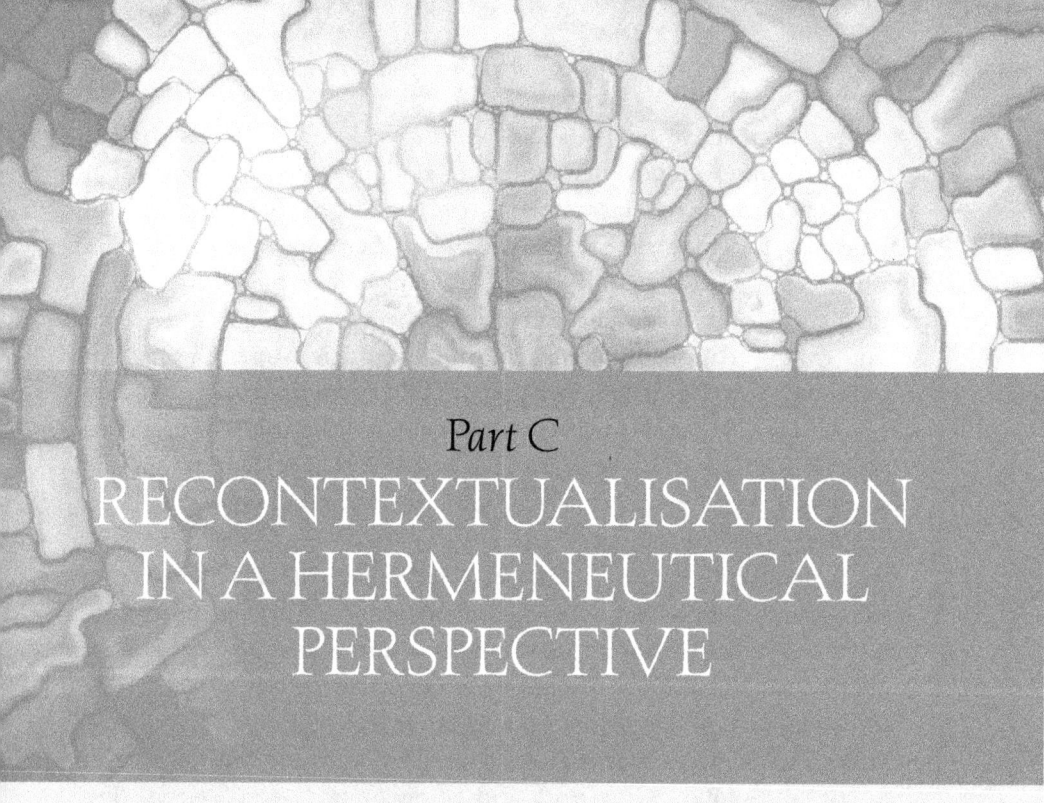

Part C
RECONTEXTUALISATION IN A HERMENEUTICAL PERSPECTIVE

In Part B we began by exploring the way in which contextualisation and recontextualisation arose as crucial elements in the Church's cross-cultural missionary experience of recent centuries, and the links that exist between this experience and anthropology. In the process of doing this we highlighted the roles that culture and worldview play in the process of meaning-making at a personal and a societal level.

Interest in anthropology grew, driven largely by the usefulness of its insights in dealing with people of other cultures. As the world became more globalised, a shift in emphasis occurred within the discipline from 'How other peoples behave' to 'Why they behave in the way that they do'. This raised the question as to whether anthropology was an empirical science or an interpretive one. Both anthropologists and missionaries became interested in the 'webs of significance', to quote Clifford Geertz, that bound a society together. Anthropology took a hermeneutical turn.

In the late 18th century, a number of European scholars began to investigate the rules governing the understanding of ancient texts, beginning with the Bible. They posed such questions as: what did the author of the text mean? How did his audience understand what he wrote? What did the author take for granted in writing his text? How much of this was shared with his audience? What does the text mean for us today? What limitation does the fact that we live in a different cultural and historical context impose? How do we know that our interpretation of the text is correct?

Such questions may seem esoteric to many readers, but they took on real meaning for citizens in the USA recently when applied to the nation's constitution and how the Supreme Court judges interpreted it in overturning the Roe v Wade decision. They also take on importance when we are confronted with literal readings of the Biblical text. The field of hermeneutics, developed initially as a study of the 'rules' that apply in reading the Bible, quickly evolved into the legal field and the study of literature. When the author is no longer available as a resource in determining the meaning of a text, how do you arrive at the correct meaning? Is there even such a thing as a 'correct meaning'?

By the mid-20th century it was recognised that texts include what we 'read', but also people and events. Accounts of events that purport to be 'objective' are told from a particular perspective, that is they are *interpretations*. In the Donald Trump era it became especially obvious that facts can be 'spun' depending on the interests of the people interpreting them, with the notion of 'truth' itself, relativised to 'your' truth and 'my' truth. Whatever does not correspond to 'my truth' can be discounted as 'fake news'! Just as biblical hermeneutics raises the question of correctly interpreting the Bible and the limits that apply to this process, philosophical hermeneutics attends to the question of correctly interpreting events and arriving at their meaning. This opens a broader conversation about what I mean when I say I 'understand' a text or 'interpret' my own, or other people's actions.

Hermeneutics raises a number of issues for both the endeavours of contextualisation and recontextualisation. Contextualisation seeks to preserve the essentials of the Christian message as *it crosses cultural boundaries and enters the meaning system at work in this new space*. Recontextualisation seeks *to maintain the essentials of the Christian message when the meaning-making framework that operates in a cultural space undergoes a significant change.*

In Chapter 9 we explore some basic hermeneutical insights dealing with how people make meaning and the limits that cultures and worldviews impose on this process. In Chapter 10 we apply these to the worldview of faith and its relationship to other worldviews. Both contextualisation and recontextualisation seek to open the worldview of a culture to the possibilities offered by the worldview of faith. How these possibilities are interpreted depends on the understanding of the worldview of faith that people bring to the task.

Some of the themes explored in Part 3 will be taken up again in Part 4, which examines recontextualisation from a theological perspective.

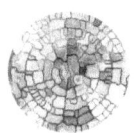

9

HOW PEOPLE CONSTRUCT MEANING:
AND WHY THIS MATTERS IN THE RECONTEXTUALISATION OF FAITH

People construct meaning with reference to their personal worldviews. Meaning-making is a complex process that occurs partly within our awareness, but mostly outside of our awareness, due to the ways in which cultural learning occurs. Meaning-making is not an exclusively rational process in that it cannot be reduced only to what people consciously know or believe. It depends also on what they value and on the sensibility they bring to the processes of meaning-making. Together these are of central importance to those who seek to develop faith through formal or informal education.

In this chapter we explore the process of meaning-making from the perspective of what has been termed 'moderate hermeneutics'.[1] This is the school of thought pioneered by German philosopher Hans-Georg Gadamer and developed further by the French philosopher Paul Ricoeur.

The process of meaning-making deals with how we come to understand that which is unfamiliar. We always interpret the unfamiliar in the context of the familiar. That is to say we always start from somewhere and bring something to the task of understanding. Gadamer calls what we bring to the task 'the forestructure of knowing'. It is what we have called in the previous chapter a personal worldview.

HERMENEUTICAL CIRCLE

New meanings open up for us in interaction with what we already know. They appear in our consciousness as new insights. When the connection is made, we have a 'eureka' moment. Expressed in popular language, 'we

---

[1] See Shaun Gallagher *Hermeneutics and Education*. *New York*: University of New York Press, 1992, 9-10.

get it'. The aim of all pedagogy is to facilitate such moments in a student's learning.

When the unfamiliar is seen in the context of the familiar, a student's understanding of the familiar expands. This in turn gives him or her a deeper insight into the unfamiliar. This deeper insight then further expands understanding and so on. The cyclical nature of the process by which insight grows is why the process is called 'the hermeneutical circle', even though in practice understanding grows more as a spiral than a circle.

Take the process of understanding a poem or story as an example.

The Six Wise Men from Hindustan; a Hindu Fable[2]

It was six men of Hindustan
To learning much inclined
Who went to see the Elephant
(Though all of them were blind)
That each by observation
Might satisfy the mind.

The First approached the Elephant
And happening to fall
Against his broad and sturdy side
At once began to bawl:
'Bless me, it seems the Elephant
Is very like a wall.'

The Second, feeling of his tusk,
Cried, 'Ho! What have we here
So very round and smooth and sharp?
To me 'tis mighty clear
This wonder of an Elephant
Is very like a spear.'

The Third approached the animal,
And happening to take
The squirming trunk within his hands,
Then boldly up and spake:
'I see,' quoth he, 'the Elephant
Is very like a snake.'

---

[2] John Godfrey Saxe (1816-1887) *The Poems of John Godfrey Saxe Vol 1*. Boston: James Osgood and Co, 1876, 259-6.1. This fable exists in multiple versions.

The Fourth reached out an eager hand,
And felt about the knee.
'What most this wondrous beast is like
Is mighty plain,' quoth he;
''Tis clear enough the Elephant
Is very like a tree!'

The Fifth, who chanced to touch the ear,
Said: 'E'en the blindest man
Can tell what this resembles most;
Deny the fact who can,
This marvel of an Elephant
Is very like a fan!'

The Sixth no sooner had begun
About the beast to grope,
Than, seizing on the swinging tail
That fell within his scope,
'I see,' quoth he, 'the Elephant
Is very like a rope!'

And so these men of Hindustan
Disputed loud and long,
Each in his own opinion
Exceeding stiff and strong,
Though each was partly in the right
And all were in the wrong.

So oft in theologic wars,
The disputants, I ween,
Rail on in utter ignorance
Of what each other mean,
And prate about an Elephant
Not one of them has seen!

On first reading, this poem appears to be about a range of people mistaking the part of the elephant that they could experience for the whole that they could not see. That is, until the reader reaches the final verse which sets out the 'moral' of the story: that religious thinkers mistake their partial understanding for the whole. It turns out that the meaning of the poem is not really about the wise men from Hindustan after all!

THE HERMENEUTICAL CIRCLE IN OPERATION: GENESIS

The diagram below simplifies a more complex reality. In the diagram, what we bring to the task of understanding is called 'the familiar'. As we have noted above, this familiar is our personal worldview. We make sense of the unfamiliar in terms of our personal worldview which expands in consequence. This in turn enables us to see what was originally unfamiliar in a new and more critical light.

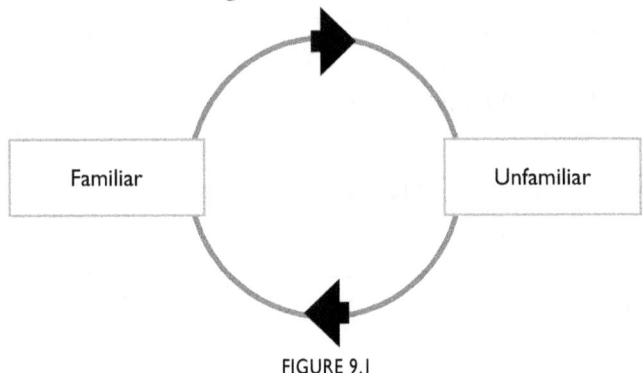

FIGURE 9.1

A good example of this process in action is how teachers work with young people in regard to the account of creation found in the *Book of Genesis*. A literal reading of the text seems clearly at odds with a scientific account of creation. Students naturally take a critical stance to a literal interpretation of the story since it runs counter to what their culture tells them is true.

What needs to be explained to students is that the Genesis account was written well over 2000 years ago at a time when people's understanding of the cosmos was quite different from our understanding. The authors of Genesis operated from a worldview in which the earth was the centre of the created world. Of course, working with insights provided by recent scientific exploration, that is not how we see things today. Their intent, however, was not a scientific but a mythological one, that is, they were laying down a foundation story of the world. In other words, whatever the limits of their account scientifically when judged in terms of today's accepted knowledge, in the final analysis theirs is not, and was not, written as a scientific account of creation. Rather, it is a story with theological intent that today's Christian faith leaders must retell within the framework of contemporary understandings. As we seek to recontextualise this Genesis account, we do well to bear in mind that, as scientific theories and explanations develop further, even today's accounts will be modified; but for people of faith now as then, the central truth of the story of God as creator of the universe remains.

In Israel's foundation story there is one God, not the many gods associated with their neighbours or with their conquerors. The text affirms that their God was responsible for creation and their experiences of God led them to believe certain things about what it means to be human and to be a community under *the God of all*. The Genesis story is a mythical account about the beginning of the world. As we have it in the version finally adopted by Israel's spiritual leaders, it exists as a *prequel* to the main story of the Old Testament, that originates with the Exodus. This is an account of God liberating Israel from slavery in Egypt to become the people with whom God made a covenant, and who exist under God's protection and care.

The Genesis story attempts to explain things within a worldview that is quite foreign to us today. By studying the context in which the text was produced, we are able to gain insight into the worldview it projects and so draw from the story some conclusions about the religious truths it contains.[3] This involves engaging with the story critically rather than literally, utilising the various widely accepted forms of Biblical criticism available, for example, literary criticism and historical criticism. The model of the hermeneutical circle discussed above needs to be expanded to take into account the impact of culture on our personal worldview. This leads us to the more complex relationship illustrated below.

THE PROCESS OF MEANING-MAKING: A MODEL

The worldview of our culture (as we comprehend it) stands behind our personal worldview. If the unfamiliar does not make sense to us immediately, we look at it in the light of the worldview of our culture and the assumptions that hold that worldview together.

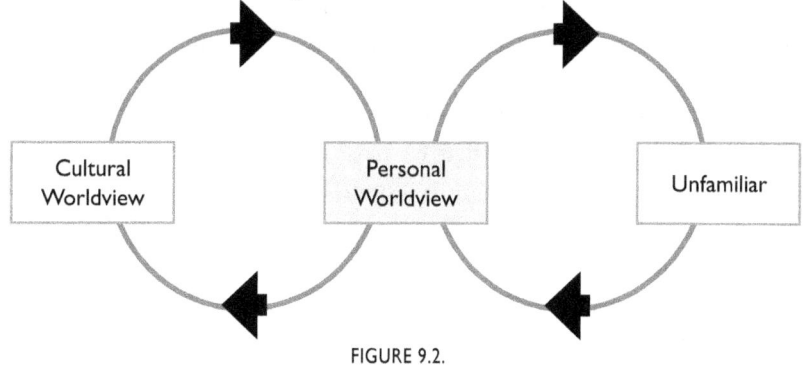

FIGURE 9.2.

---

3 In the post-Vatican II period, it is recognised that the same principle applies to all major Church teaching. Its context must be recognised

If things do not make sense within this wider framework, then we have three options:

1. To reject the unfamiliar as not worth understanding.
2. To question our understanding of the worldview of culture.
3. To question the assumptions on which the worldview of our culture depends.

While the worldview of our culture tells us much about the physical sciences, it also tells us a good deal about the social science of anthropology as well. In understanding the Book of Genesis we need to include insights from both the physical sciences and anthropology if we are to make sense of what it has to tell us about God. As a social science, anthropology provides us with tools to look at the story critically, in much the same way as the physical sciences provide insights into physical phenomena.

The case study addressed above indicates a number of things about how we make sense of the unfamiliar. The first port of call in understanding the unfamiliar is our personal worldview. This can be especially demanding for young people as their personal worldview is only partially formed by the processes of both cultural learning and faith learning.

We always try to make sense of the unfamilar in terms of our personal worldview, and in the light of our culture. If we can do this, then our worldview expands via the operation of the hermeneutical circle. If we cannot make sense of the unfamiliar, then we either reject it as not worth understanding, or even question the adequacy of our personal frame of reference. Because our frame of reference is shaped by our culture, we will put questions to this, assuming that the unfamiliar is worth the effort of understanding. We may even question the assumptions on which our culture rests, assumptions that we have previously taken for granted.

If the worldview of the age changes, rendering the worldview of our culture unstable, then we have a problem since the frame of reference we have so far taken for granted becomes unreliable in making sense of the unfamiliar. The question then becomes: How can we stabilise the worldview of our culture? The answer is that we have to make wise choices to restore the balance between theme and counter-theme that has been upset. In Chapter 8 we featured some examples of easily recognisable themes and counter themes which may become unbalanced, with the pendulum seemingly swinging too far one way or the other in a change of era.

In postmodern culture the need to choose in regard to balance points is not an option; it is a necessity if people are to live meaningful lives. The need to consciously choose is part of the new 'normal' in our cultural situation.

RICOEUR: DEVELOPING A CRITICAL UNDERSTANDING

Ricoeur sees the process of understanding moving from a naive stage in which people take things more or less on faith to a second stage that Ricoeur calls 'the second *naïveté*'. This involves a more critical appreciation of the unfamiliar because it has been assessed against a wider frame of reference. For him, understanding comes in a hermeneutical spiral rather than in a hermeneutical circle because each iteration of the circle expands a person's worldview. This goes on for as long as the person seeks to make meaning.

Ricoeur's insight has moved to centre stage in religious education as teachers invite students to look at the faith of their religious community critically rather than naively. This means exploring their faith within not only the frame of reference provided by culture and by their own faith tradition, but also against the frame of reference provided by other religions as well.

It is in this respect, that the ECSI project's goals may seem somewhat controversial. ECSI was initially developed in Flanders where in some suburbs and towns up to 95 per cent of students in a Catholic school can be Muslim. This is a situation familiar in many non-European countries, for example in Asia, where Catholic schools may cater for many or a majority of students of other religious faiths.[4] The presence of large numbers of Muslims in Catholic schools in a European country such as Belgium creates a major challenge for Catholic educators, particularly in delivering religious education. The solution developed at KU Leuven, and being implemented in schools in Flanders and elsewhere including Australia, is premised on the assumption that the variety of worldviews that students bring to school can be viewed as *a resource rather than as a problem*.

The purpose of religious education in this highly pluralistic context of Catholic schooling is to mobilise this resource to assist students to affirm their religious identity as Catholic, Muslim or other. If a student identifies as having 'no religious faith', the aim is to help them to develop as persons 'open to faith' – that is, not to close off faith as an option in their lives.

The ECSI methodology relies on the value of *empathic dialogue* between teacher and students but, more importantly, among the students themselves. In dialogue, students seek to understand not only the worldview implicit

---

4 See Thomas Groome *Educating for Life: A Spiritual Vision for Every Teacher and Parent*. Allen: Thomas More, 1998, 9-11. Groome narrates a visit to Pakistan where the understanding of a 'Catholic Education' that he encountered was very different from that in the USA. This led to some serious re-thinking about his philosophy of Catholic education. The sisters conducting the school in Pakistan had had to delve deeply into their faith tradition and find there a vision of God at work in the world – a project in which they could participate in a very different, but authentic way, from that of North American Catholic schooling.

in Catholicism which sponsors the school, but also that which underpins the Muslim faith and other worldviews held by students. The aim is to promote mutual understanding which in turn produces challenges not only in discussing religious beliefs, but also in working together on common projects that transcend faith boundaries. In this process the hope is that students come to recognise the values not only that underpin the Catholic tradition, but also those of other religious traditions and worldviews. In this way students come to a critical understanding of what is particular to their own faith tradition.[5]

WORLDVIEW OF THE AGE AND MEANING-MAKING

The picture we are painting can be taken one step further to include the worldview of the age.

The worldview of the age shapes the cultural worldview of a society in much the same way as the latter shapes a person's worldview. If there is a major change in the worldview of the age, then this has a ripple effect that spreads to the worldview of culture and so to the personal frame of reference that people access in making sense of life events.

People who are native to the new situation take the new understandings largely for granted as a result of growing up in an enviroment that also takes them for granted. For example, most people growing up in the early modern era assumed that God created the world directly. They also assumed that the world operated according to the laws of nature that God had created. They therefore found it hard to believe in miracles since, by definition, miracles break the rules of nature. As a consequence, the sections of the New Testament dealing with Jesus perfoming 'miracles' were called into question. This left people with a abstract concept of God rather than the concrete picture of Jesus' healing ministry that the gospel writers set out to create. In the worldview of these writers many things that we would now interpret in medical terms were understood as 'miracles' by the people to whom Jesus ministered. However not all of Jesus' 'signs'[6] can be explained in this way.

---

5 This model of religious education was formally adopted by the Catholic Education Office for Flanders while the authors were on sabbatical at KU Leuven in 2016. It was received with some consternation by the local secular press who had some difficulty in accepting that Catholic schools sought to help their Muslim students become better Muslims!
6 In John's Gospel, Jesus' miracles are called 'signs'.

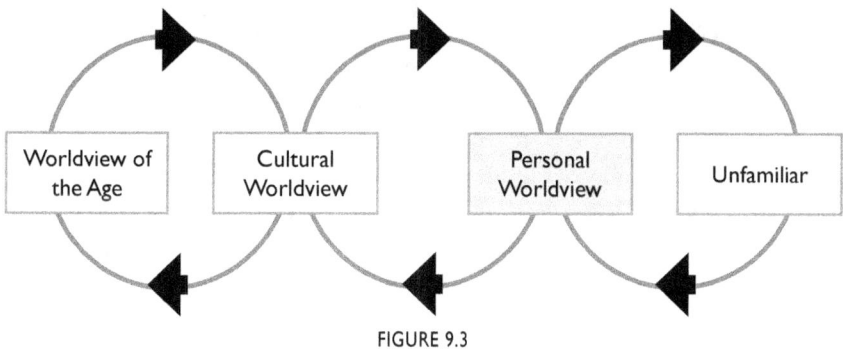

FIGURE 9.3

From the diagram above it should be clear that, if the worldview of the age undergoes major changes, or becomes unstable, then this will ripple through to the framework that people use in making sense of life. Similarly, developments in a cultural worldview can reshape the worldview of the age. This happened with the development of science and technology in Europe that was exported globally in the 18th and 19th centuries. Science was understood as a meaning-making framework that could replace religion. Science depends on validating insights by testing them against the available evidence. This contrasted with the previous model for validating knowledge in Europe that depended on appeal to the authority of the great figures in a particular field of knowledge. Science validated knowledge by inductive reasoning. Philosophy and theology, for instance, used deductive reasoning. Today it is recognised that the major academic disciplines each has its own methods of validating new insights as correct and therefore as knowledge. Science and theology now both employ inductive and deductive methods in creating knowledge.

CULTURAL WORLDVIEW AS DEFAULT FRAME OF REFERENCE

Hermeneutics holds that people make sense of life using the *worldview of their culture as a default frame of reference*. This is not a conscious decision on an individual's part, but a consequence of their enculturation – of growing up in a particular cultural milieu that is taken for granted.

This situation creates problems for religious educators specifically, because the majority of students and many of their parents are now 'native' to a highly secular Australian culture. They take this culture for granted in making sense of their lives. Growing up in a secular culture means that explicitly religious language is foreign to people, so they generally lack a basic element needed to identify or articulate their religious experiences.

If students are to make sense of such experiences in terms of Christian faith, then at a minimum, teachers need to *recontextualise the language of faith* in order to create a linguistic frame of reference that is meaningful for their students. Simply assuming language that was once meaningful is still meaningful in today's situation is foolhardy. Something similar can be said for many of the symbols of faith.

Once the worldview of the age changes, its impact on cultural and personal worldviews is such that it can no longer be assumed that religious symbols retain their meaning. In the Catholic Church, for example, many devotions and practices that were once meaningful, and commanded support among the Catholic community as expressions of faith, have clearly lost their salience. New expressions will inevitably arise that are more meaningful to a contemporary faith community. For instance, it is a well-established empirical fact that the vast majority of Australian Catholics today no longer interpret attending Mass every Sunday as an essential marker in defining themselves as Catholic.[7] This is a major change in outlook from that of the middle of the last century. The change raises the questions: how do the majority of Catholics now define their identity as 'Catholic'? How might they be assisted to deepen and enhance their Catholic identity given the current milieu in which they live?

---

7 Bob Dixon 'The Science of Listening: Contexts and Challenges for the Catholic Community in Australia', sets out the data-sharing that 95% of Catholics no longer meet five basic criteria of 'being Catholic' applicable in the 1960s. *Australasian Catholic Record*, Vol 91, Issue 3, 2014, 264–280.

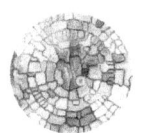

10

THE WORLDVIEW OF FAITH AS AN INTERPRETIVE CATEGORY

As we have noted previously, the worldview of faith is a public worldview and as such it is sponsored by a community – in this case a faith community. The worldview held by the Catholic community depends on how that community understands its identity and mission, and the areas of legitimate difference that exist within this understanding. This is important to our exploration of recontextualisation because it is through the worldview of our shared faith that we choose to make sense of our human experience.

Following the Reformation that occurred in 16th century Europe, the leaders of the Catholic Church sought to differentiate Catholic faith communities from other Christian faith communities, believing that only the former constituted the 'true Church' founded by Christ, and that other Christian faith communities were in error. They argued that error had no rights and that, therefore, governments in so-called 'Catholic countries' should support the Catholic Church and, at best, tolerate other faith communities.[1] Unsurprisingly, this stance invited retaliation in 'Protestant countries' resulting in the bitter denominationalism of the 18th, 19th and early 20th centuries, that played such a pivotal role in the history of white settlement in Australia, and the development of the Catholic faith community here. A similar situation occurred in many other societies.

VATICAN II: RENEWED UNDERSTANDING OF WHAT IT MEANS TO BE 'CHURCH'

A thaw in relationship among the Christian churches began in the mid-20th century. The encyclical letter of Pope Pius XII, *Mystici Corporis* 1943, which focused on the spiritual nature of the Church, opened the way for a

---

1 This understanding of the relationship between Church and State was abandoned at Vatican Council II, that is, only in the mid-20th century.

deeper consideration of unity, without in any way denying the importance of visible unity under the successor of St. Peter. In the decree on ecumenism published at the Second Vatican Council (*Unitatis Redintegratio*), a decree that explained elements of, and so complemented, the Constitution on the Church *(Lumen Gentium)*, the Council focused on Christian *communions*, that is churches, rather than individuals. It solemnly taught that the Christian churches existed in various degrees of communion with each other because of the acceptance of baptism through which members 'put on Christ' (Rom 13:14). These churches were acknowledged as salvific for their members. Although the Council taught that the fullness of Catholicity 'subsists' in the Catholic Church,[2] it moved away from fully identifying the catholicity of the Church with the Catholic Church as we know it, leaving the path open for various ways of achieving unity in plurality in the decades ahead.

All this occurred against the background of a growing realisation within the Christian churches of their *common responsibility* to carry forward within human history God's mission as incarnated in Jesus Christ. These new understandings created a foundation for regarding other Christian churches not as adversaries, but as *potential partners in this common mission*.[3] This led to the Christian churches' becoming aware of the need to carry forward 'the mission of God' in human history rather than to focus exclusively on promoting the mission of particular churches. The net effect was that, in the second half of the 20th century, 'mission' was re-construed. The churches began to look outwards to the needs of the context in which they were situated, rather than looking inwards, focused on concerns related to their own maintenance. The new perspective created the need for dialogue, not only among the Christian churches, but also with other religions and various groups within secular society to advance the 'Kingdom of God' within human history.

The new perspective interpreted the identity of the Catholic Church as a *communion of local churches* and identified the need to develop relationships among them at the national and international levels.

DIALOGUE AS A MODE OF ENCOUNTERING OTHERS

Vatican II also led Catholics to a new understanding of the relationship between Christianity and other world religions, leading to the call for *dialogue* between members of different faiths. It became possible for people

---

[2] *Unitatis Redintegratio* #4. https://www.vatican.va/archive/hist_councils/ii_vatican_council/documents/vat-ii_decree_19641121_unitatis-redintegratio_en.html
[3] An obvious area of endeavour lies in mission studies, where a fruitful scholarly collaboration among Christian scholars is occurring in many societies across the world.

of faith to explore what had previously been seen as *mutually exclusive religious worldviews* and co-operate with one another on a range of common projects based on shared values, if not on shared beliefs. Education is one of these shared projects.

In this new 'condition of faith',[4] the way in which Catholics think about themselves as a 'Catholic faith community', and the way in which they think about their relationship to other Christian and non-Christian faith communities, has undergone a major change. This development caused the Catholic Church to adopt a wider understanding of its mission and, within this, the mission of local faith communities.[5] The development also led to the Church re-construing its relationship with secular agencies, including governments. Christian faith was seen again as having a legitimate 'voice' in the 'public square' in the development of policies that impacted the lives of citizens, and not something that can easily be relegated to the 'private sphere' as happened in the modern period.

The legitimating scriptural basis for this change in self-understanding is a reclaiming of the core element in Jesus' teaching – 'the Kingdom of God'.[6] That is, that through the Incarnation God's kingdom, or reign, has broken decisively into human history. Its emergence, under the guidance of the Holy Spirit and with the responsiveness of the Christian churches, continues to play a role in the unfolding of human history. Salvation history is seen as continuing in actual history. The Church's role, therefore, is to be an agent of God's mission in history[7], advancing God's offer of salvation to all, but especially to those who are marginalised and to those who live under various forms of oppression – political, economic or social – that dehumanise them.

As a part of civil society, the Christian Church has a role to play in the public square and a contribution to make to what Pope Paul VI called 'the evangelisation of cultures'.[8] By this he meant embedding Christian values

---

4 The condition of faith in the contemporary world is an area of focus of Charles Taylor or for example, in *A Secular Age*, 2007, and also from a different perspective, that of the relationship between faith and reason in the work of Joseph Ratzinger. See for example his first encyclical as Pope Benedict XVI *Deus Caritas Est* (God is Love 2005) https://www.vatican.va/content/benedict-xvi/en/encyclicals/documents/hf_ben-xvi_enc_20051225_deus-caritas-est.html.g

5 cf *Nostra Aetate* #2, 'Let Christians, while witnessing to their own faith and way of life, acknowledge, preserve and encourage the spiritual and moral good found among non-Christians, as well as their social and cultural values.'

6 As noted in Chapter 3, the renowned Australian scripture scholar Francis Moloney prefers the translation 'the reigning presence of God', not least because in the common translation, the dynamism of the original has been suppressed in favour of a more static and geographical evocation.

7 The Church no longer sees itself as the sole agent in this project. God also acts through other intermediaries.

8 'All this could be expressed in the following words: what matters is to evangelize man's culture and cultures (not in a purely decorative way, as it were, by applying a thin veneer, but in a vital

into a society's culture and into the social structures that give expression to that culture, and so into a people's story. This is a very positive role.

The Church also has a critical role to play in challenging social structures when these create victims. Given the variety of cultures that are embraced by a global church, these are responsibilities that can be undertaken *only by local churches* in collaboration with others and are likely to take different forms in different cultures. This mission projects the Church into playing an active role in civil society as well as in the public square.

Pope Francis has in many forums highlighted the ways in which the structures of a society can marginalise people, creating streams of refugees that can easily overwhelm the support structures of another society. Having experienced this situation firstly in his native Argentina, and then more recently in Italy, Pope Francis speaks on the basis of real experience and not from a theoretical perspective. In *Evangelii Gaudium* he calls the Church into dialogue with civil society, the state, and with other believers. Such dialogue is both a means of making the Gospel present (evangelisation), but also the only fruitful – or indeed possible – modus operandi in many areas of our troubled world:

> Evangelization also involves the path of dialogue. For the Church today, three areas of dialogue stand out where she needs to be present in order to promote full human development and to pursue the common good: dialogue with states, dialogue with society – including dialogue with cultures and the sciences – and dialogue with other believers who are not part of the Catholic Church. In each case, 'the Church speaks from the light which faith offers', contributing her two thousand-year experience and keeping ever in mind the life and sufferings of human beings. This light transcends human reason, yet it can also prove meaningful and enriching to those who are not believers and it stimulates reason to broaden its perspectives (#238).

DIALOGUE AND MISSION

For Pope Francis, as with his immediate predecessors, dialogue is seen as the means by which the Catholic Church can facilitate a broader understanding of its mission and engagement with the cultures within which this mission is to be accomplished. It is also the means for engaging with people who hold other religious and secular worldviews. What dialogue means in

---

way, in depth and right to their very roots), in the wide and rich sense which these terms have in *Gaudium et Spes*, always taking the person as one's starting-point and always coming back to the relationships of people among themselves and with God.' (*Evangelii Nuntiandi* #20)

practice for the Church, and its place within the broader understanding of mission noted above, are spelled out most clearly in the Pontifical Council for Inter-religious Dialogue's 1991 document, *Dialogue and Proclamation*.[9] In discussing the nature of dialogue, the document notes that dialogue can be understood in three different ways:

1. At the purely human level, it means reciprocal communication, leading to a common goal or, at a deeper level, to interpersonal communion.
2. Dialogue can be taken as an attitude of respect and friendship, which permeates or should permeate all those activities constituting the evangelizing mission of the Church. This can appropriately be called 'the spirit of dialogue'.
3. In the context of religious plurality, dialogue means 'all positive and constructive interreligious relations with individuals and communities of other faiths which are directed at mutual understanding and enrichment, in obedience to truth and respect for freedom. It includes both witness and the exploration of respective religious convictions.'[10]

The document goes on to outline four 'forms' that inter-religious dialogue may take:

1. *Dialogue of life*, where people strive to live in an open and neighbourly spirit, sharing their joys and sorrows, their human problems and preoccupations.
2. *Dialogue of action*, in which Christians and others collaborate for the integral development and liberation of people.
3. *Dialogue of theological exchange*, where specialists seek to deepen their understanding of their respective religious heritages, and to appreciate each other's spiritual values.
4. *Dialogue of religious experience*, where persons, rooted in their own religious traditions, share their spiritual riches, for instance regarding prayer and contemplation, faith and ways of searching for God or the Absolute.[11]

---

9 This document acknowledges that there is a broad and a narrow concept of mission at work in Catholic teaching. The narrow concept focuses on proclamation, the broader concept includes the many ways in which a faith community engages with the world around it. It is in this context that the document places inter-religious dialogue. The document was produced as a clarification of points made in Pope John Paul II's encyclical *Redemptoris Missio* that was written at the same time.
10 Pontifical Council for Inter-religious Dialogue. *Dialogue and Proclamation* 1991, #9. https://www.vatican.va/roman_curia/pontifical_councils/interelg/documents/rc_pc_interelg_doc_19051991_dialogue-and-proclamatio_en.html
11 Ibid #42.

These four forms of dialogue are seen as interrelated:

> Contacts in daily life and common commitment to action will normally open the door for cooperation in promoting human and spiritual values; they may also eventually lead to the dialogue of religious experience in response to the great questions that the circumstances of life do not fail to arouse in the minds of people.[12]

The understanding of dialogue formulated above applies to inter-religious dialogue but has a wider significance when applied to settings such as a Catholic school. It marks an important move towards a dialogical understanding of what it means to be Church, a major theme in Pope Francis's teaching that ultimately finds its validation in the dialogical God who is Trinity.

This evolution in the self-understanding of what it means to be Church, and the mission that flows from it, has taken many Catholics by surprise. It challenges the rather passive stance that Catholics, in particular, have taken regarding their place in society and the responsibilities that flow from their baptism. It has initiated a major shift in the Catholic worldview that even many clerics seem to have difficulty accommodating. It is this evolution that we are seeking to trace in this chapter.

This development has highlighted competing versions of the 'worldview of faith' each claiming allegiance within the Catholic faith communities. These seem to represent paradigms or 'ideal types' defining a spectrum of views with those of Catholics spread out between the poles each represents. As a consequence, the 'worldview of Christian faith' now has a number of possible configurations. This complicates our understanding of what 'being Catholic' means today.

The older of the two paradigms relies on classicist assumptions. It holds that Catholic faith exists outside culture and history in a timeless form and can be set out as a series of propositions and practices. In missiological terms this model sees Catholic faith as having a 'kernel' that can be transmitted unchanged from culture to culture or from age to age within a given culture.

The 'timeless propositions of faith' are invoked to make sense of new situations by applying them using deductive logic. In this perspective there is only 'the Catholic worldview' that has a *definitive form* and is universally valid. The underlying assumption is that 'one size can fit all'. The model has a long provenance within the Catholic faith community, but now struggles to account for the range of human experiences encountered there, and runs

---

12 ibid #43.

counter to the Church's missionary experience as discussed in Chapter 4. The model is hegemonic and interprets God's revelation as a closed book.

Its supporters believe that scripture articulates 'God's truth' in an absolute form. In this worldview, Catholic practices, such as those associated with the sacraments, constitute non-negotiable markers defining Catholic identity.

In this perspective the present situation of the Catholic Church is one of obvious decline that can be addressed only by renewed fidelity to 'Church teaching' as understood within an acultural and ahistorical framework. Catholics and Catholic leaders holding this perspective see 're-confessionalisation' as the key to Church renewal and community vitality. As the data from the ECSI project clearly demonstrates, this position has very limited support among Australian Catholics.[13]

RE-ORIENTATION IN THE WORLDVIEW OF FAITH

The alternative paradigm is an open-story perspective that holds that the above position is theologically and hermeneutically unsound. All human understanding must be articulated in language in order to be meaningful, and so is necessarily limited, not only by the cultural framework within which the articulation occurs, but also by the worldview that underpins that framework. Since cultures and their associated worldviews are the product of history, then so too are all theological understandings. *It is therefore not possible for Catholic beliefs to be expressed in absolute terms.* The fact that many Christians think that this is possible is due in part to their misinterpreting the scriptures, in part due to their misinterpreting the thrust of human history, and in part due to their not understanding the limits that culture places on human understanding.

In pre-critical Europe[14], under Christendom, both the cultural framework and worldview of the age were nominally Christian, so life was interpreted mainly in terms of Christian categories. Many Catholic leaders seem to look back to this period naively as a 'golden age' of Catholicism. This pre-critical worldview was formally abandoned at the Vatican II.[15]

As we have noted previously, in the modern period, a new worldview emerged that discouraged Christian beliefs and practices but ironically still

---

13 Pollefeyt and Bowens *Identity in Dialogue.* Zurich: Lit Verlag, 2014, 57.
14 Western history is often divided into eras. 'Pre-critical' represents the time before the European Enlightenment when people were largely unaware of the factors in their society that created victims and discriminated against people judged to be 'different'. Society as such was not the focus of rational inquiry. Critical thought developed in the modern period and reaches its high point in the postmodern era (c1970-2000).
15 James McEvoy *Leaving Christendom for Good: Church-world dialogue in a Secular Age.* New York: Lexington Books, 2014, 170ff.

clung to Christian values.[16] Catholic leaders of the period rejected modern culture and its worldview outright with the result that many Western faith communities found themselves isolated from their surrounding society.[17] The situation proved catastrophic for the Catholic Church. It lost members who shared the aspirations for a better world implicit in the modern worldview. As members over-represented in the poorer classes, Catholic parents wanted something better for their children, if not for themselves. Catholic education was to play a decisive role in realising their hopes.

The experience of rebuilding Europe after two world wars saw the emergence of a new form of awareness there, much more attuned to the ways in which the structures of a society impacted both positively and negatively on citizens. The emergent 'critical consciousness' called the modern worldview into question, as well as many of the assumptions on which its hopes were based. This questioning became explicit with the publication of Jean Francois Lyotard's *La Condition Postmoderne: Rapport sur le savoir* (1979) and its publication in English in 1984 as *The Postmodern Condition: a Report on Knowledge*.[18]

Lyotard criticised the destructive power of what he called 'the grand narratives of modernity' (also referred to as 'meta narratives') – by which he meant *totalising accounts of the human condition* in particular, communism and liberalism.[19] He argued that people should be wary of all ideologies that make totalising claims, as these commonly overstate their case, and are forms of reductionism.[20]

Lyotard was also critical of the hegemony that science had on knowledge, holding that by the 1970s science was no longer concerned with the construction of knowledge for its own sake, but with the creation of wealth for those sponsoring scientific research.

The new emphasis on what Lyotard called 'performativity' meant that the construction of knowledge was now directed by commercial interests,

---

16 Frederick Nietzsche pointed up the irony that in modernity Europeans had 'killed God' in the sense that they had abandoned Christian beliefs, but still wanted to organise their lives according to Christian values.
17 In Australia, for instance from the 1920s until the 1960s Catholics were expected to send their children to Catholic schools, play for Catholic sporting teams, socialise together, and to marry other Catholics. The parish was the centre of Catholic social life as well as Christian life.
18 Jean Francois Lyotard. *The Postmodern Condition: a Report on Knowledge*. Manchester: Manchester Unity Press, 1984.
19 In a book length essay KUL theologian Lieven Boeve poses the question whether the totalising claims made by the Christian churches on 'truth' mean that Christianity itself falls in the category of a 'metanarrative'. See Lieven Boeve *Interrupting Tradition: An essay on Christian faith in a postmodern condition*. Louvain: Peeters Press, 2002.
20 Reductionism can take many forms. The underlying idea is that all of life can be accounted for from a single perspective be that science, theology, history, economics, biology, psychology, etc. The main theorists of human development – Piaget, Kohlberg, Erikson and Fowler – assume that their theories are true for all people. In this sense they are totalising, and potentially reductive. This is the critique Lyotard is making.

meaning that, in practice, governments and corporations now played a key role in determining what is determined as knowledge, because they hold power. Power was seen as defining knowledge, rather than knowledge defining power as had been widely held previously.[21] Lyotard recognised that in the postmodern era (1970-) a major change had occurred in 'the condition of knowledge'.

Any 'closed story' interpretation of Christian beliefs and practices falls into the category of a metanarrative because of its totalising orientation.[22] This has important implications for how a Christian church understands its identity and its mission. If it possesses 'the truth', then others can join it only on its terms. The missionary experience of the Catholic Church, as we have noted in earlier chapters, renders such a position untenable.

THE CATHOLIC STORY AS AN 'OPEN STORY'

As noted above, the core of Jesus' teaching is that God's Kingdom (or reign) has now broken into human history *in a definitive way* and will therefore continue to be part of that history. The Church, and the faith communities that comprise it, are called on to be agents of God's mission. In Jesus' lifetime the 'Kingdom of God' became evident in a number of ways: through his teaching, through his healing ministry, by means of his forming a community of disciples to carry on his mission, and by his sending the Holy Spirit to continue that mission in human history.

Jesus' ministry was not simply a spiritual ministry; it challenged both the situation of those who were marginalised within his own society, as well as challenging the reasons for their marginalisation; it involved healing the sick and comforting those who grieved; it sought to place the notion of God and Israel's covenant with God in a new light. Jesus drew on the images and symbols of his culture in conveying his message about the 'Kingdom of God' which has two dimensions: the 'now' and the 'yet to come'.

The 'now' dimension is God's offer of salvation in history which finds expression in liberation from all that oppresses, degrades, and dehumanises people. This is a mission that Christian faith communities are responsible for carrying forward.

The 'not yet' dimension of the Kingdom of God reminds people that human effort alone cannot realise the fullness of God's Kingdom which is not only completed within time, but also beyond human history. The efforts

---

21 Jean-Francois Lyotard, 1984.
22 Jean-Francois Lyotard criticised the Christian narrative as it was presented in the 1970s as a 'modern master narrative of 'love'. See Lieven Boeve's *Lyotard and Theology: Beyond the Christian master narrative of Love*. London: Bloomsbury, 2014, 49,ff.

of people in the 'now' validate belief in the 'not yet'. In other words the Christian story cannot be interpreted in closed terms within human history, since of its nature the Christian experience and story remain open to the creative action of God's Spirit within that history.

Secondly, while the Church is an agent in God's mission, *it is not the sole agent.* The Spirit is at work in all peoples and their cultures and so in the aspirations that drive their development. In pursuing its mission, the Church needs to discern the actions of the Spirit in cultures and in history and to align itself with those actions. This means appreciating God's creative action in the Catholic community, in other Christian denominations, in other religious faiths, and among people of goodwill who hold secular worldviews. It also means working with them to create 'kingdom spaces' in the lives of those on the margins of society. In the words of Jesus as presented in Matthew's gospel (Matt 16:2-3), it means 'reading the signs of the times', and discerning the Holy Spirit at work in human history just as authentic Christian leaders have done during and since biblical times.

Implicit in this realisation is the need for dialogue with people who are 'other', as well as for dialogue within the Christian community itself to address areas of tension there.

For the above reasons, recent popes have called for a 'dialogue with the world'[23], pioneered inter-religious dialogue, and established departments in the Vatican charged with carrying forward this dimension of the Church's mission. Pope Francis has brought the matter full circle with his call for a 'synodal Church', that is for dialogue *within the Church*, dialogue as *the way of being Church*.

If Christian faith is interpreted as a closed story there is always a degree of suspicion held about those who are 'other'. However, as Pope Francis notes, this is not what is called for:

> Without encountering and relating to differences, it is hard to achieve a clear and complete understanding even of ourselves and of our native land. Other cultures are not 'enemies' from which we need to protect ourselves, but differing reflections of the inexhaustible richness of human life. Seeing ourselves from the perspective of another, of one who is different, we can better recognize our own unique features and those of our culture: its richness, its possibilities

---

23 Pope Paul VI articulated this call in his first encyclical *Ecclesiam Suam* promulgated in 1964 during Vatican II. It led subsequently to the creation of the Pontifical Council for Inter-religious Dialogue (1964) and the Pontifical Council for Dialogue with Non-Believers (1965).

and its limitations.²⁴...

Authentic social dialogue involves the ability to respect the other's point of view and to admit that it may include legitimate convictions and concerns. Based on their identity and experience, others have a contribution to make, and it is desirable that they should articulate their positions for the sake of a more fruitful public debate. When individuals or groups are consistent in their thinking, defend their values and convictions, and develop their arguments, this surely benefits society. Yet, this can only occur to the extent that there is genuine dialogue and openness to others. Indeed, 'in a true spirit of dialogue, we grow in our ability to grasp the significance of what others say and do, even if we cannot accept it as our own conviction.²⁵

From such considerations Francis concludes:

What is important is to create processes of encounter, processes that build a people that can accept differences. Let us arm our children with the weapons of dialogue! Let us teach them to fight the good fight of the culture of encounter.²⁶

For the present pope, 'building a culture of encounter' and accessing the 'weapons of dialogue' provide important means by which recontextualisation will occur.

DOUBLE JEOPARDY: RECONTEXTUALISING FAITH IN A POSTMODERN SETTING

The change in 'the condition of knowledge' noted by Lyotard corresponds to a change in 'the condition of belief' observed by Canadian philosopher Charles Taylor. By this Taylor means that, today, belief in God is *one option among many* in constructing a personal worldview and, for many people, not necessarily the easiest to embrace.²⁷

It is these two major changes *occurring concurrently* that creates the need for Catholic educators to recontextualise faith both for themselves and for their students. These changes make the task difficult because of the instability

---

24 Pope Francis *Fratelli Tutti* 2020, #149.
    https://www.vatican.va/content/francesco/en/encyclicals/documents/papa-francesco_20201003_enciclica-fratelli-tutti.html
25 ibid #203.
26 ibid #207.
27 Charles Taylor *A Secular Age*. London: Harvard University Press, 2007, 3.

each introduces into the processes, discussed in Chapter 7, by which people form a personal worldview.

Interpreting the worldview of faith as an open story makes it somewhat easier to address the instabilities in the worldview of culture caused by the struggles that people native to a postmodern world have with such questions as: *What constitutes truth?'* and *'Will you please tell us what the rules are now?*

As we noted earlier, to escape the relativism accompanying the movement from the modern to the postmodern world, it is necessary to make wise choices. One of the choices lies in how we interpret the worldview of faith. This seems to be a choice between the false certainty of the closed story and the ambiguity associated with living within an open story.

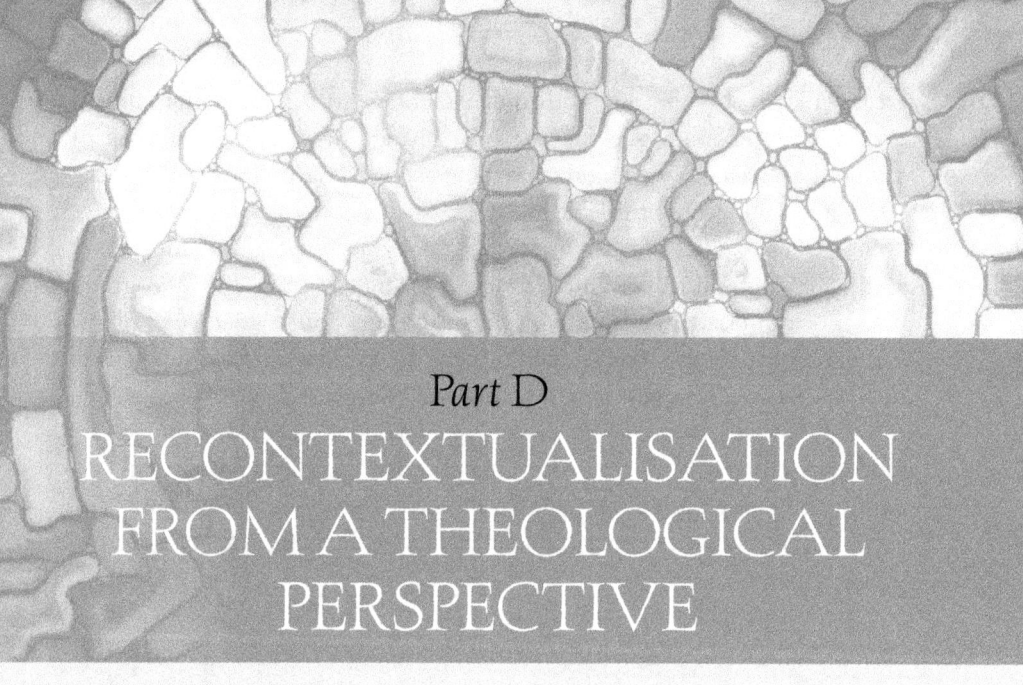

Part D
RECONTEXTUALISATION FROM A THEOLOGICAL PERSPECTIVE

As noted previously, recontextualisation has two interrelated meanings within the Catholic tradition. In the context of cross-cultural mission it refers to the need to re-interpret faith understandings when the dominant meaning system within a culture differs from that of the community who is sharing faith with another from a different culture. Independently of this formulation, recontextualisation is seen by some theologians, including those behind the ECSI project, as the dynamic by which the Catholic faith tradition evolves as history moves forward and human experience expands or contracts as the case many be. Key figures in this second theological understanding are Belgian theologians Edward Schillebeeckx and Lieven Boeve. Part 4 consists of a single chapter (Chapter 11) which addresses this second formulation of recontextualisation that arose in Europe following the advent of postmodern thinking in the late 20th century.

While Schillebeeckx does not use the word 'recontextualisation' in formulating his thinking, he does identify the dynamism by which the Catholic tradition evolves, and relates this to how people make meaning. It is his colleague Lieven Boeve who co-opts the word 'recontextualisation' to name this dynamic. Since the Christian faith had already been contextualised in Europe from earlier times, recontextualisation in this context means understanding the evolution of Christian faith as the dominant meaning system as consciousness of Europeans changed from *pre-critical* (late medieval) to *critical* (modern) to *post-critical* (postmodern-postsecular). Catholic theologians trained in a classicist understanding of theology had great difficulty in adjusting faith understandings to this changing cultural milieu, nor did many see the need for change. It was their ahistorical-acultural understanding of faith that the *Nouvelle Théologie* movement of the 1950s and 1960s sought to attack.

Schillebeeckx became an important spokesperson for this movement at the Second Vatican Council (1962-5). The *Nouvelle Théologie* group not only criticised the lack of pastoral concern found in the scholastic approach to theology, but also demonstrated the links between theological developments of the past and the context (culture and history) in which these developments took place. They undermined any interpretation of Christian faith as a closed story and emphasised that 'salvation history' continues in real-time history. Boeve develops this theme in his works and this has become an essential element in the ECSI framework discussed in Chapter 13.

11

RECONTEXTUALISATION: FROM SCHILLEBEECKX TO BOEVE

The way in which the worldview of Catholic faith is interpreted plays a major role in how people understand faith in Jesus and how they live it out in practice. As Bishop Geoffrey Robinson has pointed out, Christian faith is about *a person, an ethic* and *a story* lived out within a *community of faith*.[1] How one understands the story of Christianity throws light on how one encounters the person, the ethic, and the Christian community. Theologies tend to place different emphases on these four elements and the relationships that exist among them.

For instance, many forms of Christian activism tend to emphasise the Christian ethic as set out in Catholic social teaching, but fail to encounter the person, as accessible through the sacramental and prayer life of the community, and so misinterpret the Christian story and the place of the Christian community within that story. As a result, a person's faith can easily become individualised, secularised, and dissociated from that of the Christian community.

In this chapter we explore how theologians Edward Schillebeeckx and Lieven Boeve seek to bring the four crucial elements together and the place that recontextualisation holds within this synthesis. In doing so we acknowledge the major theological influence on both theologians of Johann Baptist Metz and his fundamental theology of memorial and interruption.[2]

---

1 Bishop Geoffrey Robinson, a reflective theologian and biblical scholar of note, was an auxiliary bishop in the Archdiocese of Sydney and headed the Sydney Archdiocesan Catholic Schools Board there. He generously devoted a good deal of his time to the in-service of teachers in the archdiocese, particularly in the use of scripture. This theme was central to his presentation of the worldview of Christian faith.
2 In terms of the philosophical frame to ECSI, we acknowledge Lyotard, his view of the end of the closed meta-narrative and proposal of the model of the open narrative. In terms of the ECSI instruments, we also acknowledge Gadamer and Ricoeur. Regarding ECSI's sensitivity to 'the other', the strong influence of the philosopher Emmanuel Levinas is acknowledged.

The hermeneutical perspective developed by Lieven Boeve responds to the critique of knowledge offered by postmodern philosopher Jean-François Lyotard.[3] Boeve's theology has its theological foundations in the work of Edward Schillebeeckx.[4] The latter's perspective is important because, while Schillebeeckx does not use the term 'recontextualisation', his theological understanding implies that recontextualisation is *the dynamic by which Christian theology develops*. It is Boeve who names the dynamic 'recontextualisation'.

SCHILLEBEECKX AS THEOLOGIAN

Edward Schillebeeckx (1914-2009) was a product of the 20th century, and his theology was shaped by the experience of growing up in that context. His family had to flee their home to Antwerp shortly prior to his birth to avoid the German advance during World War I. His theological studies were interrupted by the advent of World War II. His thinking was later sharpened by his engagement with the secularism he encountered during a lecture tour of the USA in the 1960s, was challenged by attending all four sessions of Vatican II (1962-5) as an advisor to the Dutch bishops, and again by his interactions with liberation theologians from Latin America from the 1970s.

Schillebeeckx' major works on Christology seek to interpret the gospels from the perspective of Jesus' disciples focusing in on how, as a result of their experience of living with Jesus, seeing him in action, and hearing his message, they came to understand him as 'the eschatological prophet of Israel'.[5]

As a theological student Schillebeeckx, like other key figures in the *Nouvelle Théologie* movement of the mid-20th century, was critical of the

---

3   Lieven Boeve *Lyotard and Theology: Beyond the Christian Narrative of Love*. New York: Bloomsbury T&T Clark, 2014.
4   Schillebeeckx began his doctoral studies in Paris after being ordained as a member of the Dominican Order in 1941. There he came under the influence of fellow Dominicans, Marie-Dominique Chenu and Yves Congar, both leaders of the *Nouvelle Théologie* movement. His academic career began at KU Leuven in 1943. In 1957 he was appointed professor of dogmatic theology and history of theology at the Catholic University of Nijmegen, a post he held until his retirement in 1987. Schillebeeckx was an influential figure at Vatican II because of his connections to the *Nouvelle Théologie* movement and his readiness to offer seminars to bishops on this topic. This put him at odds with some members of the Roman Curia who were heavily invested in the Neo-scholastic approach to theology. Schillebeeckx was of the view that this approach did not treat the teachings of Aquinas in their proper historical context and so were misguided. As a theologian, Schillebeeckx positioned himself close to the border of legitimate difference as orthodoxy was construed in the mid-20th century. On three occasions his writings were called into question by Vatican officials. However, no action was ever taken against him. Schillebeeckx died in 2009 aged 95.
5   Schillebeeckx' major work is the trilogy *Jesus: an experiment in Christology* (1979), *Christ: the Christian experience in the modern world* (1980), and *Church: The human story of God* (1990).

neo-scholastic approach to theology,[6] then deemed normative by Catholic authorities and mandatory in all Catholic seminaries. Under the influence of his Dominican mentor, Marie-Dominique Chenu, Schillebeeckx came to understand the value of studying the historical and cultural context in which Catholic theologies developed. This led to his involvement in the *ressourcement* (back to the sources) movement that developed in France in the years prior to Vatican II.

This movement aimed to 'retrieve' the pastoral emphasis found in the Christian teachings of the Patristic period (circa from the end of the 1st century CE to as late as the 8th century CE). Theologians of the *Nouvelle Théologie* school critiqued the neo-scholastic approach on two principal grounds:

1. It failed to consider the historical or cultural context in which the works of Aquinas were written, and so misinterpreted them.
2. It lacked the *pastoral emphasis* found in patristic theologies and so had become disconnected from the faith experiences that it sought to explain.

Schillebeeckx was also influenced by developments in European philosophy including phenomenology and hermeneutics, both of which sought to interpret human experience.[7] The way in which people choose to interpret human experience is a major theme in Schillebeeckx' theology.

THE *HUMANUM* AND CONTRAST EXPERIENCES

An important concept in Schillebeeckx' theology is what he calls the *Humanum – the possibilities inherent in being human.* It is not possible to explicitly articulate the *Humanum*, which we intuitively sense, because we are embedded in both a particular history and culture and these place limits on the imaginal horizon we bring to making sense of our experiences and so our interpretation of what it means to be human.

---

6 Neo-Scholastic theology is theology originally developed by Thomas Aquinas in the 13th century. *Nouvelle Théologie* theologians critiqued the form given to this theology by its 20th century Catholic interpreters.

7 A phenomenological approach explores human experience from a first-person perspective. For instance, it is possible to observe a teacher at work in a classroom and so to describe what he or she is doing during a lesson. This may or may not align with the lesson *as experienced by the teacher* who is constantly monitoring the class for clues as to whether what is being presented is understood by the class and adjusting the lesson in light of these clues. It is the experience of the teacher, his or her interpretation of what is going on in the process of teaching, that phenomenology seeks to catch. It focuses on what the teacher is *conscious of in the process of teaching* – the *pre-reflective processing of experience*. This is different from the experience recalled in hindsight, when models are accessed, explicitly or implicitly, to interpret the experience of teaching.

Our experiences, however, make us aware of *what is not the Humanum*, that is, what degrades, dehumanises, and oppresses people, and so prevents them from reaching their potential. Schillebeeckx names such experiences *contrast experiences*. Experiences of injustice, oppression, repression, and exploitation, all fall into this category. While we cannot explicitly articulate what the *Humanum* is, we can certainly recognise its absence. Schillebeeckx interprets God's offer of revelation and salvation as inviting humankind to liberation from the negative effects of contrast experiences and so more fully enabling the possibilities implicit in being human to emerge. Such experiences are foundational to religious faith.

SALVATION AND REVELATION OCCUR WITHIN HISTORY

For Schillebeeckx, God's offer of revelation and salvation is recognised only in the interpretation of historical experiences that, to the religious outsider, may appear as purely secular events.

As an example, he suggests that in ancient Egypt a group of Semites decided to rebel against the harsh conditions imposed on them by the Pharoah and escaped into the desert. This was the secular historical event. However, the subsequent interpretation of this event by the Jewish faith community, was of 'salvation' offered to their ancestors by God. The prophet Moses interpreted this event as God leading God's people from slavery to freedom, thus inaugurating what for the people of Israel would become 'salvation history' and the foundation on which their religious identity was constructed.[8]

The emergence of a critical consciousness within Israel's religious tradition acknowledged the prophets as individuals capable of interpreting the community's collective experiences as the unfolding of God's 'salvation history' within what, to their contemporaries, was secular history. The prophets understood that God reveals God's self in the events of human history. Israel's prophets were able to identify God's offer of salvation and revelation in these events.[9]

The challenge for the Jewish people was to live with the consequences of being embedded in God's 'salvation history'. This experience carried with it inherent ambiguities. Experiences that some members of the community interpreted as God at work in human history, others might interpret in more secular terms. Consequently, Israel's rulers had a testy relationship with Israel's prophets. This reached its climax in Jesus' life and ministry.

---

[8] The return from captivity in Babylon was later interpreted as God's further offer of 'salvation'.
[9] See Jose de Mesa & Lode Wostyn *Doing Christology: The re-appropriation of a tradition*. Quezon City: Claretian Publications, 1993, 38ff.

Prophets are often associated in popular understanding with foretelling the future. In fact, their role was often *to offer hope in uncertain times* by reminding people of the salvation and liberation wrought by God in their history and the responsibilities associated with living within this hope.

Jesus continued this prophetic tradition with his announcement that, with him, the 'Kingdom of God' had broken into human history *in a definitive way* and that God's offer of salvation was made, not just to the people of Israel, but to all people. If this hope was to be realised, then the Christian community bore the responsibility of witnessing to it in the various societies in which its members are present.

In Schillebeeckx' theology, the essential mission of the Christian faith community is to be a liberating presence within a society, working to redress the contrast experiences that limit a people's aspirations to realise the *Humanum* in their personal and collective lives. This implies two things:

1. the *capacity to identify contrast experiences* that limit a people in realising their potential as human ('reading the signs of the times')
2. *strategies to 'liberate' people from this condition* (experiences that can be interpreted by them in terms of 'liberation' or 'salvation').

He links this mission to the model set by Jesus.

People's capacity to believe in the Kingdom of God depends on their being able to interpret efforts to liberate them from the impact of contrast experiences as a form of salvation *in history* that points to the fullness of this salvation *beyond history*. The *Humanum* cannot be fully realised in history, just as the Kingdom of God cannot be realised fully in history, nor can either be realised by human effort alone. However, neither can they be achieved without human effort! This is a central dilemma of Christian faith.

Schillebeeckx emphasises the historical contingency of all human experience, including the experience of interpreting events in human history as 'salvation history'. For him, revelation is the interpretation of experiences occurring in history that have been reflected on deeply by the Christian community to ascertain their meaning. There can be multiple layers to this interpretive process as it engages with the contexts in which it occurs. As he observes:

> ... faith in God's revelation always has a starting point in this world of ours: there are historical mediations. The mediation of revelation varies, depending on place, society and period, but it nevertheless enters into the interpretation of faith which is presented on each occasion. Thus any possible understanding of faith takes place on

the basis of and through the medium of the human understanding of reality – distinctive to a particular culture in which the gospel is proclaimed and heard. This understanding of reality is historical and cultural; thus it is there only as one culturally determined, limited and special understanding of reality (despite a universal human element present in it, itself above all, a logical and largely unconscious basic structure). Therefore the question of Christian identity through the centuries can be answered only by comparison of differing cultural forms of the Christian experience of faith, interpretation of faith, and praxis of faith, as an answer to God's offer of revelation. The only difference between the past Christian tradition and the new Christian traditions that we shall have to hand down and make, lies in the fact that we can make comparisons with the past only after the event; that past has, as it were, already behind it the risk of the interpretation of faith to be made in its own time. By contrast we still have it ahead, and are in the middle of the process of interpretation with all the uncertain dangers of success and failure, of guesses and mistakes and, ultimately, of orthodoxy or 'heresy …[10]

The consequence is that there is a degree of ambiguity in what is passed from one generation to the next as a religious tradition develops, since danger lurks in interpreting a new situation from a perspective that is out of touch with the realities that it seeks to explain. This phenomenon is certainly evident in the 'newer' books of the Old Testament where Israel's leaders reflected on the impact that Greek culture was having on their tradition. Some leaders rejected this form of acculturation outright, while others sought accommodation because it expanded the imaginal horizon with which the Jewish tradition could be understood.[11]

Schillebeeckx poses the question: how do we know that the meanings central to the unfolding of 'salvation history' are preserved as times change? His reply is that as times change, the contrast experiences that limit humans from being what they can be in a given era also change, so experiences of liberation and salvation, and the framework within which these are interpreted, will change too. Using an older articulation of the tradition in a new context does not necessarily preserve its meaning.

Schillebeeckx argues that there is a proportionality between new human experience and its interpretation that needs to be preserved if God's message of salvation is to be understood.

---

10 Edward Schillebeeckx *Church: The human story of God*. London: t&t Clark, 2014, 38.
11 Lieven Boeve *God Interrupts History: Theology in a Time of Upheaval*. New York: Continuum, 2007.

The problem of the interpretation and transmission of faith is thus: How do we build bridges between the past tradition of faith and our existence as Christians in new situations. In the last resort the Christian message is preached *now*, no longer to the old citizens of Corinth, Ephesus and Thessalonica; it is preached to men and women who are our contemporaries with their own understanding of themselves and the world, living in an almost postmodern social and economic social system and labour system, with their own, albeit uncertain, political plans. Consequently, believing now means bringing the Christian tradition of faith and experience to life and making it understandable in the present, in other, different historical situations and with other categories of thought and experience.[12]

What Schillebeeckx is suggesting here is that, to understand the worldview of faith in any age, the meaning of the gospel has to be interpreted in relationship to both the cultural worldview and the worldview of the age, since both shape the personal worldview within which people make sense of their lives.

The important insight that Schillebeeckx offers is that it is the *relationship* between how the Christian message is interpreted, and the context in which this takes place that confers a recognisable Christian identity on members of the faith community making the interpretation. There are four things involved in this relationship:

1. the Christian message
2. the context that creates the need for meaning
3. the interpretive framework that enables meaning to be articulated
4. The community making the interpretation.

His discussion can be expresses schematically as follows:[13]

Jesus' message = **New Testament Message** = **Patristic Understanding of faith**
socio-historical   social-historical of the NT   social-historical context then
context of Jesus

Medieval understanding of faith = **The present understanding of faith in 1990**
socio-historical context then   socio-historical and existential context in 1990

Schillebeeckx identifies an important dynamic in how the Christian tradition continues to unfold as history moves forward and as cultures appear and disappear. Boeve, strongly influenced by the theology of Schillebeeckx

---

12 Schillebeeckx, ibid, 39.
13 ibid 40-53.

and writing in the postmodern European context, names this dynamic 'recontextualization'.[14]

Schillebeeckx' model of recontextualisation clearly links 'message' and 'context' in a relationship that unfolds through the mediums of 'interpretation' and 'community'. This helps explain what happened in modernity. In the transition from the medieval world to the modern world, Catholic leaders sought to maintain the medieval understanding of faith via their endorsement of neo-scholasticism. So the situation was:

$$\frac{\text{Medieval understanding of faith}}{\text{medieval socio-historical context}} = \frac{\text{Medieval understanding of faith}}{\text{socio-historical and existential context in the Modern period}}$$

This leadership stance lasted until Vatican II when it was realised that it was no longer a tenable position. A *particular recontextualisation* of Christian faith had, over time, been mistaken for its *definitive expression*.

The problematic facing Christian faith in a change of era is that the new forms of experience and new questions that come to define a new context tend to be interpreted using the interpretive models of a previous era and this results in confusion for people native to the new era, even while it makes sense to those brought up in an older era.

It takes time to develop new models to account for new experiences and history seems to demonstrate that these tend to appear in the secular realm before they are adapted in the service of faith. As a result the new models are initially regarded with suspicion. There is therefore a *lag time* between the new experiences of people belonging to faith communities and the meaningful interpretation of those experiences within the perspective of faith. In this liminal period various interpretations, and the frameworks within which these are made, are matters of dispute within the community.

As Boeve has pointed out in the last chapter of his 2003 essay, interpreted as an open story, the Christian tradition is always incomplete in human history. We simply do not know:

- what contrast experiences lie ahead as history moves forward
- how 'salvation history' will play out to liberate people or
- the interpretive schemas that will be needed to make sense of historical events as 'God's offer of salvation'.

---

14   Lieven Boeve *Interrupting Tradition: An Essay on Christian faith in a Postmodern Context*. Louvain: Peeters Press, 2003, 24–26. In this Boeve is employing ideas adapted from the political theology of German theologian Johann Baptist Metz (1928-2019).

Further, Boeve notes that the ongoing temptation among religious leaders is to close off the story of God's salvation, just as Israel's leaders did in Jesus' time – that is, by giving it a definitive form. This attempts to provide certainty, but ultimately fails, because it is not possible to remove the uncertainties inherent in interpreting the Christian narrative as 'salvation history'. Attempts to do so are counter-productive and thwarted as 'God interrupts history'.[15]

Within the Catholic tradition it is the Christian community itself, under the guidance of the Pope, that ultimately decides how the worldview of faith is to be constructed and who is responsible for this task. In theology this is referred to as 'the sense of the faithful'.[16] Often this source of wisdom has been ignored by clerical leaders and it is this issue that the present pope seeks to address in his espousal of the Church as 'synodal'. He clearly seeks to reframe the relationship between the Christian community and its designated leaders as a way of dealing with dysfunctionalities that have led Catholics in their thousands to abandon the worldview of faith as a source of meaning in their lives.

The theological perspective offered in this chapter opens up the approach to recontextualisation that underpins the ECSI project that we return to in Chapter 13.

---

15 Boeve develops this theme fully in *God Interrupts History: Theology in a Time of Upheaval*, 45ff.
16 In 2014 the International Theological Commission published a paper entitled 'Sensus Fidei in the life of the Church' to clarify the meaning of this and related terms. https://www.vatican.va/roman_curia/congregations/cfaith/cti_documents/rc_cti_20140610_sensus-fidei_en.html

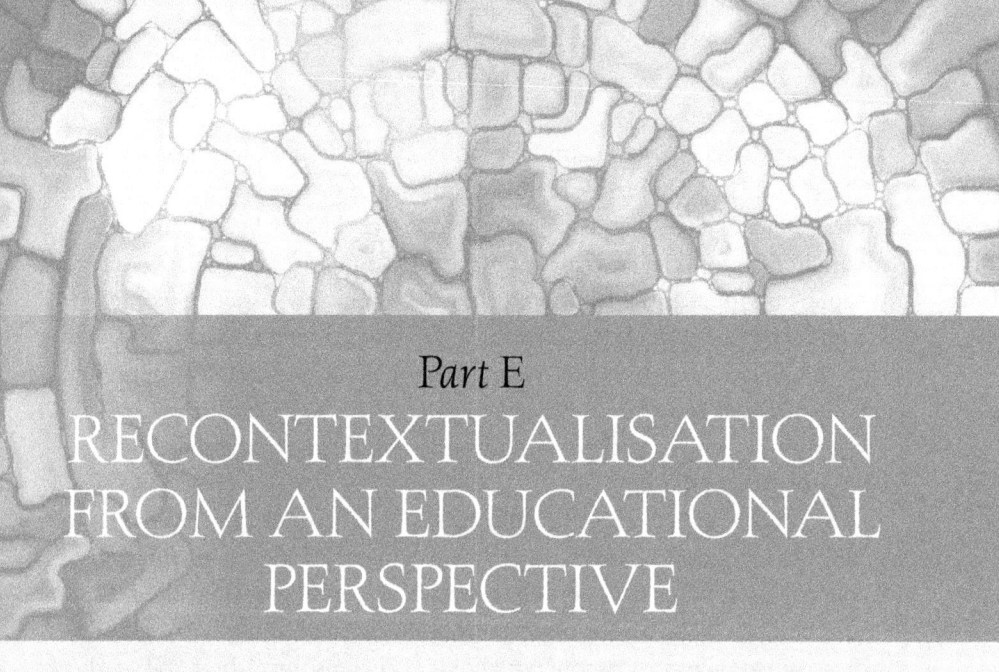

Part E
RECONTEXTUALISATION FROM AN EDUCATIONAL PERSPECTIVE

In Parts A, B, C, and D of this study we have explored the notion of recontextualisation from biblical, missiological, hermeneutical, and theological perspectives. In Part 5 we continue the exploration from an educational perspective where the focus changes from 'What is recontextualisation?' to 'How do you recontextualise faith and/or culture in the classroom or the adult education setting?'

In Chapter 12 we examine recontextualisation from a secular perspective, in particular how the idea arises in the work of educator/sociologist Basil Bernstein. Bernstein's work on the sociology of knowledge is extensive. We consider two important connections he makes:

1. the links between context, language, and learning
2. the role of the teacher as mediator between the language in which knowledge is constructed and the language in which it is taught and learned.

Recontextualisation in Bernstein's thought seeks to reframe knowledge created in the academy so that it is meaningful in the context of the classroom (or seminar). For schools, this is an across-the-curriculum issue with a bearing on all forms of pedagogy. It therefore has relevance for religious education.

Chapter 13 examines the challenges recontextualisation presents for students living in the Australian cultural context with its strongly secular worldview. In this context there are specific challenges for teachers and parents whose faith was contextualised in another era, whether here or overseas.

This leads on to discussion of recontextualisation as it appears in the ECSI project in Chapter 14. Here we look at the degree of fit between this project and the Australian context, where the challenges lie, and limitations inherent in adopting and adapting ECSI within the Australian context. Chapter 14 focuses on recontextualisation within a particular context – Catholic school systems in Victoria and what has been learnt from the experience to date. Since the development of ECSI was initially contingent on the support from these Australian systems, it seems reasonable to ask: How well do leaders in these systems understand the 'What' and the 'How' of recontextualisation?

The final chapter brings the study to a conclusion by returning to biblical themes that emerged in Part 1. The chapter examines the role of leaders in presenting faith to people native to a new era using the Gospel of Matthew as a model for how the transitions from 'the old' to 'the new' were contextualised or recontextualised, as the case may be, in an earlier era of great change. Matthew highlights the role of the community in both the contextualisation and recontextualisation of faith. This is an aspect of leading others in a faith community that needs further development. The findings of the *Recontextualising Pedagogy* research seem to confirm this assertion.

12

RECONTEXTUALISATION FROM AN EDUCATIONAL PERSPECTIVE – TRANSFORMING WORLDVIEWS

In previous chapters we have argued for the importance of recontextualisation as a significant element in the Church's recent cross-cultural missionary experience, and as an important dynamic in the development of theology. We have also explored its significance in the process of meaning-making that underpins learning.

The recontextualisation of faith is always linked to the way in which faith was contextualised in the first place. It is shaped by this history. One must deal with contextualisation, how faith makes sense for people living in a particular context, before one can recontextualise these understandings to cope with a changed context. Thus, recontextualisation is essentially an *intra-cultural* phenomenon rather than a *cross-cultural* phenomenon. Its essential concern is, to quote mission anthropologist Paul Hiebert, 'transforming worldviews'. The key question we raise in this chapter is: What does 'transforming worldviews' mean in educational terms? More particularly, what does it mean for pedagogical practice, or put more bluntly: how do you do it?

Viewed from a pedagogical perspective, recontextualisation exists within two distinct traditions – the sociological tradition and the religious education (RE) tradition. English sociologist Basil Bernstein (1924-2000) initiated the first of these traditions in the 1970s.[1] The second has developed around the ECSI project and reflects the theology of Lieven Boeve and Edward Schillebeeckx. We deal with each in turn.

---

1 From 1963 Bernstein worked at the Institute of Education as the University of London until his retirement as head of its Sociological Research Unit. His critique of pedagogy was that it was understood in an a-sociological way and that this presented major problems for teachers, particularly in the assumptions they held about the nature of the pedagogical relationship they had with students.

RECONTEXTUALISATION: THE SOCIOLOGICAL TRADITION (BERNSTEIN)

Bernstein came from a lower socio-economic family and had some difficulty in funding his education through teachers' college. His early experience was in teaching students from a similar background. He later studied at the Institute of Education at the University of London and during his long tenure there headed the Institute's Social Research Unit where he developed a number of sociological theories, some associated with the sociology of knowledge.

Based on his own research and that of his PhD students, Bernstein proposed that the reason students from low socio-economic backgrounds often fail to perform well in school is not so much a matter of their background but is due to their inability to master the language used in schools. In other words, he saw their poor performance to be a consequence of poor pedagogy! This suggestion created something of a stir among educators.

Bernstein argued that the knowledge created in the academy uses specialised forms of discourse that are largely unintelligible to ordinary people who use a 'common sense' form of discourse. The latter is the taken-for-granted language used by students embedded in a social context. This context determines their access or lack of access to the language of the academy. The lower their socio-economic status, the poorer their access. Teachers therefore have an important role in mediating the gap that exists between academic discourse and the access students have to common sense discourse. They meet this responsibility by employing 'pedagogical discourse'. This use of language seeks to 'recontextualise' the discourse of the academy so that it becomes accessible and meaningful for students, given their varying degrees of access to common sense discourse. The essential skill in effective pedagogy lies in being able to do this.[2]

This sociological tradition regarding recontextualisation has a strong linguistic orientation. It involves mediating language and the meanings generated in the academy, for people living in a 'common sense' world.[3] Consequently, the worldview of students is expanded. This not only means that they know more, but they acquire the values and sensibility that go

---

[2] Bernstein's proposal raises the question: Can teachers from a middle-class background, who have ready access to the language of common sense that they take for granted, overlook the disadvantage that students from lower socio-economic backgrounds work under with respect to the use of language? The way teachers construct the 'pedagogical language' of the classroom can make a bad situation worse, but if they discern the issue impacting the students, they can also make it much better.

[3] Basil Bernstein's major work outlining this perspective is *The Structuring of Pedagogic Discourse (Class, Codes and Control)*. New York: Routledge, 1990. See also Ana Morais; Isabel Neves; Brian Davies; Harry Daniels (editors). *Towards a Sociology of Pedagogy: The Contribution of Basil Bernstein to Research*. London: Peter Lang, 2001.

with such knowing. Students studying literature come to appreciate its performative value by seeing theatre presentations or films of the works being studied. Students of biology not only learn about living systems, but also learn how to dissect animals and master other basic biological techniques. They quickly learn that there is a 'right' way to go about procedures that need to satisfy ethical criteria. The same applies to students studying other physical sciences, social sciences, economics, and legal studies. Students learn that academic disciplines not only have a content, but they also have a way of validating new knowledge and that this involves developing both values and a sensibility.

In practice, teachers often unthinkingly delegate the recontextualisation of language that lies at the heart of learning, to the writers of textbooks and developers of digital content, without asking questions about the social context of these authors and how this affects their products. The unstated assumption is that 'one size fits all'. The pedagogical challenge to develop a form of language that is accessible to all students is missed. Recontextualising the discourse of the academy for the classroom gives students from a variety of backgrounds increased access to knowledge.

Bernstein's insights are particularly relevant to religious education, but this does not exhaust the application of his insights to education more broadly.

RECONTEXTUALISATION IN THE RELIGIOUS EDUCATION TRADITION

Recontextualisation in the RE tradition carries broader connotations than proposed by Bernstein. As outlined by Boeve, and expanded here, the tradition deals with meaning-making in the context of a change of era in which the worldviews of faith and culture are each undergoing major change. Consequently, the taken for granted frameworks within which most people make meaning becomes unstable. People react to this situation in a variety of ways: denial, loss of perspective, return to a framework that has passed its 'use by' date, canonisation of tradition, feeling lost in the new context, fascination with the new, etc.

In discussing the theology of Schillebeeckx (Chapter 11) we outlined his 'norm of proportionality' expressed in equation form as:

Jesus Message	=	**Paul's Understanding**	=	**Church Fathers Understanding**
1st Century Jewish Context		1st Century Greek Context		Their Socio-Historical Context

This process can be carried on up until our own time:

Vatican II Understanding	=	**Post-Vatican II Understanding**
Modern Socio-Historical Context		Postmodern-Postsecular context

The point that Schillebeeckx and Boeve make is that, if faith is going to be intelligible to people living in a particular age, it must be expressed using the meaning system with currency in that age because this is what people take for granted as meaningful.

As history moves forward, meaning systems evolve and important aspects of a culture's worldview change, particularly what people take for granted, what they value, and what is accepted as a truly human sensibility. Recontextualisation seeks to address the impact of this change in worldview so that faith remains meaningful in the new cultural context. The dominant influence at work here is a major change in the worldview of the age that people unreflectively take for granted.

It seems a fact of history that there is a lag between developments in the worldview of a culture (prompted by change in the worldview of the age that impacts many cultures) and developments in the worldview of faith. Catholic leaders have been slow to understand important developments in the worldview of a culture as eras change. As a result, they have clung to a meaning framework that has lost its hermeneutical force. Jesus' advice to his disciples that they should 'read the signs of the times' (Matt 16, 2-3) has simply not been taken to heart![4]

Faced with the postmodern-postsecular context, the temptation is to interpret new developments in our culture using the meaning framework of a previous recontextualisation of faith. This makes little sense particularly to young people native to this new context and who take its assumptions for granted. Brought up on a diet of classicism, Church leaders have too often failed to understand the hermeneutical dynamic at work in recontextualisation.

Cultural change is driven by the re-interpretation of ideals embedded in cultural narratives. These create the need to re-prioritise cultural values and to affirm new aspirations. This is the area where we believe the Spirit has scope to act in all cultures. The 'seeds of the word'[5] are to be found there, if only we have the eyes to see. This is as true of Australian culture as it is for any other culture. Unfortunately, this is not an issue generally pursued in RE curricula, that too often tend to adopt an understanding of faith strongly influenced by classicism.

---

4   While Church leaders thought within a classicist framework, context was largely irrelevant. Once the contextual nature of all knowledge was recognised, thinking had to change. This shift in paradigm began to be publicly and officially acknowledged at Vatican II and has continued into the post-Vatican II period. Most papal documents today begin with an acknowledgement of the context being addressed. See for instance Pope Francis' *Laudato si'* and *Fratelli Tutti*.

5   'Seeds of the Word' is a phrase attributed to an early Father of the Church, Justin Martyr, philosopher and apologist 100-165 AD.

Within a faith tradition such as Christianity, recontextualisation is the dynamic by which faith retains its meaning across major changes occurring in the cultural worldview. This does not mean that the worldview of faith is static while all around it changes. The worldview of faith evolves as new cultural meaning systems challenge assumptions that are taken-for-granted elements within it. New cultural meaning systems also offer new conceptions that can enable the worldview of faith, as held within faith communities, to expand and deepen.

A postmodern-postsecular culture places great emphasis on appreciating diversity as a resource rather than as a problem. This stance challenges exclusive interpretations of the worldview of Christian faith, and so traditional Church stances on women, LGBT members, and positions on divorce for example.

To appreciate this dynamic, think of how the doctrines of creation and salvation are now understood within mainline Catholicism compared with the case two or three generations ago. We now understand salvation both in terms of a person's ability, through the saving grace of Christ, to repent and to rise above sinfulness in such a way as to enter a deep personal relationship with God but, in addition, we also now recognise social and structural aspects of both sinfulness and salvation. We also understand how groups, societies, and social arrangements (structures) may have become entangled in webs of sinfulness. Such situations render it more difficult for well-disposed people to do good, and easier for evil to be perpetrated. One has only to ponder the structural sins of racism, the destruction of biodiversity, or sustained assault on the earth itself by human decisions based on greed and self-centredness. See for example the extended discussion of Pope John Paul II in *Sollicitudo Rei Socialis* (## 35-40).[6] The *Catechism of the Catholic Church* speaks of the relationship between personal and social sins, and touches on the ongoing cycle of personal and social sin, that is sin that becomes structured into the very fabric of society:

> 'Structures of sin' are the expression and effect of personal sins. They lead their victims to do evil in their turn" (CCC 1869)[7]

---

6 Pope John Paul II *Sollicitudo Rei Socialis* (On Social Concerns), 1987.
https://www.vatican.va/content/john-paul-ii/en/encyclicals/documents/hf_jp-ii_enc_30121987_sollicitudo-rei-socialis.html

7 *The Catechism of the Catholic Church* is a compendium of doctrine promulgated by Pope John Paul II in 1992. It is available in book form from various publishers and online via the following link: https://www.vatican.va/archive/ENG0015/_INDEX.HTM

CONTEXTUALISATION PRECEDES RECONTEXTUALISATION

Theological recontextualisation is shaped by the way in which faith has been contextualised within a particular culture. In the 20th century, Religious Education (RE) took a variety of forms, but these rarely escaped their Irish origins, and so reflect the strengths and weaknesses of those origins.

From the 19th century onwards, RE inherited a catechetical pedagogy that canonised a propositional understanding of faith influenced by classicism. 'The faith' was interpreted as the answers to questions in a catechism that students were expected to memorise. Primary students (there were few secondary students in this period) learned basic prayers and experienced 'being Catholic' by participating in Catholic practices. This introduction contextualised a 'faith' that was to be handed on. Faith was understood as an object, a 'thing' that could be 'lost'. Maryknoll missionary priest John Walsh describes this mode of contextualisation as the 'faith as a football' model. The aim in life is to tuck the ball under your arm and head for the try line (death) without losing the ball or its going flat.[8]

Rote learning went out of fashion in education in the 1960s with the emergence of curriculum theories that emphasised the role of students as agents in their own learning and acknowledged that all knowledge is a human construction. As well as being criticised for its pedagogy, the catechetical model of this time was criticised for its lack of scriptural foundation. It focused on 'the Catholic tradition' divorced from the source on which that tradition depends. Finally, the model tended to ignore the fact that faith involves a relationship with God that, in turn, leads us to relationship with others. Faith is so much more than mastery of 'knowledge' in propositional form.

In Australia, in the 1960s, Monsignor John Kelly sought to address the scriptural limitation in developing a new style of catechism for primary school students (green) and for junior secondary students (red). These books were adopted widely across Australia by dioceses and religious congregations for use in their schools. Thus, the catechetical model was receiving a new lease on life around the time Vatican II was in session (1962–1965). Two decades later, Irish-American educator Thomas Groome published a seminal book entitled *Christian Religious Education: sharing our story and vision* (1980) that sought to put RE on a sound epistemological footing in the face of criticism of the Catechetical Model by educational theorists.[9]

---

[8] John Walsh M.M. *Change Search Encounter: Evangelization and Ministry Today*. Homebush: Daughters of St. Paul, 1984. (Recorded lectures).
[9] Thomas Groome *Religious Education: Sharing our Story and Vision*. Melbourne: Dove Communications, 1980.

Groome's model set out a process known as Shared Christian Praxis (SCP) that presented a general teaching strategy for RE pedagogy and curriculum development. The process had four 'movements'. These were:

1. Begin with the life experience of students.
2. Introduce students to the Christian story/Vision.
3. Facilitate students to reflect critically on their experience in light of the Christian story/vision.
4. Help students to form a personal or collective response.

Groome defines RE rather expansively as follows:

> Religious education is 'a political activity with pilgrims in time that deliberately and intentionally attends with them to the activity of God in our present, to the Story of the Christian faith community, and to the Vision of God's Kingdom, the seeds of which are already among us'.[10]

The intention of his model was to ensure that students, in the course of being introduced to the Christian story and vision, became agents in their own learning and came to realise that they can contribute to 'salvation history' as found in the unfolding Christian story.

In Australia, with the exception of the Victorian dioceses,[11] Groome's SCP Model, often in modified form, became paradigmatic for RE in secondary schools both in the design of RE curricula and in pedagogy.[12] As Groome observes, (SCP) is:

> … a participative and dialogical pedagogy in which people reflect critically on their historical agency in time and place and on their socio-cultural reality, have access together to the Christian Story/Vision, and personally appropriate in community with the creative

---

10   ibid, 25.
11   The major influences in Victorian schools were the first and second editions of the Melbourne Guidelines featuring the four-point plan. The Guidelines grew out of visits to Victoria in the 1970s of Br Herman Lombaerts FSC from what is now KU Leuven, and Fr Amalorpavadass from the National Biblical, Catechetical, and Liturgical Centre (NBCLC), Bangalore, India. Archbishop Pell discarded the Guidelines and adopted a textbook approach which began to be published in 2000 and subsequently. At this time the other Victorian dioceses moved into a different RE project based on the curricula of Parramatta and Canberra-Goulburn dioceses which were influenced by the SCP approach.
12   In a paper presented at the 1996 Annual Conference of the Australian Association for Religious Education entitled 'Shared Christian Praxis as a basis for Religious Education Curriculum: The Parramatta Experience' Michael Bezzina et al (Peter Gahan, Helen McLenaghan, and Greg Wilson) outline the extensive influence of the Shared Christian Praxis among Catholic religious educators across Australia in the early 1990s. https://eric.ed.gov/?id=ED401266model

intent of renewed praxis in Christian faith towards God's reign for all creation.[13]

Groome's model contextualised faith in the *experience of students*. It changed the nature of the RE texts used in schools. It introduced students to a contextualised understanding of faith at a time when the worldview of their culture and the validity of strategies used in knowledge construction that had been developed in the modern era were, in late modernity, coming under challenge by postmodern critics.

The widespread use of Groome's RE model made it an easy target for critics seeking to explain the existential crisis facing the Australian Catholic Church – an ongoing decline in Mass attendance leading to the pending collapse of an institutional structure built around the local parish. Catholic schooling was seen as somehow 'failing the Church'. Catholic schools no longer seemed capable of producing regular Mass-goers (as it was presumed to have done in earlier times).

The school's expressed goal of 'passing on the faith' (understood principally in propositional terms) was becoming increasingly untenable in the face of the multiplicity of faith stances held within the Catholic Church in the post-Vatican II era – this, even though the purpose of Catholic schooling has never been defined officially in terms of church attendance. Its purpose has been articulated, in the foundational post-Vatican II magisterial document on Catholic schooling, *The Catholic School* (1977) in terms of meaning-making (integrating culture and faith in making sense of life) and character formation (aligning personal values with the values underpinning the Christian vision).[14]

The politicisation of RE within the Catholic community in the late 20th and early 21st centuries resulted in several developments such as: a 'back to basics' movement led by those brought up in a propositional understanding of faith; an evaluation of the Shared Christian Praxis Model;[15] and the search for a new model that could address challenges in understanding the worldview of faith in the context of postmodern-post secular approaches to meaning-making.

The assessment of Groome's model conducted by the Catholic Education Office Parramatta in reviewing its RE curriculum in 1996 highlighted

---

13 Thomas Groome, *Sharing Faith: A comprehensive approach to religious education and pastoral ministry*. San Francisco: Harper, 1991, 135.
14 Congregation for Catholic Education. *The Catholic School*, 1977 #37. https://www.vatican.va/roman_curia/congregations/ccatheduc/documents/rc_con_ccatheduc_doc_19770319_catholic-school_en.html
15 The most notable evaluation of this model was conducted by the Parramatta Diocese in NSW. Groome himself in several later publications attempted to provide greater clarity around the method of shared Christian praxis. See Sharing Faith 1991.

both the strengths and weaknesses of the model. In addition, it provided an important insight into the context in which most current RE teachers were educated and trained.[16]

Bezzina *et al* summarise the benefits of the model as follows:

- The praxis approach is regarded as a strength of the Parramatta RE curriculum.
- The collaborative process used in developing support documents based on shared Christian praxis contributed to the growing confidence and sense of ownership of the curriculum by RE teachers.
- Local modification of Groome's praxis approach gave RE teachers a sense of security in implementing the model.

The study also highlighted weaknesses in the use of the approach:

- The tendency for RE teachers to view the model as prescriptive (particularly so among teachers new to RE) leading to their adopting a lock-step approach to RE pedagogy and becoming dependent on support documents.
- Lack of understanding of the 'critical reflection' step in the process and so difficulty in implementing it.

This finding highlighted the fact that inexperienced teachers did not realise that the step depends on their capacity to explain and reflect on scripture and the Christian tradition in setting up this step in the process, and their capacity to lead students in reflecting on life and the Christian story. These tasks are obviously difficult if teachers have not appropriated the story themselves.

The lessons learnt from eight years working with Groome's model indicated, in the view of Bezzina et al, that the shared Christian praxis approach is best regarded as a meta-approach that is highly adaptable, a valuable tool in the construction of RE curriculum, and a process in which 'knowing' cannot be separated from 'being'.

EDUCATION IN FAITH VERSUS EDUCATION IN RELIGION

The work of Bezzina et al also highlights an important debate then underway in RE, namely, how to balance *education in faith* and *education in religion* within the RE curriculum. Education in faith seeks to achieve two aims of a Catholic school – to inform and to form students. Education in religion is

---

16 See P. Malone, P. Chesterton, M. Ryan, and M. McDonald *Report on review of Sharing Our Story* Strathfield: Australian Catholic University, 1996.

oriented towards teaching students *about religion* and is more informational than formational. The debate centred on the fact that increasingly students in Catholic schools, although baptised, demonstrated very weak links to either a Catholic community or Catholic beliefs since faith seemed no longer transmitted in the home.

The formative work of the 'Catholic home', long used as a justification for Catholic schooling, had fallen into decline as Catholics in Australia lost their 'ghetto' mentality and became fully integrated into the fabric of local culture.[17] Catholics no longer married Catholics, and this changed the nature of the homes from which Catholic schools drew their students. Religion in the home could no longer be taken for granted. This raised the question of whether RE classes were coercive in attempting to 'form' students, and whether RE should follow other disciplines and focus on learning *about religion(s)* so that students were better prepared to become citizens in a multi-faith society.

This question became more pressing as the number of students from other religions began enrolling in Catholic schools. At the beginning of the 21st century the changed demographics of Catholic schools re-ignited the issue of identity: What makes a Catholic school 'Catholic'?

As indicated previously, this question was not new. In the 1960s and 70s lay educators began to replace religious as teachers in Catholic schools. The assumption prior to this time was that the presence of religious conferred a 'Catholic' identity on schools. The identity of Catholics schools was deemed so secure that its mission was taken for granted. By the 2000s this assumption has proved to be false and the need arose to explicitly articulate the mission of Catholic schooling.

While the presence of 'students of other faiths' in Catholic schools dissipated the secularist argument that Catholic schooling is socially divisive, it left the identity and mission issues unresolved. At the heart of these issues was whether Catholic schools should be inclusive or exclusive with respect to the students they enrolled. The question led to new queries about where the boundaries of Catholic identity lay.

In 2007 the Bishops of NSW addressed this question in a paper *Catholic Schools at a Crossroads* by declaring for inclusion over exclusion. Many senior Catholic educators supported the stance taken in *Catholic Schools at a Crossroads*. However, opting for inclusion also raised the question of how to teach RE in the situation this created. The mix of students in a classroom included those with strong Christian belief (even if sometimes literal in

---

17   It is worth remembering that up until the 1950s it was not uncommon for job advertisements to carry the line 'Catholics need not apply'.

nature), those antagonistic to belief *per se*, those who embraced a different faith, and importantly, those holding a relativistic position.

In the context of an increasingly pluralist and postsecular society that accepts, albeit reluctantly, that religion is a fact of life, what form should RE take in Catholic schools? Could the Shared Christian Praxis model handle the rapidly evolving situation? What other models are available? These were the questions being debated among Catholic educators at the time that a delegation from the CECV visited KU Leuven to explore how RE was being addressed there. This led to them throwing their financial and moral weight behind the ECSI project in 2006. The adoption of the ECSI project and its hermeneutical approach to RE was judged as more likely to be effective in dealing with the increased pluralism in Catholic classrooms than the epistemologically sound Shared Christian Praxis model then in place. This was a leap of faith. Whether it was justified remains an issue for serious reflection sixteen years on.

At the beginning of this chapter we suggested that recontextualisation can be understood as transforming personal worldviews in the context of a plurality of religious beliefs and other worldviews. Groome and many Catholic diocesan authorities argued that the shared Christian praxis model helped students develop the 'critical consciousness' needed to live in such a world. The questions today are: Does the ECSI model do it better? How much is gained by combining the best insights of both models?

In the next chapter we explore the strengths and weaknesses of the ESCI model against the background outlined above. We assess some of the assumptions on which this model rests, both at the theoretical and practical levels. We explore the issues that arise when teachers seek to use the ECSI framework in the RE classroom and whether it is capable of transforming worldviews.

Given the nature of a personal worldview, 'transforming worldviews' implies the religious formation of students. Education in faith is integral to this task.

13

THE ECSI PROJECT: REFLECTIONS ON AN AUSTRALIAN EXPERIENCE

We have made several references to the *Enhancing Catholic School Identity* (ECSI) project as our discussions have unfolded. This project provides the context in which most teachers in Australian Catholic schools encounter the notion of 'recontextualisation'. It is now time to feature this important project more specifically.

CHALLENGES ADDRESSED BY ECSI

Many Australian Catholic school systems have adopted the ECSI project because it seems to address in an authentic way three major issues:

1. Affirming the identity of Catholic schools as 'Catholic', given the increasing pluralism evident in how Catholics understand the worldview of faith as a resource in making sense of their lives both within the Church and within the wider Australian society.[1]
2. Addressing the range of worldviews that are alive in Australian society and are therefore present in Catholic schools.
3. Developing a pedagogy suitable for religious education (RE) classrooms when the students, teachers and parents all tend to reflect the pluralism of the society and often demonstrate some degree of alienation from institutional Catholicism.

What 'being Catholic' means in the context of a postsecular, multi-cultural, multi-faith society, and a post-Vatican II Church, is now a major

---

1 In previous chapters we have pointed out that religious pluralism is as much a part of the faith scene today within the Catholic Church itself as it is within society. However, the mono-cultural understanding of faith associated with classicism has tended to mask intra-faith pluralism in some settings.

issue for all Catholic educators. The second major issue is concerned with how to prepare students to live both as effective citizens and as members of a faith community within the contemporary context. The third addresses the narrower challenge of teaching RE in this context.

KUL AS A SOURCE OF PRACTICAL WISDOM

Katholieke Universiteit Leuven (KUL) was initially seen by senior Australian Catholic educators as a source of practical wisdom in dealing with these three issues. It had been wrestling with questions of its own institutional identity as 'Catholic', and with the 'identity issue' as it arose for Catholic schools in Flanders, in the face of the increasingly secular social environment.

The authors of this volume visited KUL as visiting scholars in 2016, when a move to remove the term 'Katholieke' from the university's name had recently been defeated, and the Director of the Faculty of Theology and Religious Education, Lieven Boeve, had just taken up a new position as the Director of Catholic Education for Flanders. Boeve's brief was to assist Catholic schools to retain their identity as 'Catholic' in the evolving postmodern and postsecular context. KUL had a long history of empirical research in practical theology to call upon in addressing these challenges, and strong links existed between the Faculty of Theology and Religious Education and Catholic Education in Flanders. These factors made the ECSI project seem a viable option for Catholic education authorities in this country as well.

Like many renewal projects implemented before it, ECSI has both a *framework* and a *process*. The framework suggests what changes should be made, and the process suggests how these changes might be effected. The ECSI framework seems more durable than the ECSI process for reasons discussed below.

The ECSI project seeks to deal with the Catholic identity issue in two ways: by proposing what a Catholic school *is not,* and by providing a profile of what a Catholic school *should be*. It seeks to spell out a preferred future for Catholic schools.

ECSI seeks to address the broader cultural issue of pluralism by proposing a pedagogy that emphasises the place of 'dialogue' in addressing the challenge that radical pluralism poses *across the curriculum* in Catholic schools. It addresses the RE issue by proposing a specific pedagogy (discussed below) – the Hermeneutical-Communicative (HC) model. The model was developed, prior to ECSI, by Professors Herman Lombaerts FSC and Didier Pollefeyt.[2]

THE ECSI PROCESS

Within the ECSI process, data is collected from a school using three major survey instruments whose results, taken together, map the perspective held by different sections of the school community on three issues:

1. how they (students, parents and staff) understand faith
2. what they see as the preferred means of communicating faith
3. what each group sees as the school's preferred future as a Catholic school.

All three issues, to differing degrees, remain the subject of some controversy with the Australian Catholic community at the present time.

The aim of ECSI is to initiate a conversation that surfaces both areas of agreement, and areas of difference in perspective, that exist within a Catholic school community with a view of moving to some resolution of the latter. The goals are that the school can *more clearly define the particularities of its mission,* and *set clear directions with respect to the values that it promotes across its curriculum programs and within its community life.*

As the ECSI project has evolved in Australia, the most common use of ESCI data seems to lie in providing limited, but important, input to school improvement initiatives.

Catholic school (and system) leaders now face a major challenge in moving school communities – students, parents, teachers, and administrators – from where the ECSI data indicates they are currently with respect to the issues indicated above, to where they might prefer them to be once members of the school community understand what the options are. In this way ECSI provides important elements to both a school's and a school system's improvement agenda and strategic planning. It also provides a form of discourse in which these issues are to be addressed.

'Recontextualisation' appears in ECSI as the preferred model for interpreting Christian faith and ECSI offers the 'dialogue school' as the preferred future for all Catholic schools.[3] We discuss this option in more detail later in this chapter.

---

2 As indicated in our introductory chapter, Herman Lombaerts FSC visited Australia in the 1970s, a visit that generated great interest in and practical initiatives flowing from his insights and approaches in the area of religious education in the post-Vatican II era.
3 In an article entitled 'Dialogue as the future: a Catholic answer to the Colorization of the Education Landscape' (2013) the authors Didier Pollefeyt and Jan Bouwens begin by adding the caveat: 'We suggest that the international reader keeps in mind that the educational contexts

The development of the ECSI project is tied both to the 'story' of the Catholic Church in Belgium and Catholic education in Flanders. It seems an unstated assumption that the experience of Australian schools has much in common with the latter 'story' because it shares a similar context. The story of the Church in Belgium tends to proscribe the use of the term 'mission' in discussing the future shape of Catholic schooling.[4]

THE 'STORY' OF CATHOLIC EDUCATION IN FLANDERS

The promoters of ECSI analyse the context in their country in terms of a weakening of Catholic identity told against the background of the growing secularisation and the detraditionalisation[5] of culture in Belgium. As they note: 'Up until the 1950s, the confessional identity of schools from the Catholic network in Flanders was guaranteed'.[6] In Australia at this time it was also guaranteed by the presence of religious – sisters, brothers, and a smaller number of priests – teaching in Catholic schools. However, since that time, the forces of secularisation, detraditionalisation and pluralisation have placed pressure on the identity of Catholic schools as the gap between the worldview of culture and the worldview of Catholic faith varied – making the integration of faith, life, and culture problematic. Put in other words, the weight people give to the worldview of culture as opposed to the weight they give to the worldview of faith, both seen resources in making sense of their lives, has shifted markedly towards the former.

In response to developments in European cultures, Catholic schools there developed *Christian values education* as a strategy to bridge the perceived gap between faith and culture. Christian values education 'involves an attempt to link a generally shared awareness of 'a good life' to the Catholic faith'.[7]

---

abroad are likely to be different from the context proposed in the text'. We propose that this caveat be applied to the ECSI project in toto.
https://theo.kuleuven.be/apps/press/ecsi/files/2019/04/7.-Pollefeyt-Bouwens-Dialogue-as-the-Future.pdf

4   The story of the Church in Belgium includes the experience of Catholics in Rwanda where missionary policy and practice contributed significantly to the genocide of 1994 in which members of the Tutsi tribe were massacred by Hutus. Most of the Rwandan population were Tutsi and marginalised by the ruling Hutu elite. When Belgium withdrew and democratic elections were held, the Tutsis came to power and this change led to the Rwandan civil war in which tribal allegiance overshadowed all other values, indicating the shallow depth of evangelisation by the Belgian missionaries. While many Catholics, including Rwandan clergy, were victims of the genocide, many were also its principal perpetrators. This experience was traumatic for the Church in Belgium. One consequence seems to have been that 'mission' has become a proscribed term in KUL discourse.
5   'Detraditionalisation' is a term used by Boeve to indicate that traditions (religious and cultural) can no longer be transmitted uncritically from one generation to the next in the form in which they were received.
6   Pollefeyt and Bouwens *Identity in Dialogue*. Zurich: LIT, 2014, 52.
7   ibid.

The focus in RE classes moved from the values found in the Christian story to the ethics of 'doing good'.

The deficiencies in adopting this approach emerged only slowly over time – 'doing good' is clearly not the prerogative of Christians alone. The values being proposed in Christian values education *had secular counterparts as well as counterparts in other religious traditions.* As religious pluralism evolved in Catholic schools in Flanders, and along with this, multiple ways of interpreting religion, a specifically Christian approach to values education became increasingly untenable.[8]

For Christians, the failure of this RE strategy lay primarily in not maintaining links between 'Christian values' and the 'Christian story'[9]. Students of other faiths had their own frame of reference in which to make sense of 'values'. The authors of *Identity in Dialogue* suggest that, rather than enhancing Christian values, the Christian values approach to RE contributed to the secularisation of Catholic schooling.[10]

The push-back against the Christian Values education within Catholic Education in Europe took a number of forms. One was a 'back to basics' movement that sought to re-promote the *confessional identity* of Catholic schools. The approach sought a return to a propositional understanding of the worldview of Christian faith as it existed in the 1950s and earlier. However, the cultural props that had made this possible for earlier generations no longer existed in the post-Vatican II period which witnessed the death of 'cultural Catholicism' in Europe.[11] This 'back to basics' movement resulted in the *re-confessionalisation* of a small number of Catholic schools. Schools taking this path are described in ECSI as 're-confessional'. ECSI data indicates that there is quite limited support among parents, students, and teachers for this model as a preferred future for Catholic schools.

---

8   While the story of RE is somewhat different in Australia, something similar has happened with Christian service learning as a component in RE programs. Students could appreciate the value of service *as an end itself* without identifying with its Christian inspiration or motivation.

9   The evolution of RE in this country has not followed the same path as happened in Flanders. In the 1970s many primary schools in NSW adopted the *Vision and Values* project developed by the National Catholic Education Association in the USA. In the 1990s some Catholic schools took part in the Australian Values Project. Many secondary schools in NSW adopted the *Sense of the Sacred* project as an across-the-curriculum model for embedding 'Catholic values' within school programs using the values infusion methodology. In mainstream RE, Groome's Christian Praxis model discussed in the last chapter has remained dominant.

10 A second factor that aided secularisation is Europe's long association with Christianity and the ambiguities this has introduced into cultural and social life. As one senior student expressed the issue to the authors: 'The Catholic Church here has colonised the notion of God. This is not a good idea'.

11 'Cultural Catholicism' refers to the fact that people accepted a particular interpretation of the worldview of faith uncritically as the result of having been born into a 'Catholic family'. The growing pluralism in society meant the number of families where both parents were practising Catholics rapidly diminished.

Another response to the changing cultural situation, very common in Flanders, was for the school to retain the name 'Catholic', but to relinquish the identity and mission that this name invokes. The 'Catholic school' then becomes an uncritical agent in the transmission of the dominant culture and interprets its purpose from this perspective. The ECSI framework classified this model as *institutionalised secularisation*, and schools following the model are described as 'Colourless'.

A third approach was to see the Catholic faith as one option among many and to treat it as being on the same level as other faiths and secular worldviews. The result is that students come to take a relativistic view to meaning-making and religion. While this approach attempts to address the issue of pluralism in the name of tolerance, the particularity of the Christian faith is lost. In ECSI language, the result is a 'Colourful School'.

The preferred stance for dealing with the worldview of faith within the ECSI project is named 'recontextualisation'. A major problem for ECSI is that this notion is not sufficiently clarified to be put to practical use. In seeking to convey the meaning of the term in *Identity in Dialogue* the authors write:

> (A recontextualising school) is deliberately in search of a renewed Catholic profile in and through conversation with plurality. It tries to understand the Catholic faith re-interpreted in a contemporary cultural context. On the one hand, plurality is recognised and valued as such; on the other hand, the focus on Catholic identity is maintained. After all, the evangelical message remains relevant for people of today and tomorrow. But the changing cultural context should be integrated into 'being Catholic' (recontextualisation) so that it (ie 'being Catholic') remains recognisable, credible and meaningful for contemporary people (tradition development). The question then is how to live a Catholic life and how to be a Catholic school in the middle of contemporary culture.[12]

In seeking to clarify the concept of recontextualisation, Pollefeyt and Bouwens add:

> It is important to understand that the recontextualisation of Catholic school identity starts from a pluralisation paradigm. In fact, Catholicism is **one** option among a multiplicity of philosophical and religious positions. Catholics believe that God in his (sic) own way, is near to all people in search of value and meaning. This plurality

---

[12] Pollefeyt and Bouwens, 56. Material in brackets added by Jim and Therese D'Orsa.

is not only formally recognised, but also appreciated as a positive challenge and a chance to enrich one's own Catholic identity.[13]

The focus here is not on recontextualisation as a hermeneutical issue, but on recontextualising the identity of Catholic schools. Featuring the Hermeneutical-Communicative (HC) model, the authors continue:

> Openness to and dialogue with otherness (including non-Catholic) is encouraged without aiming at the greatest common denominator. Multiplicity is played out; multi-vocality needs to resound. **Recontextualisation** is not substantiated by an attitude of consensus (as in Values Education) but is propelled by dissimilarity. Young people are taught to relate to other religions and philosophies of life from a personal profile (whether Catholic or not). In dialogue with otherness they learn to know themselves, and how to take responsibility for personal choices. Show your individuality in tension with dissimilarities – precisely out of respect for the other. This way the Catholic faith is treated as the preferential perspective … A recontextualising school environment challenges people to give shape to their personal identity in conversation with others, against the background of dialogue (with) and sometimes in confrontation with the Catholic tradition.[14]

A prerequisite for the HC model to work is the presence of 'a significant minority of Catholics who are recognizable as such and who want to enter into dialogue explicitly.'[15]

THE HC APPROACH TO RE

The HC method of teaching RE was developed to address the growing pluralism of worldviews found in classrooms in Catholic schools in Flanders.[16] A major assumption of this model of RE is that students coming from different religious backgrounds can grow in understanding of both the worldview of their culture and the worldview of their particular religious meaning-making tradition (be it Catholic, Muslim or secular) by being led through a process of dialogue that respects particular worldviews while sponsoring the worldview of Catholic faith (as understood by the teacher).[17]

---

13 ibid
14 ibid
15 ibid, 57.
16 The situation there with respect to the numbers of Muslim students in some classes has been commented on previously.
17 It is worth noting that the HC model of RE does not correspond to inter-religious dialogue as usually understood where all traditions have equal standing.

The model ascribes three major roles to the teacher: that of *witness* to the Catholic faith; that of *'expert'* in the Catholic faith; and that of *moderator* of a critical dialogue among religious and secular worldviews. As a witness to the Catholic faith, the expectation is that teachers will relate with students within the Christian ethos of the school. Naturally, the 'expertise' that a teacher brings to the classroom with respect to Christian faith depends on his or her grasp of the worldview of Catholic faith. As we have seen in previous chapters, this worldview is now open to multiple interpretations, even given the guidance provided by Church leaders.

School and system leaders need to acknowledge the situation faced by teachers with limited expertise and nurture them through teacher formation programs that model the skills that teachers need to be *moderators of dialogue*. This is a difficult role for teachers operating in a Church institution with a poor record of engaging in dialogue even with its own members. To be effective, teachers need to set clear rules so that the dialogue process can run productively.[18]

The sections above outline the *ECSI framework*. In summary, the framework identifies the pluralism found within society at both the cultural and religious levels as its dominant feature. While the consequences of what this means are still being worked out at the societal level, what seems clear is that we no longer live in the modern world or within its limited construction of secularisation that placed the secular and the religious dimensions of life into separate, mutually exclusive spheres. *We live in a postsecular world in which these dimensions are once again seen as interrelated.* This situation creates new types of controversy, but it has also created the possibility of constructive relationships not only between the secular and the sacred, but also among the major religions. The legacy of the postmodern era still haunts the emerging postsecular culture, making people suspicious of institutions and those who lead them. It also breeds a suspicion about over-reaching claims on 'truth'.

In a postsecular world people must be able to deal with those who are 'legitimately other' and to appreciate the value of their being 'other'. A constructive way to address this challenge is through dialogue that, as we have noted previously, can take several forms.

What is true of society in general, is also true of Catholic schools. Pluralism in society results in pluralism in Catholic schools. This comes about in two ways: the presence in Catholic schools of students from other religions and secular ideologies, the gradual detraditionalisation

---

18 The Global Institute for Change provides an important primer for leading dialogue in a pedagogical context. *Essentials of Dialogue,* https://institute.global/advisory/essentials-dialogue

and secularisation of students and the effect this has on their attitudes to religion, even when those students are from Catholic family backgrounds. It is through critical dialogue with traditions, religious and secular, that students begin to appreciate the *particularity* of their own religious tradition or secular worldview. An important purpose of Catholic schooling is to develop this appreciation while at the same time demonstrating what the Catholic tradition has to offer as a trustworthy source of meaning.

The ECSI framework did not emerge out of thin air. While it is clearly a response to the pluralism experienced in Catholic schools in Belgium, it is also part of the response by Catholic educators to counter the impact of the detraditionalisation that can result from pluralisation and secularisation. Thirdly, it is a response to the impact that Vatican II has had in reformulating the worldview of faith. This impact is most notable in the Vatican II document on revelation and its interpretation (*Dei Verbum*) and those dealing with the Church's stance to people of other faiths and no religious faith (*Ad Gentes* and particularly *Nostra Aetate*).

The connection between ESCI and hermeneutics as mediated by the thinking of French philosopher Paul Ricoeur is also important. The latter proposes that interpretation is an iterative process that passes through several stages of critique in which a 'surplus of meaning' is generated. This concept of 'iterative process' has important bearings when exploring sacred texts. A result of this process is what ECSI terms *post-critical belief*. This stands in opposition to literal belief.

KUL researcher Emeritus Professor Dirk Hutsebaut developed a survey instrument that operationalised the two-dimensional model put forward by Emeritus Professor David Wulff of Wheaton College Massachusetts to measure people's approach to religious belief. The KUL model proposed that people's attitude towards religion can be measured by reference to two mutually exclusive axes. The X axis records the degree to which they are open to religious belief or not. The Y axis determines their stance to belief or disbelief.

The KUL model is set out in the diagram below:

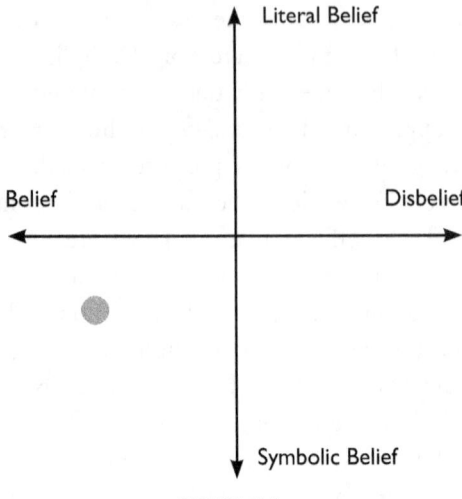

FIGURE 13.1

Literal belief takes religious texts at face value. Symbolic belief assumes that all texts need to be interpreted relative to the context in which they were written in order to assess their meaning. Hutsebut's *Post-critical Belief Scale* determines where a respondent sits in this model. The survey was developed using students at KUL as samples. It was validated in a number of research projects in Europe prior to its adoption for ECSI. Post-critical belief corresponds to the bottom left-hand quadrant. The preferred Catholic position on this model is marked by the circle in the diagram above. That is, it is characterised by strong belief as well as the recognition of the need for interpretation to assess the meaning of religious truths.

Post-critical belief corresponds to a stance towards faith that American Catholic theologian James Whitehead describes as 'befriending the tradition'.[19] That is recognising that the Catholic religious tradition, like all religious traditions, comes with both strengths and limitations, and acknowledging both. The aim of an authentic religious education program is to produce a post-critical understanding of the Catholic tradition, one that enables the student to 'befriend' it without being totally put off by either its limitations or its ambiguities.

A CRITIQUE OF ECSI FROM AN AUSTRALIAN PERSPECTIVE

Catholic RE teachers in Australia are generally familiar with the Christian Praxis model of RE even where a particular system has not adopted it formally. Given that both the Christian Praxis and HC approaches to

---

19 James and Evelyn Whitehead *Method in Ministry*. Revised and updated edition. Kansas City: Sheed & Ward, 1995, 5.

RE seek to help students develop a critical dialogue between faith and contemporary culture, it may be asked: Are they equivalent?

The answer to this question is that they are not. The Christian praxis model seeks to develop a dialogue between contemporary experience and the Catholic tradition. In this respect it is *mono-focal*. The assumption is that the Catholic tradition can make sense of all contemporary experience. However, any critical engagement with this tradition makes it evident to many students today that this is not the case. The Catholic tradition, as currently embraced officially, struggles to deal, for example, with the equality of women in the Church, and the place and role of members of the LGBT communities. The tradition is viewed as patriarchal and clericalised, and the Church's poor handling of clerical sexual abuse has undermined the credibility of religious leaders and with them the worldview of faith as a resource in making sense of life. All of these issues are interpreted as 'own goals'.

The HC model places a high value on 'otherness' and dialogue with 'otherness', that is on voices that have not been part of the conversation by which culture is shaped, and so have not been heard. This includes not only refugees, minority ethnic groups, but also LGBT persons, the disabled, and women, particularly those who have been the subject of domestic abuse. The experience of persons who are 'other' often highlights limitations in the way the dominant culture functions, as well as limitations in the way the Christian tradition is interpreted. Dialogue with otherness therefore offers the students the opportunity to critique both culture and religion from multiple perspectives seeing both the good and the bad that each produces. An assumption is that students have sufficient grasp of their own tradition to engage in a critical dialogue.[20] The model places considerable onus on teachers to manage the type of interaction presupposed by dialogue in the classroom. If, as noted earlier, teachers in Catholic schools have found it hard to manage the critical dialogue component of the Shared Christian Praxis model, it is difficult to see how they will manage the more complex critical dialogue component of the HC approach without considerable support.

The strength of the ECSI project lies in opening up a discourse about Catholic identity – institutional identity and personal identity. The hope of the project is that being 'Catholic' will take on new significance in the context of plurality, and that students will develop a personal identity open to the faith dimension of life.

Although ESCI has been in place since 2012 in some dioceses, there seems to have been no major attempt to evaluate it in terms of its goals.

---

20 'Critical' here means identifying what is good and bad in a tradition.

The reason for this is that the model comes with a pedagogy that teachers are poorly equipped to implement in the classroom. A further factor is that dioceses implement the project in their own ways and timeframes so that developing a framework to evaluate the project is now highly problematic.

For most teachers and parents, it is intuitively obvious that the Catholic faith needs to be presented to students in a way that is meaningful for them. However, parents find this difficult to achieve at home and hope that the teachers in Catholic schools know how to do it.[21] However, with 'recontextualisation' so poorly defined within the project and the limited support available to teachers in using the HC model, this seems a messianic hope.

ESCI AND THE ISSUE OF OVERREACH

ESCI has been conceptualised within an imaginative and ambitious framework. The question is whether its process can deliver on its goals. A danger with ambitious projects is over-reach. That is, that a project claims to deliver more than it can. With ECSI this appears to be the case in two specific areas: its use of survey methodology with young children, and the tendency to interpret synchronic data diachronically.

Using survey methodology with primary school students (and even junior secondary school students) can result in unreliable results. In ECSI's case the results from the adapted form of the PCB scale used with primary school students seem counter-intuitive. Primary students score more highly on the PCB scale than do most secondary students! Given the former's level of cognitive development this should raise questions either about the reliability of the results, or whether the adapted form of the PCB scale used with primary students measures the same variables as those explored with older students, or with adults. The results for primary school students seem to sit awkwardly with Fowler's theory of religious development that is often invoked in developing the scope and sequence chart for the design of RE curricula.[22] This is not to deny the reality of the religious experiences among primary school children, but to question the interpretation put on the results by its ECSI interpreters. It could be that secondary students as they develop their critical skills simply reject naive conceptions of faith to which they have been exposed or seek to keep their options open by

---

21 The aim of an earlier project adopted in some schools, the *Vision and Values* project, was to develop co-operation between home and school in promoting six 'Gospel' values for primary school children. The resources developed to support this program sought to instruct the parents as well as the students about the values being introduced so that school life and home life stood as a witness to those values.

22 It is worth noting that Fowler's sample in developing his theory of religious development did not include young children. Thus it, too, has problems.

adopting relativism as a stance to faith. Without proper longitudinal studies this issue cannot be resolved.

The second problem is more technical in nature. *Identity in Dialogue* presents data from trials of the ESCI process in Victoria in the period 2006-2012. Data was collected from several groups in this period: Years 5-6, Years 7-8, Years 9-10, Years 11-12, parents, teachers, and school administrators. These were then cumulated by group to arrive at Victorian averages for each group.

Data collected at a point in time is described as *synchronic*. It provides a snapshot of what people think *at that point in time*. When such data is cumulated across time, the tendency is to interpret it as if the results provide a moving picture of what is happening across time, that is, to identify trends. But this is not legitimate, since the one group of students, for instance, is not being followed year by year which would provide a *diachronic perspective* from which trends could be inferred. Interpreting synchronic data as if it were diachronic means the interpretation is little more than a hypothesis to be tested. The 'trends' so identified can be quite misleading. This mistake seems to occur in some of the interpretations offered in *Identity in Dialogue*, but may not occur in the reports presented to schools as part of the ESCI project. KUL certainly has the data to identify longitudinal trends for many schools and school systems, but this has yet to be reported.

ESCI AND INSTITUTIONAL IDENTITY

The 'identity question' is not new to Australian Catholic education. By the 1990s the answer to this question centred on the issue of 'mission', an issue that had largely been presumed while religious congregations sponsored Catholic schools. Schools began to engage in the process of developing mission statements and strategic plans to implement the vision that this process produced.

The thrust of such initiatives was largely compromised as state governments began to mandate 'school improvement' using the goal of 'continuous improvement' to justify public expenditure on schools. By the early 2000s, the focus on mission seems to have dissipated as schools pursued a largely secular agenda driven in part by competition for students. In addition, with the introduction of NAPLAN[23] and the decline in the capacity of senior grades to function as a bridge between the world of schooling and the world of work, the situation was exacerbated. Whereas in the 'era of the religious' the implicit mission of Catholic schools had been

---

23 See Australian Government NAPLAN website for details of this Commonwealth government initiative. https://www.nap.edu.au

to 'pass on the faith' and 'create life chances for students', in the postmodern setting neither of these objectives are guaranteed. Does the Catholic school any longer have a mission other than to have students do as well, if not better, than students in other private or public schools? If so, what is it? In reaction to this trend, congregational schools began to re-interpret their educational goals in terms of the charism of their founder. [24]

In Australia, ECSI has helped to stimulate a new form of discourse about the issue of identity by broadening the conversation about the purpose (mission) of Catholic schools to include institutional identity as 'Catholic', something that has been largely lost in Flanders. It has done this in the context of radical pluralism[25] and outlined what a Catholic school has to offer in this context.

> (In a Dialogue Catholic school) The multiplicity of voices, views, and perspectives, is recognised as a positive contribution to an open Catholic school environment. Receptivity and openness to what is different is a chance to re-profile the Catholic faith amidst contemporary plurality (**recontextualisation**). A preferential option for the Catholic message sets the tone for this dialogue. The conversation among philosophical views is conducted with a preferential option for Catholicism in mind. In the midst of plurality, one is looking to be Catholic: from being a Catholic, one lives in plurality.[26]

ECSI, however, seems to operate under some constraints:

- ECSI does not acknowledge the importance of an institution already being able to *articulate its mission* even as it discusses the question of identity. Identity – *who we are* – cannot be separated in practice from mission – *what we do, that is, what we are actually committed to regardless of what we say.*
- ECSI creates a vision – the Dialogue School – but provides quite limited practical ways to achieve it.
- ECSI highlights the importance of *students' agency* in the formation of their personal worldview. It does this by emphasising the need for students to take responsibility for forming their personal worldview in alignment with or distinctive from that of their peers. This is a very

---

24 This development is charted in Jim and Therese D'Orsa *New Ways of Living the Gospel.*
25 The 2021 Australian Census indicates that people born in Australia are now in the minority, and that less than half of Australians identify themselves as Christian.
    https://www.abs.gov.au/statistics/people/people-and-communities/snapshot-australia/latest-release
26 Pollefeyt and Bouwens, 2014, 63.

credible vision, but the support needed for it to be successful is very demanding on a school's personnel and resources.

The first constraint seems to flow from the history of mission in the Belgian church. Australia does not share in this history, meaning that 'mission' has a different resonance in Australian church history; certainly, it has a different place in Catholic education in this country. However, more recently awareness of the struggles of First Nations people, and the mixed story of Christian mission in regard to them, has comes to light and hence into reflective consciousness, and strong critiques of mission in this country as well.

The final constraint opens ECSI to the critique that, if poorly handled, the HC approach to RE leads to 'relativism', and results in a Colourful School rather than a Dialogue School, that is to the relativistic beliefs that:

1. All religions and worldviews are equivalent.
2. It is possible to construct a personal worldview by cobbling together elements taken from different public worldviews. Part of the expertise needed by teachers is knowing how to dismantle these positions.

TAKING A HOLISTIC VIEW

In developing a personal worldview that is Catholic, we have approached the task largely from an anthropological perspective. This perspective assumes that in a situation of plurality most students take the worldview of their culture as a default frame of reference in making sense of their experiences. This taken for granted stance is weighted towards the secular, even though other elements are currently being included because of the changing profile of Australian society. The task of the Catholic school is to wean students off a predominantly secular frame of reference.

As we have noted earlier in discussing the work of Hiebert (Chapter 7), this involves some *transformation of the personal worldview of the student*. To transform a worldview it is necessary to challenge it at three levels:

1. What the student *knows and believes*.
2. The *values* that underpin their worldview and sustain its norms.
3. Nurturing *a personal sensibility that reflects the aspirations inherent in the vision* that their worldview proposes as a preferred future for themselves, that is, one that is *open to faith* (seen as a trustworthy meaning system).

An important goal of a Catholic school in the context of plurality is to encourage student agency in the formation of a personal worldview *open to faith*. The school approaches this task in the classroom formally in RE; it also approaches it in the values that it articulates and the norms it develops for guiding school life; finally, it approaches this task by ensuring that the quality of the community life experienced in the school reflects the vision that underpins its values. If student agency is valued, then this means including students in the task of articulating and pursuing a mission that justifies the name 'Catholic'.

ECSI only partly realises its potential in this respect. It leaves the issue of 'recontextualisation' largely unexplained. It proposes the HC model of RE as *one model that can be effective in some contexts.*

As the history of theology attests, when a change of era occurs, there is often a lag between the actual recontextualisation of faith and the development of processes by which this occurs. Such is people's need to make sense of their lives that recontextualisation often happens as a matter of necessity rather than as a matter of intention. We live in such a period. The ECSI proposal, that recontextualisation occurs in dialogue with those who are 'other', may not represent the last word on how recontextualisation can occur. It could well be that the contribution of Australian teachers to ECSI realising its vision lies in finding additional methods of recontextualising the worldview of faith in the context of Australian postsecular plurality.

In the penultimate chapter that follows we discuss the progress that has been made on this front in Victoria.

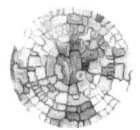

14

RECONTEXTUALISATION IN PRACTICE: VICTORIA – A CASE STUDY

When senior leaders in Catholic education in Victoria decided to sponsor the ECSI project in 2006, its promoters in KU Leuven had developed its theological framework, but were still developing its methodology and the support infrastructure necessary for it to function effectively on the international stage.

A large-scale trial was undertaken in schools of the Melbourne Archdiocese in 2008 and on the basis of the promise this showed, support from the Catholic Education Commission of Victoria (CECV) was extended for another two years. In 2010 a second trial was implemented, involving all four Victorian dioceses in validating the ECSI methodology and removing any 'chinks' revealed by the first trial. By 2013 ECSI had been used in 244 primary schools, 57 secondary schools and 6 Catholic Education Offices (CEOs) involving some 56,000 respondents. This made it the biggest data-driven project to be undertaken in Catholic schools in this country.[1]

In this chapter we trace the ways in which local leaders endeavoured to use the findings of the project to develop policies and practices leading to new developments in Religious Education. The chapter concludes with Professor Didier Pollefeyt's assessment of the issues now confronting religious educators in Victoria.

---

1 Prior to this, the CEO Sydney and CEO Parramatta adapted a data-driven program developed for Christian Brothers schools in Victoria and Tasmania to help schools develop a mission statement and strategic plan. In 2008 the CEO Brisbane commissioned the Australian Council of Educational Research (ACER) to run a survey process entitled *Who's Coming to School Today?* to assess the context in which Catholic schools in the archdiocese of Brisbane operated. The 2009 ACER report on this project was released in summary form, rather than in detailed form. Neither of these projects had the support, infrastructure or technical expertise on offer from KU Leuven in the ECSI project.

INITIAL IMPLEMENTATION IN VICTORIA

The implementation of a major project usually occurs in a series of interrelated steps. Michael Fullan, for instance, suggests these are three phases in these projects: *awareness raising, formal adoption,* and *formal implementation*.[2] Each step needs to be planned and may involve different people or groups of people. Those leading school systems tend to be the people responsible for adopting the 'new way' when it comes to major projects. Often, they work closely with those responsible for raising awareness about the need for the proposed project. Once convinced of its viability, then system leaders formally adopt it. Implementation happens mostly at the local level. It is the local response that ultimately determines whether the 'new way' has an impact and effects change.

In the awareness-raising phase of ECSI, Catholic educators in Victoria initially had difficulty with the form of discourse used in the project, many dismissing it disparagingly as 'Leuvenese'.

A major step forward occurred in 2014 when Pollefeyt and Bouwens released their book: *Identity in Dialogue*[3] and toured Australia to promote its findings.[4] This study subsequently served as a key reference for school and school system leaders in dealing with both the ECSI framework and the ECSI methodology. The book uses data collected from Victorian Catholic schools in 2012 to illustrate how the project functions, how ECSI data is presented, how it is interpreted, and how the findings of the ECSI process can be of help in policy development at the school and system levels.

The difficulties with ECSI language are evident in how Pollefeyt and Bouwens set out the research questions that the project sought to address:

- **Descriptive research question:** How does a Catholic organisation shape the religious and specifically Catholic components of its institutional identity in a cultural context characterised by increasing secularisation, detraditionalisation and pluralisation?
- **Evaluative research question:** Based on the assessment of the perceived current practice in the Catholic organisation and the ideal perspectives of its members, what does KU Leuven recommend to the leadership of this organisation, in case it wishes to maintain and enhance the religious and specifically Catholic components of its institutional identity, in order

---

[2] See Michael Fullan *The New Meaning of Educational Change* 5th Ed New York: Teachers College Press, 2015.
[3] The full title of the book is *Identity in Dialogue: Assessing and enhancing Catholic school identity. Research methodology and research results in Catholic schools in Victoria Australia.*
[4] Since this time, Pollefeyt and Bouwens have been regular visitors to Australia.

to Recontextualise it in a hermeneutical-communicative theological perspective in a pluralising context?[5]

People familiar with the theological works of Boeve and Schillebeeckx would understand the references here. In 2014 this group did not include most Victorian Catholic school principals! Visits to the four Victorian dioceses by Pollefeyt and Bouwens have played an important role in the awareness-raising phase of the ECSI project. They raised awareness about the need for Catholic educators to address the threat posed by secularisation and pluralisation to the institutional identity of Catholic schools, and to the personal identity of students in those schools. Later visits by Lieven Boeve were also helpful in awareness-raising about the theological framework behind the project.

The adoption phase of the ECSI project occurred in the years 2010 to 2012 as it was rolled out in a sample of Victorian schools. This enabled technical difficulties with the various questionnaires and survey instruments ('scales') to be sorted out so that, from an empirical perspective, the data collected in ECSI was reliable and within the literacy capacity of the various target audiences included in the project. In this period KU Leuven developed an English-language website to support the Project (www.schoolidentity.com)

The implication of the second research question (in 2014) was that a team at KU Leuven would interpret the data and make recommendations for people working in an educational context that was quite different to that of Catholic schools in Flanders. This raised two important questions:

1. Did KU Leuven have the staff with the expertise necessary to function in the cross-cultural context that this suggestion created?
2. Was such an approach necessary?

The early experience of school leaders was that they needed someone local who could interpret (translate) the form of discourse used in reports written at KU Leuven. In the absence of this person being available, principals were left to make sense of ECSI data, too often with only a quite limited understanding of the ECSI framework. This proved counterproductive.

System leaders responded to this situation by sponsoring key school and system personnel (including some diocesan clergy) to KU Leuven to attend live-in seminars where they could familiarise themselves with ECSI's framework, methodology, theology, and, more importantly, how

---

5   Pollefeyt & Bouwens, 2014, 20-21.

to interpret the data.[6]. This not only addressed an immediate problem; it also enhanced the status of the project. Following this intervention, the empirical data produced in local schools could be interpreted by someone familiar with the Australian educational and cultural context.[7] In addition, it helped lower the 'language barrier' created by the ECSI framework. Over time, teachers became more at home in using this language and the idea of 'recontextualisation' gradually became accepted, a word symbolising a strongly held hope, even if its exact meaning remained obscure to many.

Most Catholics intuitively agree that faith needs to be presented to young people in a way that is meaningful to them. However, questions arising are: 'How do we do this?' and 'How do we mobilise the opportunities open to us in an Australian Catholic school to best effect in doing this?' Belief in the value of and need for recontextualisation leads more or less directly to belief in forms of religious education pedagogy that can achieve this goal, as well as belief that the very milieu of a Catholic school can be mobilised to support this aim.

As we have argued in earlier chapters, a perspective that restricts recontextualisation to religious education (RE) is hermeneutically quite limiting. In a change of era, educators must often recontextualise the worldview of culture as well the worldview of faith. Put in other words, recontextualisation in an *across-the-curriculum* issue, not simply an RE issue.

In Victoria, the advent of ECSI initiated a number of projects relating to the pedagogy used in RE in Catholic schools. Two are dealt with in this chapter: The *Encounter Pedagogy* model developed by some members of the RE team in the Melbourne Catholic Education Office and the *Recontextualise Pedagogy Research Project* developed through a partnership among the four Victorian diocesan Catholic education systems and the Catholic Theological College, Melbourne.

---

6   The first of these seminars was offered in 2009 and they have been offered regularly since. The authors attended the 2016 seminar while working as visiting scholars at KU Leuven. In addition to seminars in Leuven, the Australian Catholic University (ACU) offered courses at its campuses in Australia and Rome. The Catholic Theological College (CTC Melbourne) also offered courses in conjunction with the Catholic Education Office Melbourne. Over time the level of expertise in Australia grew and the need for data to be interpreted in Leuven diminished.

7   For instance, Catholic school systems in Australia exercise quite limited influence over the shape of the curriculum in Catholic schools outside religious education P-10. However, they play a major role in the governance structures operative in all Catholic schools. The opposite is true in Flanders. The Catholic Education Office, by virtue of the size of the school system in Flanders, has a major influence on the curriculum but very little control over what happens at the local school level including the appointment of local principals and boards. This difference is quite important when considering how institutional identity is maintained and enhanced.

PEDAGOGIES FOR RECONTEXTUALISATION

As a change project moves into the implementation phase, it also moves through a predictable number of steps. The Concerns Based Adoption Model (CBAM) sees the change process unfolding in line with the concerns raised by implementers beginning with 'How does it affect me?' and 'How will I cope?' and ending with 'How can we do this better?'[8]

The ECSI project proposed that the hermeneutical-communicative (HC) model for RE is a pedagogical approach that enables recontextualisation to occur. This model was developed in Flanders as a pedagogically legitimate means of addressing the religious diversity encountered in Catholic schools there, using dialogue between teacher and students as well as between students as a way of consolidating the personal identity of students and the institutional identity of Catholic schools. The fact that classrooms in Victorian Catholic schools have a different demography caused some hesitancy in accepting the model here, and this led to the question of whether it was possible to adapt existing pedagogies to achieve the same outcome in the Australian context. The *Pedagogy of Encounter* attempted to respond to this challenge.

PEDAGOGY OF ENCOUNTER

As noted earlier, prior to ECSI curriculum development and pedagogy in RE in many Australian dioceses was strongly influenced by the Shared Christian Praxis model developed by Thomas Groome. A critique of this model was that it is mono-correlational in that it attempts to account for all human experience in terms of the Christian story and vision. In the face of radical pluralism. The *Pedagogy of Encounter* was designed as a local way of implementing the HC model of religious education. The diagram below presents the model in simplified form.

The diagram makes it clear that the Christian worldview is one among many possible ways of interpreting life experiences, and not necessarily the only way. The cultural worldview holds centre stage as it provides the default frame of reference that students are most likely to use. (In a pluralist society this may have several possible interpretations). 'Other worldviews' will come into play if there are students from other religions, or other Christian denominations in the class. The question 'Why is it going on?' invites interpretation. There is unlikely to be just one interpretation. This is as true for the worldview of faith as it is for other worldviews. Action is

---

[8] This model was developed at the University of Texas in the 1970s and 1980s and has since been updated. For details of the model see
https://2012-2017.usaid.gov/sites/default/files/documents/1865/Roberts.pdf

predicated on dialogue among the various traditions represented in the class and is not captive to any one tradition. It is interaction among traditions that enables students to make judgements about 'What is the heart of the matter?' and so to determine how they might respond.

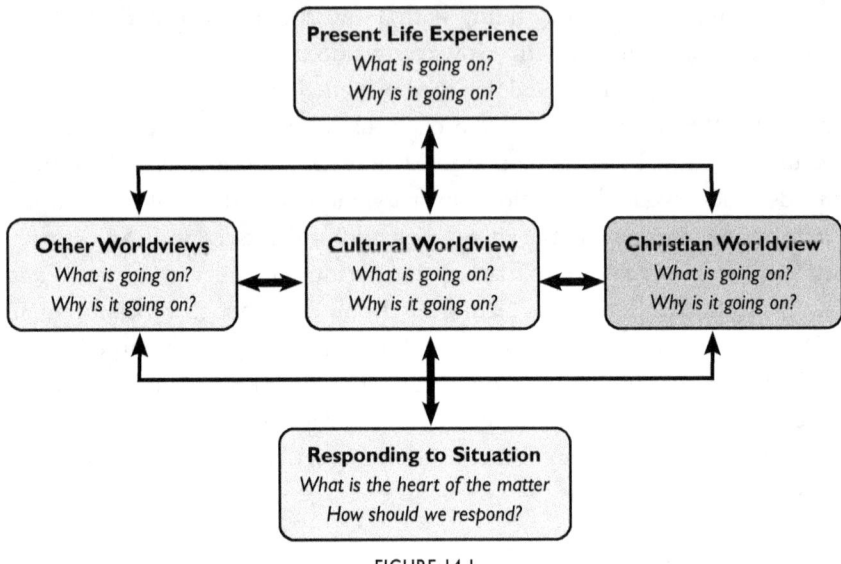

FIGURE 14.1

In presenting the model, the proponents of the pedagogy of encounter expand the roles of the teacher beyond those envisaged by Pollefeyt. In addition to the roles of witness, moderator, and specialist,[9] the pedagogy of encounter includes those of co-inquirer, designer of learning experiences, and change agent.[10]

The presentation above highlights the multi-correlational nature of the *Pedagogy of Encounter* as an interpretation of the HC model. It preserves the basic See-Judge-Act structure employed both in carrying out Catholic action for justice, and as used in the Shared Christian Praxis model (see Chapter 12).

CONTEXTUALISING PEDAGOGY RESEARCH PROJECT

In 2016 Kevin Lenehan and Rina Madden developed a position paper, on behalf of the four Victorian dioceses, in preparation for the adoption of a research project exploring what is needed at the system and school leadership

---

9 The roles of 'specialist' and 'facilitator' create the dilemma for teachers in that one can act to the disadvantage of the other in promoting 'rich dialogue' in the classroom.
10 CEO Melbourne *Horizons of Hope: Foundation Statement 'Pedagogy in A Catholic School'* Undated, 8, accessed at macs.vic.edu.au 4 Sept 2022.

levels to implement a pedagogical approach open to recontextualisation.

The paper situates RE in the context of the overall school curriculum:

In the context of a Catholic school, Religious Education is the curriculum learning area that promotes and facilitates student learning in the knowledge, practice, and self-understandings of Catholic Christianity in particular, and religious traditions in general. The contents of this learning area focuses on the sources, history, worship, beliefs, structures and roles of the faith community, and on the ways the church interacts with other religious groups and with the state in Australia and in other societies. Religious Education is deeply interwoven with other curriculum areas, since the Catholic Christian tradition has been a constitutive element of European history and the institutions of Western culture, and because along with other disciplines religion addresses the fundamental questions of meaning, identity and purpose that arise for individuals and societies. Therefore, learning in Religious Education is both practical and transforming for all involved. It challenges and equips students to respond intelligently, creatively and responsibly to their own and others' religious identities and commitments or non-religious worldviews within the non-confessional Australian state.[11]

The paper goes on to acknowledge the increasing religious pluralism that exists in Australian Catholic schools and the way in which this leads to differentiated learning outcomes. It proposes that to deal with this relatively new context, learning experiences need to be constructed around 'rich dialogue'. Referring to RE, the report goes on:

This dialogue can take many forms: between believers and their own religious tradition, between believers in different religious traditions, between religious and non-religious perspectives.

Learning through dialogue challenges students and teachers to be participants in the learning task, to move beyond self-sufficient certainty and disinterested avoidance in relation to religious knowledge and service.

The pedagogy of dialogue in Catholic schools is founded on both the capacity of the Catholic faith to provide an open and hospitable 'host-tradition' for critical and creative inquiry in Religious Education, and on the possibility of enrichment for both religious and non-religious worldviews through respectful and responsible dialogue.[12]

---

11 Kevin Lenehan and Rina Madden. *Combined Victorian Dioceses Position Paper: 'Recontextualising Pedagogy for a Distinctively Catholic Education'*. Melbourne: Catholic Theological College; (undated), 1.
12 ibid, 2.

The theological significance of dialogue comes from the way Christians understand God and God's manner of self-communication with humanity.

Religion therefore respectfully and humbly enters the world of the student as a dialogue partner that is open to the student and his or her world and at the same time keeps open the questions of God and the Gospel as the student grapples with his or her identity formation.[13]

A pedagogy based on dialogue places an ethical demand on the teacher 'to listen to the students and to ensure that all are enabled to participate and have their voice heard'.[14]

The position paper recognises that opening challenging conversations does not happen by accident; it occurs through careful planning in a process that is itself dialogical.

> Collegial planning processes focus on broadening and deepening teacher understanding of the student learning possibilities. At the same time the dialogue offers opportunities for teachers to challenge their own thinking and understanding and pursue further exploration of the concepts and theology in the planned unit of work.[15]

The notion of 'collegial planning' is significant in that it provides teachers with the opportunity to 'model the method' among themselves prior to using it in the classroom. This focus on teacher dialogue highlights the importance of an investment in ongoing teacher faith formation if teachers are to develop and implement recontextualising pedagogies.

> The paper acknowledges that pedagogical strategies such as inquiry-based learning, shared Christian praxis, rich question learning, integrated discipline learning, collaborative learning, and encounter pedagogy each aims, in its own way, to promote student learning, enabling them to progress from 'a pre-critical, literalist way of engaging with religious traditions to a post-critical, multi-dimensional interaction with the content of religious traditions'. Thus, a recontextualising pedagogy has several characteristics. It will:
> - be founded on principles of authentic student learning
> - engage the contents of the Catholic faith as the 'host tradition' for differentiated religious learning

---

13 ibid.
14 We refer the reader again to the resource *Essentials of Dialogue: Guidance and activities for teaching and practising dialogue with young people produced* by the Tony Blair Institute for Global Change (2017)
15 ibid, 4.

- involve teachers and students in collaborative processes of design in learning experiences
- develop appropriate open-inquiry, critical thinking and creative reasoning skills
- promote capacities of reflective attention, spiritual awareness and personal meaning-making
- draw on teacher roles of witness, specialist and facilitator to ensure rich dialogue between learners, the Catholic tradition and other religious and non-religious worldviews
- be attentive to the experiences of self-reflection, personal identity and worldview formation that accompany religious learning
- equip and accompany the maturing belief style from an original pre-critical **naivety** to a reflective and spiritually aware second **naivety**.[16]

The paper concludes:

Teachers and leaders build a **community of learners** that focuses on ongoing learning of all in the community. As diocesan system leaders we are included in this connected learning model, providing opportunities to learn with and from schools in the way we structure professional learning opportunities that model dialogical learning processes and faith encounters (emphasis added).

In 2018 a steering committee composed of system-level RE personnel from the four Victorian Catholic dioceses was formed to head up a research project addressing issues set out in the position paper. It was envisaged that the project would involve dialogue at several levels:

- within classrooms among students and between teachers and students
- among teachers in the same school
- between teachers and system RE personnel
- among system personnel.

Schools were invited to participate in the research. While it proved possible to gain primary participation, secondary schools were resistive to the invitation and, once the COVID pandemic struck, dropped out of the project altogether. The original hope was to complete the project in one year. However, getting ethical approval from CTC for a research project

---

16   Ibid, 6-7.

involving minors created an initial delay.[17] This was then exacerbated by the COVID outbreak in Victoria that made face-to-face teaching and meetings with teachers difficult to organise. Despite these difficulties, the steering committee continued to meet and process input from the schools and from the ongoing dialogue between school personnel and system personnel. The timeframe for the project blew out from one year to three years with a final report published in early 2022.[18]

The *Recontextualising Pedagogy Research Project* was strongly influenced by the theology of Boeve and Pollefeyt[19]. An early finding noted:

> … some system leaders involved in the project had been leading staff meeting sessions 'about' recontextualization. This meant that there was still more work to be done around the difference between **learning about recontextualization** and **experiencing a process of recontextualization (emphasis added)**[20].

This was one of a number of important 'shifts' that was identified in the initial implementation of the project. Others included: a shift from teachers identifying as curriculum implementers to curriculum innovators: a shift from approaching children as 'tabula rasa' to understanding the child as exercising agency; and a shift from fear of being judged for 'saying the wrong thing' to freedom to question. These shifts on the part of teachers were enabled by the way in which partnerships were set up within the project between school and system personnel; by the trust that this kindled; by the willingness of all involved to take risks in grappling with difficult questions; and the affirmation received in the various dialogues that took place.[21]

The major findings from the Project can be summarised as follows:

- Recontextualisation is not a product that can be handed to teachers; rather it is a process that teachers have to experience for themselves before they can lead others in it. This finding has important implications for teacher learning and professional development.
- While teachers used a dialogical model for RE within the project, the data did not indicate any major shift in students' engagement in RE.

---

17   Rina Madden, Gina Bernesconi, Bernadette Tolan, Paul Fumei, Ann Taylor. *Recontextualising Pedagogy Project: Interim Report* 2018-2020. Melbourne CTC, June 2019.
18   Rina Madden, Gina Bernesconi, Geraldine Larkin, Bernadette Tolan, Paul Fumei, Ann Taylor 'Leading Learning for a recontextualising approach in Religious Education' *British Journal of Religious Education* published online 27th Feb 2022 (Assoc Prof Jim D'Orsa acted as 'critical friend' to this team during the project).
19   Rina Madden, the principal author of these reports, had been a PhD student at KU Leuven with Pollefeyt as her thesis promoter.
20   Madden et al, 5.
21   Madden et al, 4–6.

This disappointing result could, certainly in part, be explained by the negative impact of COVID restrictions on the project.[22]
- Without explicitly grappling with what it means to be part of the 'living tradition of the whole church' (*Dei Verbum* #12) where revelation is alive and ongoing, the work of recontextualisation can be over-simplified and reduced to a focus on a product.
- The role of system leaders changes from that of expert to *co-learner with the teacher* in developing a recontextualising pedagogy. The system leader must become involved in *the process of recontextualising* with the teachers he or she leads.

THE FUTURE OF ECSI

ECSI is a process-driven project and so shares the limitations of all such projects. Surveys have a limited half-life in that over time people get to know what the 'right' or expected answer is, and this fact distorts the data. Alternatively, they tire of answering the same questions over and over, so simply cease to respond. ECSI has now been used in Victorian Catholic schools for over a decade and so is approaching its 'use-by' date. Any achievements using ECSI have yet to be formally evaluated. In a recent article Polleyfeyt provides an indirect form of evaluation by outlining findings based on school data collected in 2012-2019.[23] His conclusion is that the pedagogy used in Catholic primary schools perpetuates a mono-logical understanding of the Catholic traditions that students abandon when faced with the complexities of life as they learn more and experience more during secondary schooling. Consequently, students seek refuge in relativism as a stance to life. In taking this stance, they have the support of the dominant culture. Religion is seen as something that young people associate with 'being a child'. Currently, secondary approaches to RE do not seem capable of reversing this trend. Pollefeyt argues that the HC model of RE offers this possibility, but as Madden et al discovered, this requires an investment in the development of teachers, through the promotion of collegial dialogue and learning to make recontextualising pedagogies possible. The transformation of a student's worldview is a project that reaches beyond the RE class. It is important across the total curriculum and in the way the school functions as a community of learners.

---

22 COVID caused major disruption in education over a two-year period 2020-2021.
23 Didier Pollefeyt. *Teaching the Unteachable or Why Too Much Good is Bad: Religious Education in Catholic Schools Today.* Religions 12 810 accessed at https://doi.org/103390/rel12100810 on Sept 9th 2022.

CONCLUSION

15

THE NEW AND THE OLD:

CHRISTIAN COMMUNITY LEADERSHIP
IN A CHANGE OF ERA

In the foregoing brief exploration of the responsibilities Church communities bear to recontextualise faith in a change of era, we have chosen to shine a light on the issue of faithful recontextualisation from several perspectives. We have engaged in the task utilising the resources of both faith and culture. In regard to the latter, the disciplines of anthropology and hermeneutics have played a major part in the exploration. In the realm of faith, we have been assisted by biblical studies, mission studies, and theology, and have noted how these three areas of sacred study are beginning to flow together enriching the journey of many faith communities.

In moving to draw our discussion to a close, we wish to put the spotlight back on the issue of leadership, and more specifically the style of leadership required to recontextualise the faith of communities in the current change of era. Ours is a faith carried in *community*, so the task of recontextualising faith requires that we give attention to the nature and purpose of our community life, and how it may be strengthened so that Christian leaders, with the support of their communities, may engage fruitfully in the challenging task of recontextualisation in today's world.

There is overwhelming evidence that people yearn for community. The impoverished state of community in many sectors of church life is a major concern, given the nature of how faith is held and passed on within Christianity. The pervasive individualism of modernity, as well as the shattering of communal life under the impact of postmodernity's rootlessness and suspicion of the stories that ground communities, have played their part in the current state of societies in the West. However, the cavalier usage of the term 'community' to describe some hoped-for antidote to the current situation does little to help us to live lives of faith and service in the changed context of a globalised world. And, like 'culture', the nature, strengths, and limitations of 'community', remain a misunderstood area.

COMMUNITY: A WAY OF BEING TOGETHER

The work of the well-known husband and wife team, Evelyn and James Whitehead,[1] is helpful in providing some clarity as to how 'community' is constituted. As they point out, community is a *negotiated way of being together*. It has both psychological elements, and sociological elements in that people who consciously engage in community seek to meet their own needs via a degree of sharing and intimacy in the company of others, while at the same time endeavouring to meet the goals which are assumed to be shared by the group.

If we imagine a spectrum with intimate group life, such as that of a well-functioning family, at one end, and the impersonality of organisational life at the other, we can readily see that communities like parishes and schools sit somewhere along the continuum, drawing elements of their shared life from each of the extremes. In other words, in coming together members hope to experience elements of intimate group life characteristic of the left end of the continuum on the one hand, but also require elements from the right to achieve the other goals they have in coming together. How much of either members expect from community life in a particular case is often a cause of tension, and a degree of negotiation is necessary if the community is to survive.

Members of such groups inevitably continue to be affected by the pull towards individualism that is a feature of modern culture, as well as by the impact of the postmodern critique of all narratives including their own. All the while they also experience the impact of globalisation, not least the vast movement of people who inevitably make their presence felt within society, culture, and church, in so many ways. Consequently, when we come together in community, it is likely that there will also be an element of interculturality involved in the experience. For these reasons the Whiteheads identify the need for a 'ministry of clarification' for any group to function effectively as a community.[2] The ministry of clarification must address the different levels of expectation that exist among members with regard to six questions[3] each relating to an important area of group life:

---

[1] Evelyn and James Whitehead. *Community of Faith: Crafting Christian Communities Today*. Mystic: Twenty-third Publications, 1992.
[2] ibid, 15-25.
[3] ibid, 28-37.

- What is the major locus of the group? Group itself (maintenance) or task (mission)?
- How fully are members involved? Fully or filling a role?
- Is emotional sharing encouraged? In depth or neutrality?
- How is the group behaviour regulated? Custom/pressure or procedures?
- How are members obligated to one another? Loyalty or contract?
- How are members evaluated? 'One of us' or performance?

As we have noted, the options on the right are characteristic of an association or institution. Those on the left are those of a family-type small group. As a negotiated style of group life, the heart of the negotiation lies in determining where members stand on these issues and how to build a consensus in regard to the expectation they have of one another.

When it comes to a recontextualising pedagogy for example, whether at the cultural or faith level, if a school staff is to model the notion of becoming a learning community, then teachers have a responsibility to exercise a 'ministry of clarification' that builds community by *negotiating* answers to the questions above. The same applies to a parish. Otherwise, the educational demands of recontextualisation will quickly ensure that the challenge is relegated to the 'too hard' basket.

In terms of the Catholic faith practised in communities across the globe, it is most helpful, and certainly most accurate, to think of ourselves as comprised of a *community of communities*. While it is through the agency of a local faith group that we nourish our faith and generally contribute most to the vibrancy of the faith life of those around us, in terms of the recontextualisation of faith we must go beyond the local. This is a task carried out in collaboration with other associations of the faithful that comprise our faith community across the globe.

As always, the Holy Spirit continues to raise up leaders who function at various levels and in various ways – pastoral, educational, prophetic, theological, and missional – to ensure faithful recontexualisation occurs.

Christian community life has a toughness and resilience about it because of the commitment members have to the goals that bring them together. Even when the quality of shared life is less than ideal, there is a depth dimension in being together that results in members opting for renewal and continuance over a dissolution involving the jettisoning of chosen ways of being together. We have seen evidence of this characteristic of our shared faith life in the strength of the various renewal movements at work in this country.

As we draw this study to a close, there are certain important features of our shared Christian life that we need to note because they feature so strongly in the recontextualising process.

COMMUNITIES OF INTERPRETATION

As we have surveyed elements of the Judeo-Christian story in the process of our exploration, we have noted that faith communities have always been communities of interpretation and re-interpretation, making sense of foundational beliefs as contexts change. Israel, for example, under the leadership of prophets, kings, and learned leaders, negotiated what it meant to be a community who worshipped one God, rather than many gods, as they moved through contextual changes beginning with the movement from Egypt to Sinai where they were constituted as a people of faith in the one God who is both creator and saviour. They renegotiated this covenantal relationship with God again and again, particularly in such times of trial as the Babylonian exile of the 6th century BCE.

Early Christian leaders, including the gospel writers, continued this work, recontextualising faith in such dramatically changed circumstances as the break with Judaism following the fall of Jerusalem in 70 CE, and the foundation of faith communities within the many peoples and cultures of the Roman empire.

Today's faith communities find themselves negotiating their group life under the impact of dynamics unleashed by globalisation, pluralisation, and detraditionalisation, while contemporary pharaohs both political and economic[4] like the Egyptian pharaoh at the time of the Exodus, present themselves as alternative deities.

COMMUNITIES OF SOLIDARITY WITH THOSE ON THE MARGINS

Many of today's faith communities must relearn what it means to place the poor at the centre of each local community's consideration, just as Israel was covenanted to do, and as Jesus did in his ministry, in a signature way. This requires the capacity to analyse need, and where necessary to use the analysis provided by others. It also requires the sensitivity to encounter those in need in the circumstances of their vulnerability, and to do so in such a way as to uphold human dignity. Today's communities are learning to express their solidarity with those on the margin in terms of *dialogue,* as they discern how others feel, and how they see themselves as best helped

---

4   Students of the Old Testament scholar Walter Brueggemann will find in his books and podcasts numerous memorable references to the Egyptian pharaohs' contemporary counterparts.

in the most dignified and culturally appropriate ways. In complex societies, *dialogue is a key hallmark of our being together.* It is a modus operandi with demands and complexities that have become familiar to teachers involved in the ECSI project in Australian Catholic schools have come to know very well (see education section of this study).

MISSIONAL COMMUNITIES

Benefitting from Vatican II's implementation across the last six decades, and the far-reaching work of subsequent Roman synods, together with theological and biblical contributions from scholars across the whole Christian Church, today's faith communities are growing in consciousness of their life as *missional*. They are also coming to realise that it is God's mission, modelled for us in the mission of Jesus, that gives birth to every Christian community and shapes its communal life.

The recontextualisation of faith is itself one of the forms of mission to which all, especially leaders, are called in the current change of era. It is an invitation to expand one's imaginal horizon in retelling the Christian story. It provides a glimpse of how communities such as parishes and schools might 'do life differently', crossing cultural boundaries, re-imagining themselves as co-creators and co-redeemers, co-repairing with others of good will a degraded and broken physical and human world in which every positive contribution takes God's mission forward.

THE NEW AND THE OLD: MATTHEW MODELS RECONTEXTUALISING LEADERSHIP

> *And he said to them, 'Every scribe that has been trained for the kingdom of heaven is like the master of the household who brings out of his treasure what is new and what is old. (Matt 13:52).*
>
> *And Jesus came and said to them: 'All authority in heaven and on earth has been given to me. Go therefore and make disciples of all nations, baptizing them in the name of the Father, and of the Son, and of the Holy Spirit, and teaching them to obey everything that I have commanded you. And remember, I am with you always, to the end of the age.' (Matt 28: 18-20).*

The verse from Matthew chapter 13 above is an important key to the theology of the gospel in which Matthew develops a splendid version of the good news of and about Jesus Christ, at a time of immense change. He does so after the fall of Jerusalem by recontextualising the traditions about

Jesus against a background of his own knowledge of Jewish traditions for converts mostly of Jewish origin who had accepted Jesus as messiah. These were experiencing the situation in which others, not of similar background, wanted to join them. The verse is generally recognised as a disclosure, available to those who have eyes to see, of the way the gospel writer saw himself and his leadership role.

The second passage is the culmination of Matthew's presentation of Jesus and his mission, and contains a resolution to tensions deliberately emphasised by the author in pursuing a theological agenda by means of his narrative. Resolving tensions between the old and the new is one of each faith leader's most important and difficult challenges today. It lies at the heart of the recontextualisation of faith that must occur in a change of era.

The second passage, often referred to as 'the great mission commission'[5], expresses the practical resolution of the tension between the old Israel and the new. In due course we shall see how Matthew achieves this resolution through the way he has presented his narrative of Jesus. By paying attention to the literary approach adopted by the gospel writer, we can ascertain what that great commission came to signify for the original Matthean community/ies of Jewish Christians, and in the light of that, reflect on what it calls forth in our faith communities today.

All four canonical gospels have Jesus as their focus, albeit a focus pursued in different ways and offering different perspectives on Jesus and his mission. As with each of the gospels, Matthew's presentation of Jesus has much to offer those tasked with recontextualising his good news for a particular community or communities, in a change of era.

THEMES AND QUESTIONS

Our discussion of Matthew's gospel will be guided by the following questions and themes:

- Regarding the resolution of the tensions between the old and the new, we will ask: what is 'the old' in Matthew? What constitutes the 'new'? How is a resolution achieved in the course of the narrative?
- How did Matthew perceive the consequences of this resolution for his immediate community and for the world?
- In terms of Christian faith, the death and resurrection of Jesus was and is the turning point of human history. It is, however, more than a

---

5 This phrase reflects the pre-eminence of the Gospel of Matthew as a teaching gospel in the life of the Church. It was also seen to provide a strong rationale to the those who undertook cross-cultural mission during the first and second expansions of European peoples into the Americas, Asia, Africa, and Oceania from the 16th to the 19th centuries.

one-off event; it is also a *paradigm of God creatively at work in every faithful community in every age.*

CONTEXTUALISATION/RECONTEXTUALISATION AT VARIOUS LEVELS

In Matthew, we see contextualisation working at several levels. At the most obvious level, Jesus is depicted as contextualising his subject matter in the manner of a skilled teacher, tapping into everyday life, using familiar imagery so that people could readily comprehend the import of his words.

At the same time, while Jesus was contextualising his teaching about God, human relationships, and God's creation, he was going beyond the current understandings of Israel's traditional faith. One has only to think of how Jesus presented the Kingdom of God, and God as *abba* (intimate term for father), to see how he subverted contemporary understandings of God and of God's reign.

The destruction of Jerusalem resulted in the main pillars defining Jewish identity in Jesus' time being destroyed. Matthew is faced with telling Jesus' story for Jewish converts living in a dislocated world in which Jewish and Christian identity were both being re-negotiated. He does this by using elements drawn from a cultural world that no longer existed, and the contemporary cultural world of his audience. It is a process that involved contextualising some elements while recontextualising others. On reflection, Catholic educators – in schools, tertiary settings, and parishes – will readily identify similar key elements in their own task in the current change of era.

Dean Flemming identifies obvious contextualising features in Matthew's gospel in the way the writer assumes familiarity with Jewish language and culture. He makes reference, for example, to Jewish customs such as hand-washing at meals (Matt 15:2) and the wearing of phylacteries and fringes (Matt 23:5), without explanation. Obviously out of respect for Jewish sensibilities, Matthew substitutes 'Kingdom of Heaven' for 'Kingdom of God' as used in Mark and Luke, and includes material on Jewish concerns such as fasting, Sabbath observance, temple offerings and temple tax, and refers to Jerusalem as 'the holy city' (Matt 4:5; 27:53). In a whole range of ways, Matthew's narrative is connected into a previous story, the story of Israel.[6] His Jewish audience would have been able to attune themselves to this story religiously and culturally with a degree of ease. If we are to authentically recontextualise Christian faith in our time, in fidelity to Matthew's exemplar work we must try to understand his theology and how

---

6 Flemming, 245-6. In the latter point he is quoting from N.T. Wright. *The New Testament and the People of God*, p 385. Minneapolis, Fortress Press, 1992.

he manages to successfully resolve the tensions between the old and the new.

MATTHEW'S LITERARY METHODOLOGY

The relationship between writer and audience is important in understanding the significance of the way any narrative is constructed.[7] The Christians in Matthew's community were Jews who had come to faith in the crucified Jesus as the long-awaited messiah-king. Their fellow Jews rejected this view and were attempting to re-establish their faith communities using the synagogues as their religious centres, re-affirming YHWH as Lord and the Torah as the basis of their religion.

In due course, a fundamental split occurred between the Jews who sought to re-found the faith after 70 AD and those Jews who followed Jesus. The result was that the Christians became unwelcome in many synagogues. It became clear to them, and especially to their leaders, such as the writer of the Gospel of Matthew, that the future of the Jesus' movement did not lie with their fellow Jews, but with Gentiles who were already beginning to seek membership.[8] While we take this position for granted today, it was not so clear at the time Matthew was writing.

What is emerging as the identity and mission of this group of Jewish Christians? How can Matthew answer that question and yet speak convincingly to both the Jewish members and the Gentile would-be members? In moving more deeply into Matthew's narrative, we are guided by the work of Australian scripture scholar Francis Moloney, who provides a literary analysis of Matthew's Gospel as a way of accessing his theology.[9]

Matthew is presenting a story of Jesus with a storyline (plot) linking the beginning of Jesus' story with its roots prominently in the story of Israel, and its conclusion within the entire world. In doing so, Matthew must deal with the fact that, in his earthly life, Jesus confined the bulk of his efforts to the 'lost sheep' of the house of Israel (Matt 15:24). When he made exceptions, such as for the Canaanite woman seeking help for her daughter (Matt 15:21-28) or the centurion for his servant (Matt 8:5-13), it was an opportunity to strengthen the faith of fellow Jews, who were the principal focus of his own mission.

---

[7] A point well made by Dean Flemming in discussing the contribution of rhetorical criticism as an element of biblical study that emphasises audience-centred communication. As with many other ancient writings, the aim in addressing the audience is not just to explain, but to persuade, in this case that Jesus is the messiah-king who founds the new Israel for the sake of the world. ibid, 239.
[8] Donald Senior *The Gospel of Matthew*. Nashville: Abington, 1997, 72-84.
[9] A helpful resource is Francis J. Moloney. *The Shape of Matthew's Story*. Biblical Studies from the Catholic Biblical Association of America 9. New York: Paulist Press, 2023.

But post-resurrection everything changed. Under the inspiration of the Holy Spirit, the significance of Jesus' life, death, resurrection, and mission for the whole world became clear.

Why and how did Matthew insert such seeming contradictions into what was a well-crafted story? The answer to the 'Why?' lies in his desire to create and focus on the tension between the old and the new that will be resolved at the end of the gospel in an unexpected way. The 'How?' is via the narrator who exercises the privilege of storyteller. The narrator interjects events from the past, and the future, into the narrative for the purpose of creating tension that will ultimately be resolved and raising questions that will ultimately be answered.

Matthew is telling a story that concludes with the community sent, not to the house of Israel, but to the whole world, so what happened to change the original focus? The answer lies in the death and resurrection of Jesus. As the old order passed away, the new order dawned.

The enormous significance of this is shown symbolically through events retold by Matthew as accompanying the death of Jesus. To a Jewish person attuned to the Old Testament references on which Matthew draws, these indicate the passing from one era to the next. However, 'the next' in Old Testament terms is *the end of time* – the ultimate change of era. Let us attend to Matthew's account:

> *All at once there was a violent earthquake, for the angel of the Lord, descending from heaven, came and rolled away the stone and sat upon it. His face was like lightning, his robe white as snow. (Matt 28:2-3).*

The apocalyptic imagery on which Matthew has drawn is found in Old Testament passages describing in various ways the end of time when YHWH would return as Lord and Judge (c.f. Amos 8:9; Jer 15:9, Ezek 37:12-13; Isa 26:19; Dan 7:9; 10:6; 12:2).[10] A brief selection will be sufficient to demonstrate how Matthew is drawing on these sources, raising echoes of the familiar for his readers:

> *Therefore prophesy and say to them: 'Thus says the Lord God: I am going to open your graves, and bring you up from your grave, O my people, and I will bring you back to the land of Israel. And you shall know that I am the Lord when I open your graves and bring you up from your graves, O my people (Ezek 37:12-13).*
>
> *On that day, says the Lord God, I will make the sun go down at noon, and darken the earth in broad daylight. (Amos 8-9).*

---

10   It is worthy of note that these apocalyptic utterances are spread across several centuries.

> As I watched, thrones were set in place, and an Ancient One took his throne, his clothing was white as snow, and the hair of his head like pure wool; his throne was fiery flames and its wheels were burning fire (Daniel 7:9).

The great turnaround is from the focus on Israel (inward) to the gospel's literary and theological resolution directed to the whole world, 'the nations'(outward). This vision is to be carried forward by a new Israel entrusted with a new mission. With the death and resurrection of Jesus, the paschal mystery turning point of the ages, has occurred. Jesus has perfected the old law and ushered in the new. With the words: 'All authority in heaven and on earth has been given to me' Jesus is depicted as assuming the authority of Yahweh in issuing a new Torah and founding a new community. The Matthean community, and similar fledgling Christian communities, were indeed the new Israel, charged with a missionary mandate to the gentiles.

Matthew's perspective on Jesus as the new Moses, the founder of the new Israel, is portrayed by the way Matthew presents his narrative. Just as many people today are experiencing a crisis of religious identity as the context of society, culture and church shifts and appears menacing, so too did the Matthean community. The resolution of their religious crisis came through a focus on the death and resurrection of Jesus, the turning point of their age and every age. This paschal mystery – mystery in the sense of a spiritual reality into which we journey ever more deeply throughout our personal and communal lives – is not simply a one-off event; it is a gift at work in the life of every faith community, who from time to time will be called forth into new, uncharted territory, just as we Christians are today. As leaders, we learn that the gifts of 'the old' and 'the new' are freely available from within our Christian 'storeroom'. Just as the Holy Spirit post-Pentecost enabled the writer of Matthew, to contextualise the Christian faith for Jewish converts by linking Jesus' story to Israel's story, and other Gospel writers to recontextualise it for those of other cultures, we can be certain that spiritually-attuned leaders will continue that process faithfully.

We can make the gift of recontextualised faith available to our communities to the extent that we are prepared to enter humbly into the power of the paschal mystery, and in doing so become empowered to provide leadership to hope-filled faith communities, the co-creators of a 'new humanism', responding to the profound change of era we are all experiencing.

See, I am making all things new (Rev 21:5).

SELECT BIBLIOGRAPHY

Bauckham R, 'Mission as Hermeneutic for Scriptural Interpretation' in Goheen, M Ed, *Reading the Bible Missionally*, Grand Rapids: Eerdmans, 2016.

Bauckham R, *The Bible and Mission*, Baker Academic, Grand Rapids, 2003.

Beeby DH, 'Coe, Shoki (C.H. Hwang)' in *Biographical Dictionary of Christian Mission*. Andersen, Gerald, H. Editor. Grand Rapids: Eerdmans, 1998.

Bernstein B, *The Structuring of Pedagogic Discourse (Class, Codes and Control)*, Routledge, New York, 1990.

Boeve L, *Interrupting Tradition: An essay on Christian faith in a postmodern condition*, Peeters Press, Louvain, 2002.

Boeve L, *Lyotard and Theology: Beyond the Christian narrative of love*. Bloomsbury, London, 2014.

Casson A, *Catholic Identities in Catholic Schools: Fragmentation and Bricolage* https://www.researchgate.net/publication/322711732_Catholic_Identities_in_Catholic_Schools_Fragmentation_and_Bricolage.

Collins JJ, Hens-Piazza G, Reid B OP and Senior D CP (Editors), *The Jerome Biblical Commentary for the Twenty-first Century,* Bloomsbury, London, 2022, 1923–1949.

Coloe M, *John 1–10* Wisdom Commentary Volume 44A, Liturgical Press, Collegeville, Minnesota, 2021.

Costas O, *Liberating News: A Theology of Contextual Evangelism,* Eerdmans, Grand Rapids, 1989.

Cote R, *Revisioning-Mission: The Catholic Church and the Culture of Postmodern America,* Paulist Press, New York, 1996.

De Mesa J and Wostyn L, *Doing Christology: The re-appropriation of a tradition*, Claretian Publications, Quezon City, 1993.

Dixon B, 'The Science of Listening: Contexts and Challenges for the Catholic Community in Australia', *Australasian Catholic Record*, Vol 91, Issue 3, 2014.

D'Orsa T, 'Mission in the Gospel of John: Reflections on a unique spiritual tradition', in *New Ways of Living the Gospel*, D'Orsa J and D'Orsa T, Garratt Publishing, Mulgrave, 2015.

D'Orsa J and D'Orsa T, *Pedagogy and the Catholic Educator: Nurturing Hearts, Transforming Possibilities,* Garratt Publishing, Mulgrave, 2020.

Donovan V, *Christianity Rediscovered,* Orbis, Maryknoll NY, 2003.

Flemming D, *Contextualization in the New Testament: Patterns for theology and mission,* Intervarsity Press, Downers Grove, 2005, p 296.

Gallagher S, *Hermeneutics and Education,* University of New York Press, New York, 1992.

Geertz C, *The Interpretation of Cultures,* Basics Books, New York, 1973.

Gensiche HW, 'Warneck, Gustav' in *Biographical Dictionary of Christian Missions,* ed. Gerald H Anderson, Macmillan, New York, 1998.

Global Institute for Change: *Essentials of Dialogue.* https://institute.global/advisory/essentials-dialogue

Goheen MW, *A Light to the Nations: The Missional Church and the Biblical Story,* Baker Academic, Grand Rapids, 2011.

Goheen M, *Introducing Christian Mission Today,* IVP academic, Downers Grove, Illinois, 2014.

Goheen MW Ed, *Reading the Bible Missionally,* Eerdmans, Grand Rapids, 2016.

Groome T, *Religious Education: Sharing our Story and Vision,* Dove Communications, Melbourne, 1980.

Hall ET, *Culture: The Silent Language,* Anchor Books, New York, 1973.

Hiebert P, *Cultural Anthropology,* J.B. Lippincott Company, Philadelphia, 1976.

Hiebert P, *Transforming worldviews: An anthropological understanding of how people change,* Baker Academic, Grand Rapids, 2009.

Hofstede GJ, Hofstede G, Minkov M, *Cultures and Organisations: Software of the Mind,* Harper Collins, London, 1994. (Third revised and expanded edition published 2010).

Kraft CH, *Christianity in Culture,* Orbis Books, New York, 1991.

Kroeber AL and Kluckhohn C, *Culture: a Critical Review of Concepts and Definitions,* originally published by The Journal of Philosophy Inc., New York, 1954, this reference Pantianos Classics, 2020.

Lenehan K and Madden R, *Combined Victorian Dioceses Position Paper: 'Recontextualising Pedagogy for a Distinctively Catholic Education',* Catholic Theological College, Melbourne (undated).

Luzbetak L SVD, *The Church and Cultures: New Perspectives on Missiological Anthropology,* Orbis Books, Maryknoll NY, 1988.

Lyotard JF, *The Postmodern Condition: a Report on Knowledge,* Manchester Unity Press, Manchester, 1984.

Madden R, Bernesconi Gina, Tolan B, Fumei P and Taylor A, *Recontextualising Pedagogy Project: Interim Report 2018–2020,* Melbourne CTC, June 2019.

Madden R, Bernesconi G, Larkin G, Tolan B, Fumei P, Taylor A, 'Leading Learning for a recontextualising approach in Religious Education', *British Journal of Religious Education,* Published online, February 2022.

McCulloch R SSC, 'The Kovado Cross: Christian Presence in Pakistan before 1000AD', *The Far East,* Columban Fathers, Essendon, May 2022.

Malone P, Chesterton P, Ryan M and McDonald M, *Report on Review of Sharing Our Story,* Australian Catholic University, Strathfield, 1996.
Moloney F, *Mark: Storyteller, Interpreter, Evangelist,* Hendrickson, Peabody MA, 2004.
Moloney F, 'Mission in the Acts of the Apostles "The protagonist is the holy spirit"', *The Australasian Catholic Record,* Vol 96, No 4, December 2019.
Naugle D, *Worldview: The History of a Concept,* William B Eerdmans Publishing Company, Grand Rapids, 2002.
Nissen J, *New Testament and Mission: Historical and Hermeneutical Perspectives,* Peter Lang, Frankfurt am Main, Third Edition, 2004.
Okoye J, *Israel and the Nations,* Orbis, Maryknoll NY, 2006.
McEvoy J, *Leaving Christendom for Good: Church-world Dialogue in a Secular Age,* Lexington Books, New York, 2014.
O'Malley J, *What Happened at Vatican II,* Harvard University Press, London, 2010.
Phan P, C. *Mission and Catechesis: Alexandre de Rhodes and Inculturation in Seventeenth-Century Vietnam,* Orbis, Maryknoll, New York, 2005.
Pollefeyt D and Bowens J, *Identity in Dialogue,* Lit Verlag, Zurich, 2014.
Pollefeyt D and Bowens J, 'Dialogue as the future: a Catholic answer to the Colorization of the Education Landscape', 2013. https://theo.kuleuven.be/apps/press/ecsi/files/2019/04/7.-Pollefeyt-Bouwens-Dialogue-as-the-Future.pdf
Reed B, *Engaging with the Hope of Parishes,* Lit Verlag, Hamburg, 2019.
Rolheiser R (editor and author), *Secularity and the Gospel,* The Crossroads Publishing Company, New York, 2006.
Sanders JA, *Torah and Canon,* Second Edition, Cascade Books, Eugene OR, 2005.
Schein E, *Organisational Culture and Leadership,* Third Edition, Wiley, New Jersey, 2015.
Schillebeeckx E, *Jesus: an experiment in Christology* (1979); *Christ: the Christian experience in the modern world* (1980); and *Church: The human story of God* (1990), T&T Clark, London.
Schreiter Robert, 'Inculturation of Faith or Identification with Culture?' in Norbert Greinacher and Norbert Mette (Editors) *Christianity and Cultures* (*Concilium* 94/2), SCM Press, London, 1994.
Sivalon J, *God's Mission and Postmodern Culture: The Gift of Uncertainty,* Orbis Books, Maryknoll, New York, 2012.
Shiner W, *Proclaiming the Gospel: First Century Performance of Mark,* Continuum, London, 2003.
Schussler FE, *In Memory of Her: A Feminist Theological Reconstruction of Christian Origins.,* SCM Press, London, 1983.
Senior D and Stuhlmueller C, *The Biblical Foundations of Mission,* Orbis, Maryknoll New York, 1984.

Smith MS, 'Genesis' in Collins J J, Hens-Piazza G, Reid B OP and Senior D CP (Editors), *The Jerome Biblical Commentary for the Twenty-First Century*, Bloomsbury, London, 2022.

Shorter A, *Towards a Theology of Inculturation*, Geoffrey Chapman, London, 1988.

Taylor C, *A Secular Age*, Harvard University Press, Cambridge MA, 2018.

Thornhill J, *Making Australia: Exploring Our National Conversation*, Millennium Books, Newtown, 1992.

Wright CJH, *The Mission of God: Unlocking the Bible's Grand Narrative*, IVP Academic, Downers Grove, 2006.

Thesis

Prince AJ, *Contextualisation of the Gospel: Towards an evangelical approach in the light of Scripture and the Church Fathers*, Doctor of Theology, 2015.

Encyclopedia

St Anselm, *Stanford Encyclopedia of Philosophy*, May 2000. Revised 2020. https://plato.stanford.edu/entries/anselm/#FaiSeeUndChaPurAnsThePro

Dictionary

Gensiche HW, 'Warneck, Gustav,' in *Biographical Dictionary of Christian Missions*, ed. Gerald H. Anderson, Macmillan Reference USA, New York, 1998.

Vatican Documents

Paul III (Pope), papal bull *Sublimus Deus*, 1537. https://www.papalencyclicals.net/paul03/p3subli.htm

Vatican II *Gaudium et Spes (Pastoral Constitution on the Church in the Modern World)*. https://www.vatican.va/archive/hist_councils/ii_vatican_council/documents/vat-ii_const_19651207_gaudium-et-spes_en.html

Vatican II *Unitatis Redintegratio (Decree on Ecumenism)* https://www.vatican.va/archive/hist_councils/ii_vatican_council/documents/vat-ii_decree_19641121_unitatis-redintegratio_en.html

Vatican II *Nostra Aetate (Declaration on the Relation of the Church with non-Christian Religions)*. https://www.vatican.va/archive/hist_councils/ii_vatican_council/documents/vat-ii_decl_19651028_nostra-aetate_en.htm

Paul VI (Pope), *Ecclesiam Suam (On the Church)*, 1964. https://www.vatican.va/content/paul-vi/en/encyclicals/documents/hf_p-vi_enc_06081964_ecclesiam.html

Paul VI (Pope), *Evangelii Nuntiandi (On Evangelization in the Modern World)*, 1975. https://www.vatican.va/content/paul-vi/en/apost_exhortations/documents/hf_p-vi_exh_19751208_evangelii-nuntiandi.html

John Paul II (Pope), *Catechesi Tradendae (On Catechesis in Our Time)*, 1979. https://www.vatican.va/content/john-paul-ii/e n/apost_exhortations/documents/hf_jp-ii_exh_16101979_catechesi-tradendae.html

Pontifical Council for Inter-religious Dialogue. *Dialogue and Proclamation* 1990. *https://www.vatican.va/roman_curia/pontifical_councils/interelg/documents/rc_pc_interelg_doc_19051991_dialogue-and-proclamatio_en.html*

John Paul II (Pope). *Redemporis Missio. (Mission of the Redeemer)*, 1990. https://www.vatican.va/content/john-paul-ii/en/encyclicals/documents/hf_jp-ii_enc_07121990_redemptoris-missio.html

Benedict XVI (Pope), *Deus Caritas Est (God is Love)*, 2005. https://www.vatican.va/content/benedict-xvi/en/encyclicals/documents/hf_ben-xvi_enc_20051225_deus-caritas-est.html.g

Francis (Pope), *Evangelii Gaudium (The Joy of the Gospel)*, 2013. https://www.vatican.va/content/francesco/en/apost_exhortations/documents/papa-francesco_esortazione-ap_20131124_evangelii-gaudium.html

Francis (Pope), *Laudato si' (On Care for Our Common Home)*, 2015. https://www.vatican.va/content/dam/francesco/pdf/encyclicals/documents/papa-francesco_20150524_enciclica-laudato-si_en.pdf

Francis (Pope) *Fratelli Tutti (On Fraternity and Social Friendship)*, 2020. https://www.vatican.va/content/francesco/en/encyclicals/documents/papa-francesco_20201003_enciclica-fratelli-tutti.html

Other Sources

Australian Government Census Data, https://www.abs.gov.au/

Walsh JMM, *Change Search Encounter: Evangelization and Ministry Today*, Daughters of St Paul, Homebush, 1984. (Recorded lectures.)

INDEX

A

acculturation 87, 98
adaptation 5
anthropology 5, 12, 51, 55–8, 65, 68, 71, 73, 80, 86, 89, 92, 97–9, 100, 101, 109, 116, 189
 cultural 54, 63–5, 67, 75, 99, 202
 emperical 104
 empirical 109
 modern 98–9, 101
 social 116
ANZAC 93, 105

B

Babylonian exile 18–19, 22, 23, 192
Bauckham 23, 36, 201
Bernstein, Basil 145, 147–9, 201
 sociological tradition 148
Bible 15–20, 22, 23, 26, 30, 36, 78, 80, 100, 106, 109–10, 201, 202, 204
 mission as hermeneutical key 22
bioi 45
blessing to the nations 15, 19, 20, 21, 25
Boeve 7, 128–9, 133–6, 140–3, 147, 149, 150, 160, 162, 177, 184, 201

C

Catechism of the Catholic Church 151
Catholic Curriculum: a Mission to the Heart of Young People iv, 11
Catholic Education Commission of Victoria 4, 175
Catholic University Leuven 3, 4
change of era 3, 4, 7, 10, 12, 16, 35, 39, 46, 51, 72, 95, 116, 142, 149, 174, 178, 193–5, 197, 198
Change of Era 9, 189
Chenu, Marie-Dominique OP 136–7
Christianity as an open story 13, 142
Christian values education 107, 162–3

Church
 mono-cultural to a multi-cultural Church 82
classicism 5, 67, 70, 75, 77–80, 82–3, 150, 152, 159
 17th and 18th centuries 55
 in academia 79
 in the Catholic Church 79, 80, 82
 in the colonies 55, 78
 Medieval Europe 76
 Roman Classicism 76
Coe, Shoki 5, 201
Coloe, Mary 44, 201
Concerns Based Adoption Model (CBAM) 179
condition of faith 123
Congar 136
contextualisation 5–6, 8, 14, 16–17, 26, 28, 36, 46, 49, 51, 53, 58, 61, 63, 65, 70, 80, 85, 109–10, 146, 152, 195, 204
 as a dialogical process 36, 58
 contextualising faith in Australia 59
 rites controversy 58
contextual theologies 83
Costas, Orlando 39, 40, 201
cross-cultural mission/ary 3, 5, 14, 53–4, 58, 61, 63, 72, 83, 100, 109, 133, 147, 194
culture
 as civilisation 5
 Australian 59
 depth dimensions of 107
 descriptive models 102
 faith and culture 11
 modern concept of 55
 myths and genesis stories 105
 semiotic approaches 103–5
 synchronic and diachronic 63
 way of life 25

D

de Mesa, Joe 138, 201
de Nobili, Roberto 59
de Rhodes, Alexander 59, 203

detraditionalisation 9, 162, 166–7, 176, 192
dialogue 8, 11, 12, 24, 58, 60–1, 83, 107, 117, 122, 124–7, 130–1, 161–7, 169, 171–4, 176, 179, 180–5, 192–3, 202–3, 205
  dialogue and mission 124
  Dialogue and Proclamation 125, 205
  teachers as moderators of dialogue 166
disciple-making for the kingdom 40
D'Orsa, Jim & Therese
  Explorers, Guides and Meaning-makers 9
D'Orsa, Jim & Therese 9, 11, 13, 24, 43, 78, 164, 172, 184, 201

E

enculturation 85, 89–90, 119
Engaging with the Hopes of Parishes 3
  Reed, Brendan 3, 203
Enhancing Catholic School Identity (ECSI) 3, 72, 159
  ECSI methodology 117, 175–76
  post-critical belief scale 168
  students' agency 172
Enuma Elish 27–8
Evangelii Gaudium 9, 39, 80, 124, 205
  Pope Francis 9, 39, 80, 124, 205
evangelisation of cultures 123

F

Franklin 64–5, 67
Fratelli Tutti 9, 131, 150, 205
  Pope Francis 9, 131, 150, 205
Fullan, Michael 176
  The New Meaning of Educational Change 176

G

Gadamer, Hans Georg 111, 135
Gallagher, Shaun 111, 202

Hermeneutics and Education 111, 202
Global Institute for Change 166, 202
globalisation 8–9, 25, 61, 190, 192
God Interrupts History 140
God's mission as hermeneutical key 16, 22
Goheen, Michael 22, 23, 36, 201, 202
Gospel of John 34, 43, 201
Gospel of Luke 42
Gospel of Mark 37, 38
Gospel of Matthew 18, 34, 40, 41, 146, 194, 196
  Matthew's literary methodology 196
gratuitous education movement 78
Groome, Thomas 152–4, 157, 202
  Educating for Life 117
  shared Christian Praxis 154–5, 163, 179

H

hermeneutics 5, 14, 65, 86, 110–11, 119, 137, 167, 189, 202, 210
  hermeneutical circle 111–12, 114–17
  historical-critical method 20
Hutsebaut 167

I

inculturation 5, 59, 64, 81–2, 203–4
  Catechesi Tradendae 5, 205
indwelling the text 15
Indwelling the Text 24
integration of faith and culture 11
Israel as a 'contrast people' 21
Israel's location 17, 26
  importance in identity 18–25, 27–30, 34, 35, 38, 41, 46, 69, 93, 106, 115, 129, 138–40, 192, 194–8

J

Jerome Biblical Commentary for the Twenty-first Century 20, 27, 201, 204

K

Kelly, John (Monsignor) 152
Kingdom of God 36–7, 122, 129, 139, 195

L

Laudato si' 9, 150, 205
Lenehan, Kevin 180–81, 202
Levinas, Emmanuel 135
Lombaerts, Herman FSC 153, 161
Luke-Acts 46
 a liberating gospel 42
Lumen Gentium 122
Luzbetak, Louis 65, 68–9, 71, 104, 202
Lyotard, Jean Francois 128–9, 131, 135–6, 201–2

M

MacKillop, Mary 13
Madden 180–1, 184–5, 202
McEvoy, James 127, 203
meaning-making 6, 7, 12, 14, 42, 46, 63, 85–6, 92, 109–10, 118–19, 147, 149, 154, 164–5, 183
 and the recontextualisation of faith 35, 85, 111
 model of 95, 115
Metz, Johann Baptist 135, 142
missiology 55
 missiology and anthropology 5, 57
mission 3, 4, 5
 from monological to dialogical engagement 57
 God's mission 8, 16, 21–3, 35, 38, 72, 122–3, 129–30, 193, 210
 God's Mission 203
 mission anthropology 65, 80, 86, 100

 post-Vatican II mission project 6, 8
modernity 7, 10–13, 61, 72, 91, 128, 142, 154, 189
Moloney, Francis SDB 36–9, 42, 123, 196, 203
Mystici Corporis
 Pope Pius XII 121

N

Nehemiah 22, 25
New World 50, 76, 77
 discovery of 76
Nissen, Johannes 39, 42–3, 203
Nostra Aetate 123, 204

O

Okoye, James
 Israel and the Nations 17, 22, 203

P

Paul III 204
Pedagogy and the Catholic Educator 13, 24, 78, 201
Pollefeyt, Didier and Bowens, Jan 4, 107, 161–2, 164, 172, 175–7, 180, 184–5, 203
 Identity in Dialogue 107, 127, 162
postmodern-postsecular 12, 79, 133, 149–51
postmodern thought 7, 11, 12

R

recontextualisation 3–8, 14–18, 20, 28, 30, 34, 40, 49, 60–1, 63, 70, 75, 210
 New Testament 31
 Old Testament 14, 16, 26, 58
 recontextualisation as theological process 14, 37
 recontextualisation of faith and culture 3, 4, 8, 16, 18, 43, 63, 85
 the religious education tradition 4, 14, 72
Recontextualisation 33, 36, 53

Redemptoris Missio (Pope John Paul II) 80, 125
relativism 132, 171, 173, 185
Ricci, Matteo 59
 rites controversy 58
Ricoeur, Paul 111, 117, 135
 post-critical belief 167
Robinson, Geoffrey (Bishop) 135

S

Sanders, James 19
 Torah and Canon 19, 203
Schillebeeckx, Edward 7, 133–42, 147, 149, 150, 177, 203
 Humanum 137–9
Schreiter, Robert 64, 103–4, 203
Second Vatican Council 72, 79–80, 122, 134
secularisation 9, 13, 55, 107, 162–4, 166–7, 176–7
Secularisation 12
secularism 12, 136
Senior, Donald and Stuhlmueller, Carroll 204
 The Biblical Foundations for Mission 20, 22, 27, 201, 203
Shoki, Coe 5, 201
Sivalon, John MM 72, 203
St Columban 7
story
 Catholicism as open story 13, 129
 closed story 13, 129–30, 132, 134

T

Taylor, Charles 12, 131
 A Secular Age 12, 123, 131, 204
theology of the kingdom 13
theory of interpretation 30
translation 5, 77, 123

U

Unitatis Redintegratio 122, 204

V

Vatican II 6–8, 71–2, 83, 115, 122, 136, 142, 149, 150, 152, 154, 159, 161, 163, 167, 204

W

Walsh 152, 205
weltanschauung 86
Whitehead, James
 Befriending the tradition 168
Whitehead, James and Whitehead, Evelyn 190
 Method in Ministry 168
worldview
 cognitive themes 89
 definition of 51, 87
 evaluative themes 90
 Hiebert's model 89
 personal 85, 95, 107, 108, 111, 114–16, 120, 131–32, 141, 157, 172–4
 public 85, 121, 173
 root metaphor 89–90
 themes and counterthemes 89
 transforming worldviews 87, 147, 157, 202
 worldview of an age 85, 91
 worldview of culture 91, 95, 97, 116, 118, 132, 162, 178
 worldview of faith 14, 71, 105, 110, 121, 126–7, 132, 141, 143, 150, 151
 worldview of pre-modern Europe 92, 127
Wostyn 138, 201
Wright 22, 23, 26, 30, 204
Wright, NT 195

Z

Zeitgeist 86

www.ingramcontent.com/pod-product-compliance
Lightning Source LLC
Chambersburg PA
CBHW070252010526
44107CB00056B/2429